THE CHURCH IN AFRICA 1977

Charles R. Taber
EDITOR

PAPERS PRESENTED AT A SYMPOSIUM
AT MILLIGAN COLLEGE
MARCH 31 – APRIL 3, 1977

William Carey Library

533 HERMOSA STREET • SOUTH PASADENA, CALIFORNIA 91030

Library of Congress Cataloging in Publication Data

Symposium on the Church in Africa, Milligan College,
Tenn., 1977.
The church in Africa, 1977.

Bibliography: p.
1. Christianity--Africa, Sub-Saharan--Congresses.
I. Taber, Charles Russell. II. Title.
BR1360.S95 1977   276.7   78-14923
ISBN 0-87808-161-5

Cover photograph by Russ Busby, BGEA,
Courtesty of African Enterprise

In accord with some of the most recent thinking in the academic
press, the William Carey Library is pleased to present this
scholarly book which has been prepared from an author-edited
and author-prepared camera ready copy.

Published by the William Carey Library
533 Hermosa Street
South Pasadena, California 91030

PRINTED IN THE UNITED STATES OF AMERICA

*To those African Christians, famous or anonymous,
who have struggled, often at the cost of their lives,
to make real and effective the testimony of Jesus Christ
in Africa and through His Church*

Contents

87944

Preface

The Symposium on the Church in Africa which was held at Milligan College on March 31 to April 3, 1977 was the second in what was intended to be an annual series. The first, which was held in April 1974, produced the volume *Christopaganism or Indigenous Christianity?* (Yamamori & Taber 1975). In 1975 and 1976, financial exigencies made it impossible to realize our initial hopes. However, through the generosity of Mr. Roy True of Johnson City, a trustee of Milligan College, the Institute of World Studies/Church Growth was able to hold the Africa symposium, and it is expected that in following years similar conferences will be held relating to other regions of the world. Plans are already underway for the 1978 Symposium on the Church in Latin America.

Since Tetsunao Yamamori spelled out in detail the history and justification of the Institute and of the planned symposia in the earlier volume (Yamamori and Taber 1975:9-10), I need only summarize briefly.

The origin of the Institute at Milligan College goes back to the tenacious vision of President Jess W. Johnson, who was determined that as a Christian institution, even such a liberal arts college as Milligan should be *"a college with a missionary vision."* Through the initial generosity of Mr. and Mrs. William S. Carter of Dallas, Texas, this dream began to be realized in 1972 with the coming of Dr. Yamamori to Milligan, followed by my coming in 1973 and the Carter Symposium already mentioned in 1974. Development since has been slow, but certain signs point to the possibility of a more adequate program in the years ahead.

It should also be mentioned that since the fall of 1975, the Institute has, in cooperation with Emmanuel School of Religion, offered elective graduate courses constituting a missionary emphasis in the M.Div. or the M.A. in Religion.

After the initial symposium, which focused on a theme of very general missiological significance, it has been our intention to hold symposia--possibly four or five in sequence--dealing more concretely with the Church of Jesus Christ in the various regions of the world. Accordingly, as various persons representative of all parts of Africa and numerous church bodies were invited to speak at the 1977 Symposium on The Church in Africa, they were asked to give "as comprehensive and accurate a picture as possible of the Church in Africa: its present situation, its prospects, its problems, and the path it should follow in the next few decades." Speakers were asked to focus on four general topics: evangelism and church growth, the church's internal life, the church's total service to the world, and the future of the church.

Three persons represented each region of sub-Saharan Africa: a presenter, who was allotted 60 minutes for the initial paper, and two respondents, who were allotted 15 minutes each. The responses were followed by open discussion among the persons attending the symposium and the speakers. The speakers are presented on a preceding page.

Presenter for southern Africa (South Africa, Swaziland, Lesotho, Botswana, Namibia, Angola, Mozambique, Zimbabwe) was Mr. Thomas Moses J. Leeuw. Responding were Dr. Norman E. Thomas and a South African who has asked to be anonymous for purposes of this volume. Ato Negash Kebede presented a paper on eastern Africa (Tanzania, Kenya, Uganda, Ethiopia, Rwanda, Burundi, Sudan, Somalia), to which Fr. Vincent J. Donovan and Rev. Byrum Makokha responded. Central Africa (Zambia, Zaire, C.A.E., Chad, Congo, Gabon,.Equatorial Guinea) was represented by Mr. Mutombo-Mpanya and respondents Dr. Max Ward Randall and Dr. John E. Ross. Finally, Prof. John S. Pobee spoke for western Africa (Togo, Cameroun, Nigeria, Niger, Benin, Ghana, Ivory Coast, Upper Volta, Liberia, Sierra Leone, Guinea, Guinea Bissau, Gambia, Senegal, Mali), and Rev. Dick Darr and Dr. Charles H. Kraft responded. Dr. Norman E. Thomas presented a summary and projection at the final session.

It will be noticed that all of the presenters as well as several of the respondents were black Africans. This is no accident; I have felt for some years that we have for much too long tried to get a feel of what it means to be a Christian in Africa through the second-hand perspective of westerners who have knowledge, sometimes considerable, of Africa. But if this was ever an adequate approach to understanding, it is so no longer; there are today, as the contributors to this symposium illustrate, numerous Africans capable of analyzing their situation in biblical and existential terms and offering bold and realistic solutions to the problems they face. This is only another way of saying that the Church in Africa has come of age (it came of age, at least in some areas, many decades ago; we failed to see it because we were looking through colonial-style spectacles), that it is able to speak for itself as well as any other church in the world. Given such a reality, it would be the height of folly on our part to continue the second-hand pattern of the past. I must add, now that Africans have spoken, that it is incumbent upon us to rid ourselves of the vestiges of the colonial mentality that would see in their words something quaint but not quite serious, and certainly not to be acted upon. Rather, it is high time we accorded them the courtesy we expect others to accord us, that is to recognize them as spokesmen for their own churches and authoritative interpreters of their own reality; our role, insofar as they have need of us, is to take seriously their definitions and interpretations and to enter loyally into their hopes and plans and programs.

Since I will try in the Epilog to summarize the main thrusts of the symposium, I will not discuss here the substance of the contributions. I do wish in closing to express appreciation to a number of persons who, in addition to the speakers, helped to assure the smooth operation of the symposium. First, to Dr. Jess W. Johnson, President, and Dr. Kenneth W. Oosting, Dean of Milligan College, for complete cooperation from the administrative side. Second, to the chapel crew, to the students who drove hundreds of miles between campus, motels, and airport for the convenience of participants, and especially to my secretary Mrs. Gerri Smith, who made the logistical burden very light on my shoulders and who typed the entire manuscript.

Charles R. Taber
Milligan College

Contributors

DICK DARR (B.S., Bob Jones University)

Director of Administrative Affairs, Gospel Missionary Union; for 15 years a missionary (Gospel Missionary Union) in Mali, involved in evangelism and church planting.

VINCENT J. DONOVAN (graduate studies in theology at St. Mary's Seminary (Connecticut), Fordham University, and Gregorian University)

Roman Catholic priest, member of the Provincial Council of the American Holy Ghost Fathers, presently involved in research and writing in mission theory and theology; for 17 years a Holy Ghost missionary in Tanzania, where he served successively as Director of the Major Seminary on Mt. Kilimanjaro, Director of the Catechetical Training Center for the Diocese of Arusha, and for eight years in direct evangelization of the nomadic Maasai people; he was also on the National Catholic Liturgical Commission of Tanzania; author of articles in various periodicals.

NEGASH KEBEDE (B.S., Haile Selassie I University; graduate studies, Temple University)

Recently Associate Secretary of the Overseas Office of the Eastern Mennonite Board of Missions; formerly teacher, Dean, and Principal of The Bible Academy (Nazareth, Ethiopia); formerly Secretary, then Chairman, Meserete Kristos Church (Ethiopia).

CHARLES H. KRAFT (B.A., Wheaton College; B.D., Ashland
   Theological Seminary; Ph.D., Hartford Seminary Foundation)

Professor of Anthropology and African Studies, School of World
Mission, Fuller Theological Seminary; former missionary
(Brethren Church) in Nigeria; formerly on faculties of Michigan
State University and U.C.L.A.; linguist, specialist in ethno-
theology; prolific author.

THOMAS MOSES J. LEEUW (B.A., Cornell University; M.A., Union
   Theological Seminary/Columbia University; Ph.D. candidate,
   University of Nijmegen)

Lutheran lay theologian from South Africa; poet, writer, and
speaker at many conferences on South African religious thought,
the South African religious scene, and other topics.

BYRUM MAKOKHA (B.A., Anderson College; M.A., Asbury Theological
   Seminary; M.A. candidate, Fuller Theological Seminary)

Minister of the Church of God (Anderson) in Kenya, active in
pastoral and evangelistic ministries; recently Executive
Secretary-Treasurer of his denomination in Kenya.

MUTOMBO-MPANYA (B.A., Bethel College (Kansas); M.A. candidate,
   Mennonite Biblical Seminary; other studies in Belgium)

Formerly Mennonite minister in Zaire; formerly mathematics
teacher in Zaire and Belgium; recently Assistant Director of
the Mennonite Central Committee in Zaire; involved in economic
planning, economic and political development, project analysis
in underdeveloped countries, and African culture and history.

JOHN S. POBEE (B.A., University of Ghana; B.D., Cambridge
   University (Selwyn College); other studies at Westcott
   House)

Professor, Department for the Study of Religions, University of
Ghana; frequent lecturer at conferences and prolific writer in
New Testament studies, African theology, African church history;
guest lecturer at universities in the U.S., England, and
Holland; member of the Committee of the Theological Education
Fund (Chairman, Africa Committee of the T.E.F., 1972-1977).

MAX WARD RANDALL (B.A., Minnesota Bible College; M.A., Fuller
   Theological Seminary; D.D., Minnesota Bible College)

Professor of Missions, Lincoln Christian Seminary; missionary
of the Christian Churches in South Africa and Zambia for many
years; also involved in launching Christian Church work in

Ghana, Spain, and other countries; Author, *Profile for Victory in Zambia* and numerous articles; frequent speaker at missionary conferences.

JOHN E. ROSS (B.A., Butler University; M.D., Indiana University School of Medicine; other studies at Yale University, London Institute of Tropical Medicine, and at institutions in Belgium)

Retired missionary of the Disciples of Christ in Zaire; did medical work for many years under both mission and government auspices in Zaire; frequent speaker at conferences.

NORMAN E. THOMAS (M.Div., Yale University Divinity School; Ph.D., Boston University)

Visiting Professor of Missions, Yale University Divinity School; Staff Associate, Africa Task Force, Board of Global Ministries of the United Methodist Church; former missionary (United Methodist Church) in Rhodesia, director of New Life for All, and on staff of Epworth College; later Dean of Studies and Associate Director, Mindolo Ecumenical Foundation (Zambia); author of scholarly papers on themes related to his experience.

PART I

The Church
in Southern Africa

The Church and Human Liberation in Southern Africa: Interpretations of Current Motifs

Thomas Moses J. Leeuw

With this presentation, we intend to let the oppressed people and those who are on their side speak. We are primarly endeavoring the role of interpreter, while presenting the new images which form the vision of the creation of a new history in southern Africa. This is the history of the exodus, the pathway to liberation, where God must "make all things new" through the creative efforts of liberation by the oppressed and hated indigenous majority peoples of southern Africa and those missionaries, white church people, and other white people on their side.

The history of the indigenous people of southern Africa is represented in compendia of various academic sophistication, inspired by countable ulterior motives. These motives usually surface as justifications for the nature of black and white relations forced on the peoples of southern Africa. These motives have also in themselves come to be accepted as authoritative representations of the essence of black and white history in southern Africa, for example: colonization, christianization, deception, starvation, and extermination. The structures for facilitating this fabric or network of political and religious systems and social and economic organization and structures, are creations and impositions of the white minority at the expense of the most basic universal human principles of life. However, these motives are seldom treated in their own right as part of these compendia of the history of the indigenous people of southern Africa.

The interpretation which we are formulating here is an
attempt at an understanding of these motives. Thus the need
for letting the oppressed people and those who are on their
side speak.

They speak of the dehumanizing effects of colonization. They
speak of the generally disguised ulterior motives of christianization. They speak of the deception accompanying the imparting
of so-called Western Christian Civilization which takes form in
"trusteeship" and "guardianship", and worst of all, in "separate
development" as justifications for a racist anti-Christian
system. They further speak of the reality of child death as a
consequence of malnutrition and adult starvation. And they
speak of militarization as a self-deification by the white
minority for exercising the power of life and death over the
black majority in presently white occupied parts of southern
Africa. These voices also reveal the captivity of the church
in various forms in parts of southern Africa where black leadership and rulership still fail to free themselves totally from
foreign domination at the expense of true human liberation for
the masses.

The cries and yearnings for freedom, justice, and fraternity
express the captivity of the majority black peoples in southern
Africa in the aforementioned political and religious systems and
their accompanying social and economic organization and structures. Consequently, the call for repentance of the whites in
southern Africa and for reconciliation with the oppressed black
people of southern Africa forms a legitimate goal of creative
efforts for liberation in southern Africa. These efforts are
presently still mainly a preoccupation of the oppressed black
masses because the white masses seem to have purposely decided
that their oppression of, and separation from, all black people
in southern Africa represent a God-determined act which it is
their sacred calling to make real, with the support of *their*
interpretations of the Bible and the Christian religion.

In the light of all this, our view is that considerations of
evangelism and church growth, the church's internal life, the
church's total service to the world, and the future of the church
in southern Africa must take place within the dynamics of the
existing revolutionary stage of black and white experience
there. Each of these four concerns is featuring in present
relationships between the church and the oppressed and those
who are on the side of human liberation and the relationships
among the church and the white minority rulers and their white
supporters.

The place of the church in southern Africa is well recognized
among the oppressed black people, but the reality of the

existing revolutionary climate in which the throes of liberation take place must also not be taken lightly.

The place of the church in southern Africa is probably well represented in the following statement by "Chief" Gatsha Buthelezi when he opened the South African Congress on Mission and Evangelism in Durban in 1973:

> I have been asked as a churchman to focus our attention on the task of the Church in South Africa in the next decade. . . . The Church during our own time ought to be interested not just in soul salvation, but salvation of the whole man in his circumstance.
>
> The Church's task then, within the next ten years, is to see that it relates to the current needs of our world. The world has no choice but to participate in change. This is a matter or urgency for the Church, as it is fast beginning to be an institution of the past, and thus unrelated to the current needs of our people. . . .
>
> We must become ever more aware of those points at which the struggle for justice must be fought (Buthelezi 1975).

That reality of the revolutionary climate in which the throes of liberation take place is probably well identified in the following observation by D. D. L. Makhathini:

> He who emphasises the historical reasons for our denominational differences is, if he be Black, sleeping through a revolution, or hibernating when Spring has set. If he is white, then no black man should doubt his motive, which is to keep you black man an underling in his Palace of Benevolent Despotism at whose gates is the sign "Christian church" but on its inner doors WHITES or NON-WHITES. This pseudo-Christianity black Theology rejects and argues that if we can understand each other's speech in the kitchen or factory or garden or cane field or fowl run, we surely can worship together and be understood by God the author and Creator of human and angelic tongues (when I say "we" I mean blacks and whites).
>
> Black Theology seeks to make Christianity relevant. The Bible ought to be made alive to the twentieth century Black people. . . . Black Theology ought to demonstrate that the kingdom of God is in our

midst, *now*. In other words Black Theology must have the word
of prophecy heard and understood by the twentieth century Black
man (Makhathini 1973:11).

All these attempts, in our view, aim to witness to Dr. J. H.
Oldham's declaration in 1924 in his work *Christianity and the
Race Problem:*

> Christianity is not primarily a philosophy but a cru-
> sade. As Christ was sent by the Father, so He sends
> His disciples to set up in the world the Kingdom of
> God. His mission is a declaration of war--a war to
> the death against the powers of darkness. He was
> manifested to destroy works of the devil. Hence when
> Christians find in the world a state of things that
> is not in accord with the truth which they have learned
> from Christ, their concern is not that it should be ex-
> plained but that it should be ended. In that temper we
> must approach everything in the relations between races
> that cannot be reconciled with the Christian ideal
> (Oldham 1974:2).

With this as our introduction, we must proceed to make a
systematic study of the countries in southern Africa where the
human condition calls for urgent study and for action against
the forces of oppression. Because of the different historical
developments in these countries since the coming of Christianity, we are pursuing human liberation as a common theme, lest
it become impossible to give a sensible treatment of the relation of the church to the political and religious systems
and social and economic structures of the people of southern
Africa.

We emphasize various aspects of human liberation in this
study; hence the absence of a sub-topical arrangement applied
generally in the study from country to country. Although this
is the case, we do discuss the different aspects of human liberation in the light of our own interpretations of Christology.

BOTSWANA

Our treatment of Botswana will be brief, mainly because the
state of the church there has not presented us with much of a
challenge. The reason may be that the church retains a strong
missionary character, and is, therefore, under much foreign
control.

The London Missionary Society pioneered the mission enterprise in Botswana during the early 19th century, around 1816.
Presently, the mission heritage of the LMS is represented in

the *Congregational Church Commission for World Mission*. The foreign control of this denomination is evidenced by the fact that it is one part of a union spreading over six to eight regions or synods or presbyteries (Setiloane 1974:1). This church joined the union in about 1968. It is united with church organizations whose missionary origin is either Congregational or of the former London Missionary Society. These organizations are: Congregational Union of South Africa (offspring of LMS), Bantu Congregation Church in Natal (offspring of the American Board of Commissioners for Foreign Mission or the United Church Mission), and with work of this same Church Mission in Zimbabwe. The union is now called the United Congregational Church of Southern Africa.

Does the Congregational Church Commission for World Mission have any connection with the Botswana government? Yes, through membership of top-ranking officials in the church; hence the relationship between this church and the government can be defined in these terms:

> It is very significant that the first Speaker of the Botswana Parliament after Independence in 1966 was, and was until three [now six] years ago, a CCWM missionary. So also was the first mayor of the capital town of Gaberone. . . .

> Congregationalism is the principal Church, almost understood as the State Church, of the whole area. . . . it is to this church that the most influential Batswana families, of chiefs and other noblemen, belong (Setiloane 1974:1).

Further, according to Setiloane, this church has also helped to shape the people's "concept of Christianity, and their general attitudes, mood and temperament as a people" (1974:1). This may mean, in our view, that, from a church point of view, the dictates of the United Congregational Church of Southern Africa, stationed and engineered in white dominated South Africa, also shape the members' "concept of Christianity, and their general attitudes, mood and temperament." How else could it be, since they decided to unite with that church—especially in 1968 when religious, cultural, and political consciousness was beginning to be on the upsurge in southern Africa?

Let us not be blamed, therefore, for judging that this church retains a strong missionary character and is under much foreign control. How do others judge this relationship between this church and a white dominated South African sanctioned and engineered body? One response:

This union, according to my judgment, has robbed the
Botswana Church of the autonomy which it needed so
vitally, as any other Church in Africa, at the time
of the attainment of political independence of the
country. Only in this way could it have helped to
give fibre to the quality of life and the struggle
for selfhood which inevitably follows such a situation of independence (Setiloane 1974:1).

The CCWM would give the impression that it is a lively force
influencing the church to witness to the people in their concrete post-colonial historical reality. This is not so, because there is nothing but harsh criticism for this church,
mainly because its incorporation into the white dominated
structures in South Africa makes it appear to be supping with
the devil, but, guardedly, with a long spoon. The demands on
the church to witness for Christ in southern Africa have become
very acute; therefore, there can be few sympathizers with those
who run the CCWM in Botswana when disappointed observers spit
in its face as follows:

> . . . one detects in the Botswana Region of UCCSA a
> lack of initiative and insight to see the need, and
> to concentrate on the special and unique problems
> of the Church in that political, social, and geo-
> graphic unit. . . . the other partners are much
> more vigorous in national (ethnic) personality, in
> numbers and church life, leaving swamped the timid,
> quiet, English-influenced Botswana ways of doing
> things. The result is that, I found, in 1971 a
> rather sad impression as to the witness of this
> section of the UCCSA to Botswana life and devel-
> opment, materially, spiritually and morally
> (Setiloane 1974:2).

It is understandable why the white South African dominated
structures must have such an effect of religious inertia on the
CCWM: the social, political, and theological/religious exigencies are weighing heavily on South Africa and Zimbabwe and
they are shaking the church out of its dodo dormancy. In these
parts of southern Africa, especially in South Africa, there is
a flux of constructively conceived theological development
which serves as the spur to the UCCSA in the Cape and in Natal.

There are the *Wesleyan Methodists*. They began work in
southern Botswana in 1823. The Methodists are also under
foreign control, from South Africa. They have not known it
any better; thus the disappointing word:

> Therefore Methodist work in Botswana has always
> been and still continues to be outpost work of the
> Methodist Church of South Africa, and its peculiar
> needs are secondary and diffused and lost in the
> needs of a huge church of more than one million.
> When I was there in 1971 the Botswana Methodists
> were agonised and feeling rather neglected
> (Setiloane 1974:2).

In fact, white dominated South African influence is manifested
concretely in the Methodist Church by racism, which rends the
church into two; "the Methodists still have a hangover inherited
from South Africa, of inability to worship across the races"
(ibid). This influence, it is maintained, is partly to blame
for attempts in the early 1960's to unite Christian witness in
the Gaborone area, at least.

There is further evidence that the Methodists are under
foreign control and domination:

> In the north of Botswana, Francistown etc., there
> has been a little overflow of Methodist work from
> Rhodesia which is still a "District" of the Methodist
> Conference of Great Britain and Ireland. So these
> few families still look to Bulawayo and Plum Tree
> (where the nearest Methodist minister in Rhodesia
> resides) for their pastoral care (Setiloane 1974:3).

The *United Methodist Church* (U.S.A.) entered Botswana in the
late sixties to begin mission work in the form of a secondary
boarding school. This project has turned out to be a dismal
failure.

There is even the *Dutch Reformed Church* of South Africa,
which came to Botswana around the 1890's. Their work has never
met with success because of friction between the Afrikaners
(whites governing South Africa) and the Botswana people. This
church has a hospital and schools, including a secondary school,
at Mochudi, where a white missionary is in charge. There seems
to be a lack of spiritual satisfaction among the Batswana
membership of this church, with the result that the African
Independent Church Movement from Johannesburg (South Africa)
is beginning to make its presence felt there. The DRC is confined to its own interests; it is said:

> The Mission here has continued the policy of non-
> cooperation with the work of the English Churches, as
> is practised by their mother body refusing to partic-
> ipate in the Christian Council of South Africa (now
> S. A. Council of Churches). Until very recently,

The Botswana Council of Churches was not existent
and questions of trans-Confessional cooperation
in Botswana were determined and decided in and by
the then Christian Council of South Africa
(Setiloane 1974:3).

The *Anglican Church* is not very visible in Botswana. They
are a good example of how mission enterprise subsisted in the
colonial adventure. When Botswana became a British Protec-
torate, the Anglicans also came, to provide for the pastoral
concerns of the British servicemen and other British officials.
But ecclesiastical control came from Bulawayo, Zimbabwe, where
the Bishop of Matebeleland had his seat. These British servicemen and their officials fell under that diocese.

The Anglicans had so much to spare--because they had so
little engagement in Botswana--that they served ecumenically
with the Methodists and Congregationalists in the Trinity
Church in Gaborone in the 1950's.

It is reported that they have no schools, hospitals or any
traditional missionary forms of evangelistic ventures in
Botswana. They do, however, have a white bishop in Botswana
because of the UDI situation in Zimbabwe.

The *Lutherans* have lately become more prominent in Botswana,
especially along the border with South Africa. It is said that
the extension of their work there is a measure of convenience:
they find it somewhat difficult to do work inside South Africa.
This is probably because the Lutheran Church in South Africa is
fast coming under African control, and because the younger
German missionaries, in many cases, express their opposition
to the racist Apartheid system in South Africa openly.

They have improved their educational and medical work lately
with support from the Lutheran World Federation. Their exec-
utives are also said to be planning their work for Namibia from
Botswana rather than from South Africa. How is their work
judged? We are told:

Although they have a very small area to work the
Lutherans appear to have made a pretty good physical
work of it. In the usual manner of Luther's theology
of the two realms they have not done much for the
moral uplift of the people, however (Setiloane 1974:4).

The *Roman Catholic Church* has a recent history in Botswana,
but it is the fastest growing community. They began 25 years
ago, and yet they are fully established, with their usual organs such as schools and a cathedral in Gaborone. This Church's
foreign element is embodied in the presence of an Irish bishop.

The Roman Catholic Church cooperates with other churches in an appreciable extent. Otherwise

> . . . like other older missions in Southern Africa they have used a dog in the manger attitude to other Protestant missions refusing to come in to help them, appealing to outdated Comity arrangements and often using doubtfully ethical means of influencing the authorities to shut would-be competitors out (Setiloane 1974:4).

When all is said and done, the doors for the penetration of other denominations into Botswana have been opened wide lately. Some speculate that it is because, as a country, Botswana is embarrassed by its strong church ties with white dominated South Africa, as evidenced by the UCCSA.

The Botswana Theological Training Programme seems to be about the only aspect of the church that is typically its own. It is a seven-year program, which aims to serve the whole country. What is this program?

> When, in 1973, it was learned that students from Botswana churches would no longer be admitted to Rhodesia for theological training, people were very worried. Since 1967 no Batswana had been admitted to South Africa by that country's government. In many churches the need for trained ministers had become critical and there was no other place to turn without enormous expense (Sales & Mbali 1975:3).

The history of the idea to have this program is summarized, and its purpose is to

> . . . combine, in the weekly meetings, good theological studies with searching investigations of their own [i.e., the students'] fields of secular employment. We have seen, in effect, lay academies being born as we meet with the highly motivated students (Sales & Mbali 1974:3).

There is an attempt to emphasize what may be called "applied ministry," for the students are urged to take seriously the stated purpose of the program:

> In this way, a layman wishing to specialise in a field of his or her own choice, could after the first year, elect the teaching ministry or the preaching ministry for specialisation, while a

person who plans to study for ordination will, as
things are planned, gain skills in each of the
skills we have isolated (Sales & Mbali 1975:3).

Furthermore,

The BTTP does not claim to prepare people for
denominational ministries, but rather for the
Christian ministry. From the beginning we have
stressed to the churches of Botswana that we
will train people from any denomination but that
every denomination must plan to teach its own
specific denominational information to its candidates. With that in mind we have opened the
door in every way possible to persons from both
"older" and "independent" African churches
(Sales & Mbali 1975:3).

There are other advantages offered by this program. Lay
workers in churches enroll in it, so that they may discharge
their duties more effectively in the parishes. Two other
significant advantages are being summarized as follows:

(a) [to overcome the idea that] Theological
Education for Ordination was for people who
were intending to work as "full time" ministers.
And at that stage of understanding, it was generally inconceivable to even consider "theological education" on its own terms; that is,
as something valid and necessary for the people
of God as such. In other words, what the two
points mentioned here in the introductory
section are saying, is that there has been a
time in this part of the world when, by and
large, theological education used to be understood as catering for a particular and rather
fixed type of ministry.

(b) As a result of the insights of the TEE
method, theological education in this part of
the world has become "available". By this we
mean to indicate that theological education is
no longer the prerogative or preserve of "or-
dinands" to this or that ministry. Now it is
open to interested laypeople, and to those who
want to exercise special ministries (Sales &
Mbali 1975:6).

Maybe a discussion on the state of the church in Botswana
should be based on an analysis of the implications of the
following:

On the whole Tswana Church life and Christianity
impressed me as listless, uninspired and unin-
spiring, and calling for very unfavourable comment
from neighbouring Christian workers e.g. South
Africa and Lesotho, with whom they are bound in
common projects like the University of Botswana,
Lesotho and Swaziland (Setiloane 1974:2).

LESOTHO

The Paris Evangelical Mission Society began the mission
enterprise in Lesotho in 1833. This mission effort later on
resulted in the establishment of the Church of Basutoland. The
aim was to make this church the national church of Lesotho.
However, it is reported that 39% of the about one million inhabitants are Roman Catholic. This is the highest percentage
church membership of any single denomination in Lesotho. It
is also being reported that the majority, if not all, members
of the National Party are Roman Catholic (Vos 1976:2).

Presently, the major church denominations are Lesotho
Evangelical, Anglican, and Catholic. Other denominations form
8% of the 82% nationally declared Christians. It was reported,
though, that: "Competition among religious groups, however,
has created tensions among Christians like those today in
Northern Ireland" (AACC 1970:33). This is a reference to the
continuing tension between the ruling Basutoland National Party
and the Basutoland Congress Party which are Roman Catholic and
Protestant, respectively (Vos 1976:2).

The policy of the Paris Evangelical Mission Society was to
develop in such a way that the Africans would undertake responsibility. This policy, however, resulted in a paternalistic relationship between the missionaries and the African
ministers because of the hierarchical structure on which the
Society was organized. There was an Assembly (called *Seboka*)
at the top, composed of sixteen missionaries and nine African
ministers; this was followed by a Conference of white missionaries, below which were a synod and consistories, successively
(SANRC 1908:217). We shall not go into the responsibilities
of each of these bodies, except to illustrate why we maintain
that paternalism was maintained in relations between the white
missionaries and the African ministers. Although the *Seboka*
was at the top of the hierarchy, it did not deal with administration of funds from overseas, and secondary and industrial
education because it contained African representation. These
matters were the responsibility of the Conference of European
Missionaries.

This paternalistic attitude of the missionaries toward the
African ministers was a common factor in the whole of southern
Africa. It has resulted in some of the intolerable relationships existing presently, especially as voiced by black pastors
in South Africa. But a close study of the countries of
southern Africa will bear out this relationship, even though
it takes varying forms. In terms of how it compared with black
and white relations in everyday life, the technique of white
domination by guardianship gives an accurate explanation. Nobody could have put it any better, in terms of church circles,
than M. Jacottet, when he wrote:

> It is said every day in South African and English
> newspapers . . . that they [i.e. the South African
> natives] are children and ought to be treated as
> children. Whilst this opinion may be true as far
> as the bulk of the heathen population is concerned--
> and even then not without qualifications--it is no
> more true of the large part of the Christianised
> population. They have advanced very quickly and
> in a remarkable way during the last ten or twenty
> years, and a large number of them have already
> given proofs of high qualifications which give
> them the right to be considered as being no more
> children, but grown-up men, able to hold their
> own in the world, and who should be treated as
> such (SANRC 1908:18).

The "unsavory" effects of this type of relationship are manifested when one examines it (in terms of white *versus* black)
in the context of the colonist and the African people:

> The Colonist himself often describes this relation-
> ship as one of guardian and ward. However incom-
> plete this conception may be, we do not doubt the
> sincerity of those who adopt it. In the work of
> the Commissions on Native Affairs we have a de-
> tailed scrutiny of the extent to which the duties
> of guardianship and trust are performed. Can it
> be said that the guardians or trustees have seen
> to the education of those for whom they act? Have
> they avoided squandering or wasting the estate of
> their ward? In the account which they render of
> their stewardship, do they show that they have
> acted for the best for their ward, and have not
> exploited him for their own purposes? These tests
> could hardly be satisfied by the policy of the
> past. Will the policy of the future conform to
> them? (SANRC 1908:233).

Whatever favorable relationship between the missionaries and the African ministers might have developed, it does not seem that the natural human factor stimulated it. There was great fear on the part of the missionaries that secessions similar to those which were occurring in South Africa would also happen in Lesotho. This history of the secessions forms a chapter unto itself in missionary and African relations ever since the colonial and missionary presence in southern Africa. Such secessions did not occur in Lesotho. The fact that the policy of guardianship combatted this process is secondary to the fact that the missionaries did not trust the African ministers. This distrust is clear from M. Jacottet's account of how the secession movement (or Ethiopianism) was forestalled in Lesotho:

> After having felt our way for a certain time with our first native ministers, not knowing exactly what special rights we should give them, we decided in 1898 to trust them entirely, and to take them into our councils on terms of equality with ourselves. . . . Our decision, which may have--in fact, has--seemed rash to some of our best friends, has proved itself to have been, not only liberal, but very wise, and even those of our number who would have criticised it at the time, are quite content with it now. . . . It is very likely this that has prevented Ethiopianism from making any headway in Basutoland, and from harming in any way our churches. We have had no secessions to speak of; all our staff, all our congregations have never wavered for a minute in their allegiance to our church (SANRC 1908:218-19).

Had the political history of Lesotho not developed the way it did, God knows what the destiny of those one million Basotho inhabitants would have been! The Voortrekker Boers might have taken them in captivity after establishing their Orange River Boer Republic. The missionaries saved the situation, and their deed is recorded in history:

> If Basutoland is today an independent and self-governing country, that is largely due to the labours of the great French and Swiss missionaries, who held the Boers at a distance, and kept alive the soul of a people under the shelter of a British protectorate which genuinely gave protection (Neill 1966:414).

It is, therefore, strange that they later on evolved this policy of guardianship with their fellow Basotho ministers.

Since this is not the occasion for us to survey the church history of Lesotho in its totality, the above account should suffice as introduction to the church in Lesotho. Let us now turn to current preoccupations of the church in Lesotho.

First of all, how is the church presently organized in Lesotho? Different denominations (of which we enumerated the major ones earlier) are affiliated with the Christian Council, which was formed in 1965. In relation to the government, this Council is apparently neutral. But church-government relationships exist in terms of government relationships with Protestant and Roman Catholic denominations. The Roman Catholic Church is portrayed as giving outright support to the present ruling Basutoland National Party, which is opposed by the suppressed Basutoland Congress Party. The strength of Protestant support for the BCP is embodied in the attitudes of the Evangelical Church to the existing political régime (Baëta 1975:4).

Apart from the political tension between the government and the Protestant church and the political alliance of the government with the Roman Catholic Church, there is also cooperation between the government and the Roman Catholic and the Protestant churches together. In 1966 the government requested the churches in Lesotho to launch a joint drought relief campaign, and in 1969 the churches held a conference at Roma University to study the problem of unemployment (AACC 1970:33). An ecumenical hostel for girls working in town has been built in Maseru. At the Southern Africa Urban Consultation of the AACC, it was reported that a post-primary school was planned for school leavers, where they could learn skills in carpentry, agriculture, and domestic science, but that: "The above mentioned post-primary school will be used also both as a Christian training centre, and as a place for 'Christian tourism' where tourists from South Africa could camp and meet with Christians from Lesotho" (ibid:34).

Lesotho lies heavily in the shadow of the white dominated government of South Africa. This is an important consideration to remember, in order to understand the significance of the existing political situation in Lesotho, which is the next matter we are embarking on. There have been the two political parties already mentioned existing in Lesotho since it became independent from Britain in 1965. In 1970 general elections were announced. It is reported that:

. . . things took a sharp turn for the worse when the Government, upon being apparently defeated at the polls in 1970, decided to cling to power and embarked upon a rule by force, backed by the police and para-military forces (Baëta 1975:2).

In light of the statement we made earlier on Lesotho's relation
to white dominated South Africa, the post-1970 events have created a very grave situation, such that some reporters say that
the present régime receives repressive dictates directly from
the government in South Africa, especially since it employs
similar methods of repression as those imposed and exercised
in South Africa (*vide* Vos 1976:2). Others call a spade a spade:

> There lies the responsibility for the near-erasure of
> civil liberties, aided by a vicious Internal Security
> Act, that has turned the police and their proteges
> loose like wild dogs (Baëta 1975:3).

> . . . by far the source of greatest resentment and
> ill-will is the existence and activities of the so-
> called *Lebotho la Khotso* or "Peace Corps". It is
> generally agreed that they are directly responsible
> for creating in the country almost intolerable con-
> ditions of unnecessary violence, persecution,
> extortion. . . . they exercise powers going even
> beyond those of the police in arresting and searching
> without warrant, beating up and detaining without
> further ado (Baëta 1975:7).

Baëta had been delegated by the All Africa Conference of
Churches to investigate the situation in Lesotho; however, what
he reports above is confirmed by A. Vos on behalf of the Reformed Church Synod in The Netherlands (1976:2). He was in
Lesotho in August 1976. *One World* magazine also bears testimony
to C. C. Baëta's report (1976). Baëta describes the concern of
the AACC in the Lesotho situation in a note on his terms of
reference when he was delegated. He says:

> In December 1974 I accepted an invitation from Canon
> Burgess Carr, the General Secretary of the All Africa
> Conference of Churches to go to Lesotho for a fort-
> night on behalf of this Council and see what I could
> do to "assist [the Christian Council there] in their
> search for unity and reconciliation" (Baëta 1975:1).

That leads to the next question: How did the Christian
Council in Lesotho become involved in a situation which seems
to be the doings of the Basutoland National Party and the
Basutoland Congress Party, both of which claim to represent
the people of Lesotho? This is *the* leading question because
the part of the churches in the situation is what has made it
so acute a matter worthy of our consideration. The answer to
the question is that the Roman Catholics and the Protestants
largely supported these two political parties, respectively.
Now that the opposition of the parties to each other has

resulted in the present situation of grave human suffering, the
people of Lesotho, generally, are calling on the Christian
Council to do something, since both denominations are members
of the Christian Council. But the Roman Catholic Church, as
alleged supporter of the Basutoland Nationalist Party, now
repressing the people, makes discussion of this matter impossible at Christian Council meetings. Consequently, an outside
mediator has been sought for. The people have suggested that
the Botswana government be invited as a mediator if the Christian Council is not bold enough to present to the Lesotho government the people's conditions of suffering at the hands of
Lebotho la Khotso ("Peace Corps") brutality. They have also
suggested that the Organization for African Unity, or the
United Nations if absolutely necessary, be invited to provide
a peace-keeping force, so that a supervisory government can be
formed under the leadership of King Moshoeshoe II.

The Lesotho situation demonstrates that when churches become
involved in political party politics (not policies as such) they
can become trapped in their own institutional reality of failing
to represent the people, as well as that of the political
parties. This leads the church to lose sight of its theological
task, which is, in our view, to be involved in socio-political
matters with a critical responsibility, and not as partners in
evil contracts. Such critical responsibility is inescapable
because the church is the community of God's people; therefore,
it must be present where God's people are because God is always
present where his people are--and the church is not present
where God is not present.

The task of the church in Lesotho will be to reconcile the
Basotho people, who interpret the political party strife as a
strife between Catholics and Protestants. This Catholic-
Protestant confrontation is what is so fearful to the people.
Reconciliation has become a factor because it is generally
feared that the Basutoland National Party is afraid of retaliation from the Protestant supported Basutoland Congress Party
should an election be called and the BNP loses.

However, the Basotho people are calling on the church to
bring about reconciliation, also, because it is church members
who are involved in each side of the party lines. The voices
for reconciliation come in different tones, says Baëta:

Because of these alleged alignments, many of those
who spoke to me laid the blame for the deep divisions
that had come about among the people, principally at
the door of the Churches. "The bitter feuds between
Catholics and Protestants in France and Canada were
transferred to our country, and we were roped in to

carry these fights", said one. Another commented:
"The Churches' frequent protestations of, and ex-
hortations to, reconciliation, come to us under a
heavy cloud of suspicion. Why don't the would-be
physicians first heal themselves? . . ." (Baëta
1975:4).

In its report about a student who had actually been tortured and
wrote a letter to his friends bearing on reconciliation, *One
World* magazine reports:

In a letter to his friends, the student wrote
"Jesus Christ was ruthlessly crucified at Calvary
for sinners. He had not done anything wrong . . .
now we are faced with the final examinations here
at school, but our minds are also troubled because
of a political situation. You may not feel what I
mean because you are like the spectators at a foot-
ball match who do not feel the toughness of the game
on the ground. . . . My dear friends, there are
only four things of fundamental importance to fight
for in this world. These are TRUTH, JUSTICE, PEACE
AND LOVE" (*One World* 1976:19).

ANGOLA

The historical developments in Angola and Mozambique regarding the relationship between the churches and the Portuguese
colonial power are very similar. In Angola as in Mozambique,
the Protestant churches were persecuted, forbidden, and re-
stricted by colonial authorities. The Roman Catholic Church
was in a privileged position under colonial rule because the
1940 Concordat between the Vatican and Portugal protected the
Catholic Church from colonial repression.

What the churches suffered as organizations does not compare
in any way with what the Angolan people suffered, as a society
and as individuals. Perhaps the account of Jose B. Chipenda
gives a better impression of the magnitude of that suffering
when he says:

It was seen, meanwhile, that this colonial situation
was not directed only against the Evangelical Mission
but against the people in their totality. The state
of things created against the total development of
the people reached such a saturation point that it
originated the explosion of the liberation movement
in Angola. But, it is important to point out that
these liberation movements are composed of elements
from the United Methodist Church in Angola, from

some other evangelical denominations and also from
the Roman Catholic Church herself (1975:2).

The liberation movements give us a direct link between the
Angolan suffering and the Mozambican struggle against the
colonial system. In Mozambique, President Samora Machel argued
that the churches were controlled from overseas and that that
limited their involvement in and commitment to the resistance
against Portuguese colonial oppression. Might this not have
been the same in the case of Angola? After serious reflection
upon the question, "What can the church do?" or the observation
that the churches were silent in southern Africa, one sobers to
the realization that the church cannot, nor could it earlier,
fulfill any of the yearnings of the people because it retained
a foreign character in the whole matrix of the African experience with colonialism and with the church itself. This awareness thus reveals another stark reality, namely, that the church
in southern Africa has been too western; therefore, when the
inhuman structures of oppression are replaced a new concept of
the church will by necessity have been created. But whether
the church will, as such, become a thing of the past like these
inhuman structures is a debatable question. In our view, the
church is presently an established cultural institution in the
African reality. Therefore, its replacement is a matter to be
considered in relation to the reality of the African religious
consciousness.

No doubt, the church as a social reality may be transformed
thoroughly. This is the light in which we must pose and discuss
the place of the church in southern Africa. We must endeavor
to fathom the similarity between the church there with the prevailing social reality which is a consequence of the political
and economic structures which have been imposed upon the people
and are being enforced with great disregard for human life.

Once human life begins to center as the hub of a people's
concerns, then they become eager to interpret and understand
what it is all about to have a church. This is how we would
like to characterize the situation in southern Africa presently.
The people seem to have gone beyond judging the form in which
the church exists; they are now concerned with its essence.
Once in this frame of mind, we must be able to grasp with
humility the liberating force and essence of what Chipenda
expresses when he affirms:

It was with great joy that the United Methodist
Church in Angola received the news of the fall of
the former regime which occurred on April 25,
1974. . . . This Church given its relevant mission
of the establishment of the Kingdom of God among all

people by the preaching of the Gospel founded on
peace and on the fraternal communion between
peoples of all ethnic groups must not be silent
in the face of the events of vital importance
which are involved the Angolan society of which
we are a part.   Therefore, we rejoice in the
freedom of the political prisoners and their
return to their homes (1975:4).

Here we find a human predicament and imagery of liberation
similar to that captured in Isaiah 58:6-7 and Luke 4:18.   This
imagery introduces a theophanic and epiphanic presence which
contrasts remarkably with the Pauline view on mission, for that
presence is not possible within the context of the "old order,"
where baptism is the symbol of liberation, but is possible
within the context of the "new humanity" or "new order."

So, here again, whether or not we like it, in order to
participate in the theophanic and epiphanic presence, we must
be drawn into the christological theological hermeneutical
exercise.   That exercise is the prerequisite to claiming that
the mission of the church is conceived on Jesus' concept of
mission and not on the Pauline view: the neighbor and the
community gain pre-eminence in Jesus' concept of mission.   In
the Pauline view of mission, we contend, importance is laid on
individual salvation through baptism.   The difference between
Mozambique and Angola, however, is that in Mozambique the
churches seemed ambivalent about initiating a relationship
with the forces of liberation which would replace the colonial
rule, while in one definite case in Angola we find just the
opposite.   This is the case of the United Methodist Church.
Chipenda made several affirmations concerning the United
Methodist Church in Angola and the Liberation Movements on his
return visit to Angola on 24 February 1975.   Three of these
affirmations are relevant, for they suggest that the church
appropriates for itself the task of carrying out a theological
hermeneutical exercise:

Without belonging to any political party or movement
or trying to inhibit the liberty of its sons and
daughters who may wish to do so, the Church affirms
the following:

1.   Recognize the valuable action developed by the
     liberation movements;
2.   Gives its unconditional support to the total
     and complete independence of Angola . . .
3.   Repudiates racism and any other form of di-
     vision (Chipenda 1975:4).

It seems that in Angola there was no need--and there may be
no need even presently--for the existing government to issue
categorical statements on the relationship between church and
state.   This was largely because the church had identified itself and asserted itself as a legitimate participant in the
Angolan people's affairs, after liberation.   Consequently, we
find that when the World Council of Churches sends a delegation
to Angola the terms of reference are not to go and determine the
status of the Church.   Instead, the terms of reference are to
the point, for the WCC clearly seems to regard the government
and the churches to be on equal footing.   These were the terms
of reference of that delegation:

1.   To establish or pursue contact with the churches
     in Angola to discover how they contribute to
     national reconstruction and to tackle new oppor-
     tunities for service to the people of Angola;

2.   To learn from government authorities what plans
     are being made and implemented for the socio-
     economic transformation of the country; and

3.   To explain to the churches and government au-
     thorities the activities and concerns of the
     WCC (1976b:1).

Another difference between Mozambique and Angola is that in
the former the voice of the church is expressed in a unitary
body, the Christian Council of Mozambique, while in the latter
different denominations seem to continue to retain autonomy
(the Angola Evangelical Alliance had been uniting the Protestant
churches in a lose association from 1922-1974).   Therefore, in
our consideration of the state of the church in Angola we must
examine some of these denominations' commitment to the theological hermeneutical responsibility of the church, which is
necessary for creating a new christological foundation for the
church.   That new christological foundation must be taken as a
formulation of a new concept of the church.

We must also point out a similarity, in another respect,
between Mozambique and Angola, bearing on the place of the
church as an institution, or on the church as a social reality.
That similarity is embedded in what the WCC delegation reports
here:

Free, universal education will be a responsibility of
the State, The Churches have begun to seek registration
of their schools and teachers with the Ministry of
Education, and already the government has taken responsibility for paying teachers.

The Ministry of Education is reorganizing all
schools, beginning with the primary schools. The
demand for education is so great that the existing facilities are unable to absorb the school
population. In some areas buildings need to be
reconstructed and restaffed (1976b:4).

In addition, it would appear that the government in Angola and
the churches will work together in the bureaucratic structures
of the mission of evangelization, for the WCC delegation notes
that:

The government authorities have established various
schemes to reorganize activities in the field of
health, education, etc., as well as an inter-
ministerial commission to coordinate the programmes
directed toward the resettlement of the victims of
the wars, both displaced populations within Angola
and returning refugees from neighbouring countries.
This commission is located in the Secretariat of
State for Social Affairs, which is directly related
to the Prime Minister (1976b:4).

We now examine what appear to be the commitments of two denominations in terms of their relation to: (a) government
initiatives in education, (b) the mission of the church, (c)
their participation in the theological hermeneutical exercise,
which aims to illuminate the christological implications of a
new concept of the church, through the possibility of a theophanic and epiphanic presence emanating from liberation.

The *Methodist Church*: It is reported to be "optimistic"
about the future of the nation and the church. However, this
church seems to acknowledge that in the welfare of the people,
it has a common concern with the government. But it has not
yet made a theological synthesis of what participation in that
common concern represents in the light of its mission as a
church. It may be concluded, therefore, that, at the time of
the WCC delegation visit to Angola, this denomination had no
clearly expressed form of participation in the theological
hermeneutical exercise which aims to illuminate the christological implication of a new concept of the church.

Such a new concept of the church is inevitable if it is
recognized that, in its nature as a social reality, the church
demands indisputable commitment to the concrete social context
of the people's experience of life. This is the reality to
which any concept of the church must conform as an outcome of
the theological hermeneutical exercise. For if the colonial
system was considered oppressive, and thus militated against

the task of the church, then a condition of liberation must lead
to a church with a new task, one which is consistent with the
new form of the church and the society. That task must differ
from what existed under colonial rule because the human condition reflects a new social reality and the religious reality
of the liberated has its essence in the continuously self-
liberating creative community which must demonstrate its grasp
of a theophanic and epiphanic presence in the experience of
life. That presence represents the christological reality and
context of the church in that community. It is not sufficient
for the Methodist Church, as is said, to contend that: "They
are confident that the present government policy of helping
oppressed people is consistent with the goals of the Church"
(WCC 1976b:6). Such contentment suggests that the church has a
mirage-like view of the inextricability of its task from its
christological reality. Such a view does not represent a perception of the centrality of christology in the form of the
church. This form can only have its impact felt through the
theological hermeneutical exercise. In the case of the Angolan
context, the church will recognize affirmingly, that liberation
from colonial oppression is a christological form which can
only be explained in the language of prophetic eschatology.
This christological form has become possible because of the
theophanic and epiphanic presence experienced by the liberated
community. Hence, it will be accepted that the church can only
exist in its true nature--in the community--if it bears the
revolutionary character of liberation. If the dynamics of participation in the concrete praxis is still obscure it is,
therefore, theologically unsound for the Methodist Church to
contend only:

> The Church will have to seek its own role as the gov-
> ernment assumes responsibility for programmes for
> which the Church in the past felt a special concern,
> such as education, health and literacy (WCC 1976b).

If we take the WCC delegation report as the only authoritative source, then we must comment as follows on *The Evangelical Church of Northern Angola* (IENA). First, this church
continues to exist as a foreign injection in the "new order"
in Angola, since it retains the Anglical liturgy, using the
Book of Common Prayer. The liturgy is the common expression
of a community, and of its interpretation of the relation between its experience of the social reality and the religious
reality of the nature of the church. That interpretation always
seems to be consistent with the history of the community.
Within the context of liberation, that interpretation, in fact,
constitutes the boundaries within which the history of the
community becomes meaningful in the light of the demands of
prophetic eschatology.

It may, therefore, be concluded that this church has not begun its task in the theological hermeneutical exercise. To this church, liberation does not seem to have become a reality to be fathomed as a process of revelation, hinging on the centrality of the christological imperative in the mission of the church.

The following churches also exist in Angola, but we examined the above two just as an illustration of the extent to which the churches there still seem to lag behind in their critical involvement in the "new order": Baptist churches, The Council of Evangelical Churches of Central Angola, Churches in Cabinda, The Kimbanguist Church in Angola, The Evangelical Church of Southwest Angola, Plymouth Brethren, Africa Evangelical Fellowship, Assemblies of God, Seventh-Day Adventists, The Tocoist Movement, and The Roman Catholic Church.

It may be difficult for the churches in Angola to participate effectively in the "new order" as long as they are so independent of one another. This lack of unity may also prove a danger to the cohesiveness of the government and its effective impact on the welfare of the population.

MOZAMBIQUE

In Mozambique the church exists almost like any other institution which concerns itself with the social, economic and political betterment of the people of Mozambique. This is the church as social reality. The church also exists like any other institution which affirms that the independence of Mozambique must mean a radical change from the state of affairs which existed during Portuguese colonialism in Mozambique. This form of existence is that of the church as religious reality. Therefore, the church no longer exists as a separate and privileged organization or institution which was more of a social and cultural menace and hindrance to the human historical experience of the people of Mozambique than a fact of religious significance.

Immediately at the advent of independence, the subject of the place of the church became a thorough preoccupation. This was important because the church had been isolated from the Mozambican masses during the colonial era; and when the Protestant churches attempted to protest and bring the church to identify with the strife of the masses for independence, the Protestant churches and their leadership were persecuted. In this development, the Roman Catholic Church pledged support to the manner in which the colonial system treated the Mozambican masses. Hence the Concordat which was signed by the Vatican and Portugal in 1940 must be seen as the source that unleashed the

new forces of attack and counter-attack between the liberation
Mozambican government and some church people inside and outside
Mozambique after Independence Day, June 25, 1975.

When viewed from the angle of western or Latin theology, a
discussion of the church in Mozambique might be dismissed as a
subject of heresy. The discussion would be heretical, first,
because the institutional organization of the church has an un-
usual relationship with the "temporal powers." Therefore, it
could not be accepted as a church. Second, because there is a
suggestion that salvation is not possible outside the traditional framework of the church organization. But when viewed
from the angle of the mission of Jesus of Nazareth, a discussion
of the church in Mozambique is a subject of christological
significance.

The Lutheran theological dichotomy of the realm of the two
kingdoms is nullified in present-day Mozambique, and the church
institution is no longer a symbol of God's presence with humanity, justified only by faith. Rather, the church is the
manifestation of God's actual presence with humanity, expressed
in the concrete reality of neighborliness. Here we have a
contrast between a stilted or fossilized conception of revelation and a concept of a continuing forthcoming reality of
revelation. This is the cutting edge of the difference between
the heretical suggestion and the christological significance
that an unprejudiced discussion of the church in present-day
Mozambique reveals.

The contention that God's people are perpetual sinners of
whom no good can come inspires the judgment that within church
circles dismisses the church in Mozambique as a matter of
heresy. However, seen in the christological sense, God's
people are central, with the imperative that we must first
recognize them as *ecclesia* and *laos* before we claim, for example, faith as a basis for justification. This perception
is very different from the heretic condemnation which con-
ceives of God in exclusively abstract terms which correspond
only to abstract and subjective definitions of our own being,
for example, terms such as *faith*. Therefore, we are no longer
justified before God exclusively by faith, but also by the fact
that we are living actively with God, as God's creation takes
shapes and forms in his people--our neighbor. Here, the "old
order" is juxtaposed with the "new order."

It is to the ends of the christological affirmation that we
find statements about the church in Mozambique preoccupied with
attempts to distinguish between the "old order" or the colonial
era and the "new order" or the liberated Mozambique. Let us
examine some of the dynamics of this contrast and detect what
the nature of the resultant christological tension is.

In his inaugural speech on June 25, 1975 President Samora
Machel touches on the elements which constituted the framework
of the "old order," and appropriately draws on its relation to
religion or Christianity in his final forsaking of it. He says:

> One must look back to the situation which prevailed
> earlier, that of colonial domination. Why did co-
> lonialism kill people? Why did it imprison? Why did
> it deport, why did it massacre? Why were our tra-
> ditions humiliated, why were our women violated, our
> civilisation denied? Mozambicans were imprisoned for
> the merest manifestation of patriotism (Machel 1975).

There remain two striking images from the human experience in
the colonial system, namely, death and imprisonment. Why did
the word of liberation and salvation not unshackle the chains
of imprisonment? Why was there no salvation from death--not
natural death, but arbitrary death? If the formation of
FRELIMO was inspired by a commitment to take the place of the
imprisoned and the dying, does the usefulness of the church at
that time not become questionable? The church had no inspiration because its fundamental theological commitment was *faith*
oriented and not *action* or *creation* oriented. The church seems
to have put Jesus' mission in abeyance as an accomplished
mission. It lacked any prophetic eschatological vision; or,
if it had one, it lacked the courage to confront the evil
structures. The church was caught in the Lutheran theological
dichotomy of the kingdom of the two realms. The Pauline faith
oriented mission of the church was a dynamic force here,
regulating repeated new realizations of the communal dynamics
of the church. The church was not involved in God's creative
act, in which his promise that he is "making all things new"
becomes fulfilled. No, it was involved with exclusively abstract dimensions such as the soul and with evangelism whose
fulfillment rested in baptism. Thus it was possible in the
presence of the church that

> Our labour force was exploited, with millions of
> Mozambicans transformed into slaves and taken to
> other continents, where they were sold as mere
> chattels . . . and the populations were forced to
> flee, dying of hunger while the companies that
> had been granted the concessions were accumulating
> enormous profits (Machel 1975).

President Machel proceeds--whether or not he knows it--to
indicate the relation between justification and creation:

> Religion, and in particular the Catholic Church,
> contributed powerfully to this. It contributed

greatly to the cultural and human alienation of the
Mozambican, so as to make of him a subjected instrument and an object of exploitation and thereby
break any manifestation of resistance (ibid).

What President Machel says here points .to the paradox in Christian mission when it is examined in the light of God's creation.
God seems to have been present with all his people or creation
throughout history (by "his people," I do not mean the Jews).
In this history, they encountered experiences of the theophanic
and epiphanic presence of their creator, liberator and provider.
Yet, when the mission of the Christian churches came, instead of
identifying with this presence of God, it plundered and de-
nounced and shut certain human races out of God's act of
creation. For are not our religious perceptions, expressed in
our cultures, sufficient reason for claiming a degree of consciousness of God? The mission of the churches saw heathenism
in the African's culture, and set out in an iconoclastic ram-
page against all images which Africans held about God--concrete
as well as spiritual or cultural.

The christological tension resides here, in the question of
the universality of the saving act of Jesus of Nazareth. We
know that he performed concrete acts in his mission amongst his
followers. But that was a historical happening which cannot
be re-enacted in our concrete historical situations. Therefore,
the christological relevance of Jesus as Savior and liberator
lies in affirmations of anthropocentric significance. This
wider context in which God and the mission of Jesus are placed
transforms the structures of the church as a symbol of Christian
salvation and liberation. This is the significance of the prevailing strife for liberation from colonial oppression in
southern Africa, with or without the cooperation of the church
as an institution.

But the effort to break from the "old order" and usher in
the "new order," in which human beings are affirmed as partners
in God's continuing act of creation, caused great concern in
Mozambique. For example, in a Special Report to the South
African Council of Churches, Rev. Ted Smith (superintendent of
Methodist missionary work in Mozambique) says:

Most of the enquiry that has come to us about the
Church in Mozambique has been born out of deep concern for the survival of the Church, and also out
of a deep fear that the Church would not be able
to withstand the pressures that are being placed
upon it. And so, instead of saying this at the
end of what may be to you a rather dismal picture,
I want to say it now. We affirm that the Church,

the living organ and instrument of God, will not
die, and it cannot die, but the Church as an institution, the Church as an organization, will
undergo radical change if in fact, it is not
entirely dismantled (Smith 1975:1).

Here, Mr. Smith seems to recognize the distinction between the
church as a social reality and the church as a religious reality. The impact that the change of government has had on the
church in Mozambique, in our view, is that of transforming the
church, so that its nature as a social reality can enhance it
also as a religious reality. This is done by creating a wider
christological context for liberation and salvation. The
people as a whole form that context, insofar as they are recognized as God's people. Therefore, there is a shift from the
abstract *faith* basis of justification to the concrete *creation*
basis, where neighborliness is the premise of Being. That justification is concretized in the history of the new relationship with God as an *oikoumene, ecclesia* or *laos,* and not a
privileged lot who are isolated from the rest of God's creation.
The transformed state in which the church comes to exist is no
longer that in which the church identifies with forces of oppression, but that in which the church becomes creatively
involved in identifying with the everyday human reality of all
God's people. Of necessity, this must mean that even the
liturgical community of the church takes on a new context.
(Is this an African conception of the church, where the church
is the people and their history?) This new orientation to the
church also demonstrates that the church as a social reality
must remain open to change--it must be revolutionary--and that
the dynamics for the momentum of that change is provided by
balancing the orientation to the church as a social reality
with the church as a religious reality. The religious reality
is manifested in the people's perception of God's presence in
their history of liberation, as a community of *ecclesia,
oikoumene* or *laos*--and not an isolated and privileged community.
Consequently, it is notable that in his attempt to explain the
new situation and the task of the church in Mozambique, the
Rev. Ted Smith contrasts *obedience* and *faith*, which is a contrast of action and subjectivity; he says:

But we know also, that that dismantling will not
destroy the Spirit of Christ, who will still move
and work in the lives of those who respond to him,
and give to him their total allegiance. The Church
of Christ will continue to exist, but the form in
which it will exist will be determined by our obedience to what the Holy Spirit is saying to us in
a new situation (Smith 1975).

The Roman Catholic Church had signed a Concordat with the
Portuguese colonial authorities in 1940. This event took place
when some church people were beginning to assert themselves
against colonial injustice. What did that Concordat provide?

> the Missionary Concordat, signed between Vatican and
> Portugal gave the Roman Catholic Church a free hand
> in establishing and expanding its work, and at the
> same time deliberately impeding the work of the Prot-
> estant Churches. We know now of course, that this
> unhappy marriage between Church and State, has now
> left the Roman Catholic Church in Mozambique a
> rather destitute widow (Smith 1975).

The unfavorable position of the Roman Catholic Church in
liberated Mozambique because of its alliance with Portuguese
colonialism, illustrates that, generally, in southern Africa,
those institutions which were pillars of the oppressive colonial and neo-colonial system may have to be weeded together
with the colonial structures when liberation takes effect.
This has probably also happened in other parts of the world,
where the struggle for liberation was identical.

Although it may not be quite clear to some of us what is
happening to voices inside and outside the church which speak
out against injustice in South Africa, Namibia and Zimbabwe,
what has happened in Mozambique must help to illuminate the
situation:

> From the late fifties, and more particularly during
> the sixties, the Church came under a new harassment--
> in the form of the PIDE or the DGS, the ruthless
> State Security Police, whose deeds of brutality and
> torture have been exposed since the 25th April last
> year, and under their reign of terror, Churches
> were closed down, travel was curtailed, members of
> the Churches were arrested, some of them, including
> Zedekia Manganela, who was Moderator of the Pres-
> byterian Church, died in PIDE prisons as a result
> of torture (Smith 1975:2).

The agents and instruments of brutality and torture are presently active also in South Africa, Namibia and Zimbabwe.
Therefore, what are normally termed "Security Police" or
"Security Forces" are actually Oppression Police or Oppression
Forces. We must not isolate the countries in this region when
we discuss the human condition there, for there was and still
is a collusion in the forces of oppression. From the above
description of the role of the so-called "Security Police" in
colonialism, it must be clear that people of conscience were

not saved; instead they became prisoners for conscience. Where
was the Christian word of liberation whose advocacy the churches
claimed as their prerogative?

That word of liberation happened outside the churches because
the churches were shackled in their institutional chains and
were bedfellows of the oppressive structures. FRELIMO championed
that word of liberation because people of conscience outside the
church structure had come to say: NO! Their strife for liberation makes these prophetic eschatological words of liberation
concrete: "Behold, I make all things new" (Revelation 21:5).
The *coup d'état* took place in Portugal because the army was dis-
illusioned with a continuing struggle against forces of human
liberation which had the prophetic eschatological vision promising a "new order" and life. Hence true liberation came *for*
the people, generally, *and* for the mission of the churches in
particular. They could now freely begin to re-examine themselves
in the light of the vision which Jesus of Nazareth had for his
mission, namely:

> The Spirit of the Lord is upon me because he has
> anointed me;
> he has sent me to announce good news to the poor,
> to proclaim release for prisoners and recovery of
> sight for the blind;
> to let the broken victims go free,
> to proclaim the year of the Lord's favour (Luke
> 4:18-19, NEB).

Partial testimony to these words of liberation is expressed as
follows:

> For the first time as members of a Christian com-
> munity, we felt free to speak openly with one another.
> You will have no idea of the sense of strain that we
> felt for all the years, not knowing with whom one
> could speak openly even about Christian matters,
> but the moment this restraint was removed from us,
> we immediately entered into a new spirit of fellowship
> and understanding and progress (Smith 1975:2).

This change or transformation of the "old order" to the "new
order" happened in the spirit of Christ's definition of mission,
which focuses on the significance of the neighbor; it did not
happen in the spirit of the Pauline view of mission, which seems
to focus more on baptism and conversion to Christ as the premium
for participation in the "new order." Therefore, the churches
in Mozambique seem to have been placed in stride to make true
also the possibility of prophetic eschatology, according to
which liberation in this world is not only possible but is also

sanctioned by the mission of Christ. When contrasted with an exclusively apocalyptic eschatological view, aimed at fleeing from
the realities of this world this frame of reference has great
significance for the liturgical importance of the social or political community: such a community is a sign of unity. Repentance and reconciliation create that unity, for the community
is the concrete frame of reference for detecting the presence of
God. This effort to unite the oppressed and the oppressors
through commitment to liberation vitalizes the christological
dynamics at play in any liberation efforts. Such has already
been exemplified in the liberation of Mozambique colonial oppression:

> Frelimo leaders began to make reference to the di-
> visions which existed within the Church, and to the
> dividing influence which the Church had upon the
> community life of the people. We were told that
> Samora Machel said to one of the delegations, "You
> Christians claim to be united beneath a cross, but
> you are divided, we Frelimo have no cross but we
> are united," and this was a damning statement to
> make, but we knew that it was true (Smith 1975:2).

The above quotation indicates or confirms that the word of liberation and salvation is not an exclusive privilege of the institutionalized church, but of all of us who want to obey the
demand that we cannot truly meet God or be in God's presence
unless we are repentant and reconciled with our fellow beings:
that entitles us to express the word of liberation. Such a
relationship with our fellow beings commits us to creativity.
Thus we begin to participate in God's creation. This participation is imperative because repentance and reconciliation
cannot be expressed any more concretely than by rallying around
Christ's mission and his words of liberation.

It seems that testimony to another aspect of Christ's vision
of mission is born out in Mozambique by placing the institution
of the church under the Ministry of Education. What greater
task does the church have than to teach or educate? What is
happening here, in our view, is an attempt to formulate a new
conception of the church. It may even be an example of a theological hermeneutical exercise which recognizes that any theological dissertation which takes no cognizance of praxis is
pipe dreaming and un-liturgical. It places God and the people
outside their historical reality, where they must remember their
commitment to God and to themselves, while also continuing to
strive to make repentance and reconciliation real. This type of
theological hermeneutic is the key, it seems to us, to what the
church will mean to African people in southern Africa. For how
can we live in the world, in community with one another, if we

do not learn and educate ourselves in the meaning of God's continuing act of creation and revelation which can be realized
also through liberation? This type of theological hermeneutic
exercise also, it seems to us, recognizes that the world is in
continued revolutionary motion. It also recognizes that we need
a source that can both interpret that revolutionary motion to us
and articulate our relation to it. We must also discern the
creative role that we *are* playing in it or must still play in it.

It is no surprise, therefore, that the concept of separation
between church and state in Mozambique means that the church must
be under the control of the state. It does not mean that the
church will carry on its progress unattended by the state. This
is mainly because a new concept of "state" has also come into
existence. The state is no longer a bureaucracy and centralized
administration, aimed at promulgation and enforcement. Rather,
the state now means liberation, and liberation is only possible
where there is continued revolution--or change. Therefore, the
state is now a bureaucracy and centralized administration aimed
at proclamation and bearing witness because of its commitment
to the people. The church has thus been brought into a partici-
patory relationship with the state in Mozambique in its formulation of such proclamation. Similarly, it must carry out the
accompanying witness through its teaching task. If education is
open for all, it then means that the church will also now be
open for all. This leads us to a more universal concept of the
church. Regarding the relationship between church and state,
we must understand the following admission of guilt in the light
of the foregoing analysis:

> During the weeks immediately prior to Independence,
> the newspapers echoed with the speeches of the as-
> pirant President Samora Machel, as he made his
> journey from the North of Mozambique towards Lourenco
> Marques, and in his speeches he attacked the Church,
> mainly the Catholic Church, because of its exploi-
> tation of the population, using schools and hospitals
> as it were, to buy professions of faith, baptizing
> people simply so that they could receive them to a
> system from which they could not break free. But we
> all felt concern, because we felt that this was not
> an indictment only of the Catholic Church. In some
> measure we all felt a sense of guilt and we felt
> that there was a certain amount of justification
> in what the future President was saying (Smith 1975:2).

As a result of the liberation effort in Mozambique, even the
churches came to feel a need to unite. This happened in August
1975, when the Christian Council passed a resolution to have a
permanent secretariat (Smith 1975:3). This step shows the extent

to which the church as an institution was affected by the liberation event. What about changes experienced in the church as a
religious reality? It is reported:

> Because of the attacks that have been made upon the
> Church, membership statistics and attendance sta-
> tistics have been affected. Many members who saw
> in the Church during the days of oppression the only
> way of escape, who saw in the Church the only small
> area where they could find some sense of dignity,
> and some sense of belonging, saw in Frelimo the new
> Saviour, the new Messiah, and they no longer needed
> the Church for their salvation didn't go beyond
> that. But others have joined the Church during
> this period of crisis and trial and those within
> the Church, old and young alike, have found a far
> deeper faith, and a far deeper meaning in this
> faith (Smith 1975:3).

There are some people in various parts of the world who still
regard the church in terms of the presence of overseas missionaries. This is understandable because that has been the tradition of the church in southern Africa also. This concern
about the overseas missionaries became particularly animated
after President Samora Machel had criticized the churches for
being too much under the dictates of traditional missionary home
churches overseas and from South African white churches. The
President expressed this criticism on July 24, 1975 (Smith
1975:3). How do those who are presently actively participating
in the church in Mozambique view the usefulness of overseas
missionaries in Mozambique? If what Rev. Ted Smith says here
is indicative of a prevailing view, then it may be worthwhile
considering it:

> But I am becoming clearer in my mind now that the
> missionary presence in Mozambique certainly in a
> controlling capacity, is not to be desired, neither
> is it needed. If missionaries are to be there at
> all, they are to be there because they can be as
> useful there as they can be in any other place,
> and perhaps a little bit more useful there than in
> some other place (Smith 1975:5).

It seems that there are some in Mozambique who recognize
that the "new order" in Mozambique is of greater importance
to the Mozambican people than the bureaucratic organs of the
church. Therefore, it seems that if liberation is the absolute
priority in Mozambique, all those who are for that justice embodied in liberation must be prepared to make the necessary
sacrifice to see liberation prevail. For it is only through

liberation that the transformation of the "old order" can be
achieved, and that the promise for the "new humanity" can be
fulfilled. As the relationship between state and church develops in Mozambique, we may have to keep stock of how the
success or failure of that relationship can be traced to pledges
such as the following:

> I believe that we shall take what action we can take,
> not against the State, except perhaps to clear up
> wrong impressions, but the action that we must take
> must be to see how the Church can continue within the
> New Order. And it may no longer need in that new
> order, special buildings--if ever it really needed
> special buildings, it may no longer need salaried
> clergy (and I'm a clergyman myself so I can say
> this)--if indeed it ever really needed salaried
> clergy. The Church must not develop a persecution
> complex within the Revolution. The Church, and by
> the Church I do not mean the power group, but I
> mean Christians who are commited to Christ and to
> their fellowmen, must play its own active part in
> the socialistic system that there is in the cap-
> italist system. I believe that in a system which
> has as its aims the care of all its people, Chris-
> tianity can inject a very worthy motive--I will
> share what I have, I will give what I have, I will
> help you all I can, and sacrifice all I can, not
> because there is a rifle in my back, but because
> I love you, and because we love God (Smith 1975:6).

That pledge must inevitably demand a certain degree of vigilance
which will serve as a form of consciousness raising among the
Mozambican people, for the state and the church are presently
the most influential organizations determining the future of
the "new order." The vigilance needed for making that pledge
of support to the Mozambican liberation real will have to come
to terms with this fact of history:

> In Mozambique the Church has lost its credibility
> with most of the leaders and a large majority of
> the population, first of all because of the iden-
> tification of the Catholic Church with the State,
> with the oppressors, and secondly because of the
> silence of the Protestant Churches. We did not
> collaborate with PIDE; but neither did we protest
> when wrong and injustice were flaunted before our
> eyes, because it was far too dangerous to do so.
> It was dangerous personally, and we had to safe-
> guard the few privileges which we still held, so
> that we could go on preaching, go on baptizing,

go on erecting buildings, raising denominational
banners, counting statistics. Men were saved in
that period, do not misunderstand me. For a few
men God became real, but for many more our God
became irrelevant (Smith 1975:6).

This fact of history is a vivid expression of the kind of
captivity which the church in southern Africa is in, generally.
It seems that the church can only wrestle itself free from that
captivity if it is prepared to make real only these most important terms of its mission. That is necessary for it, otherwise
it cannot transform the "old order," and make the "new humanity"
or the "new order" realizable. Does not the mission of the
church have its mandate defined in the following terms:

Is not this what I require of you as a fast:
to loose the fetters of injustice,
to untie the knots of the yoke,
to snap every yoke
and set free those who have been crushed?
Is it not sharing your food with the hungry,
taking the homeless poor into your house,
clothing the naked when you meet them
and never evading a duty to your kinsfolk?
(Isaiah 58:6-7, NEB).

How do some Mozambican theologians interpret the relationship
between church and state, now that the "old order" has passed
and the "new order" is happening? We will evaluate a report on
the discussion of the Catholic missionaries of the diocese of
Bishop Dom Manuel Vieira Pinto on the role of the church in
Mozambique, a discussion which took place *because* the "new
order" is happening. The discussion was held during the first
days after Mozambique became independent on June 25, 1975.
Bishop Pinto had been expelled from Mozambique in April 1974
together with other missionaries, after the fascist régime was
toppled in Portugal. He was in exile in Portugal, but returned
to Mozambique in January 1975.

The opening words in the report, assessing the essence of
the liberation of Mozambique echo what we argued earlier to be
the terms which explain the context in which the mission of the
church is justified (Isaiah 58:6-7; Luke 4:18):

The proclamation of the independence of Mozambique
was a decisive and significant victory; a victory
of liberty over slavery, dignity over humiliation,
solidarity over imperialism, peace over war and
crime, life over death. . . . The victory of the
Mozambican People is a victory of all oppressed

people. It is, without doubt, a step forward in
the building of brotherhood. . . . It is to salute all those who in any way, inside and outside
Mozambique suffered and struggled for the triumph
of justice and its highest expression. Independence. It is to salute all those who during the
ten years of armed struggle and during the centuries of colonialism shed their lives, blood and
tears in order that the Mozambican People would
finally be able to cry . . . we are an independent
People! (IDOC 1976:2,3).

A new concept of the church in Mozambique, as a result of the
Mozambican liberation, is discernible here. The church gains
a legitimate place in the unfolding history of the people now
that liberation has happened. It is this new place of the church
which gives it a new form of universalism, a universalism which
is different from the Pauline conception which hinges on baptism.
Instead, it is one which is more in tune with Jesus' mission,
which focuses on the neighbor or the community. This new concept
of the church sanctions the church's commitment to struggles
against injustice and oppression. The report says of the
church's presence in the Mozambican society:

The Church of Jesus is the sign of integral salvation. It is a sacrament of unity, a liberating
ferment. . . . It is a reconciled People carrying
the Gospel of "life in abundance". . . . The
Church is, therefore, in the history which Mozambique builds: it is in the Revolution which
the Mozambican People lead (IDOC 1976:3).

This report also recollects the form in which the church
existed as an institutional reality during colonialism. A
recollection of the past that the church played in relation to
oppression in the "old order" inevitably magnifies that reality.
This causes the rejection of the church. In this recollection
is expressed an alleviation at the break with the past and the
need for repentance as well as the possibility of reconciliation
within the context of liberation:

In terms of *Recollection:* Yet in practice, we
verify, that the Church in Mozambique while stating
that it did not involve itself in politics, *supported* the politics of the established order; while
proclaiming an apolitical mission, *appeared* alongside the constituted powers; while affirming that
the political task belongs to laypeople, *did not
orient* evangelization and pastoral care so that the
Christian would be trained and commited to a

politics of liberation and dignity for each person
and all people. . . . The collaboration of the
Church with Portuguese colonialism, by commission
and omission, is an injury against the Mozambican
People, an injury in which is very difficult to
forget. Let us not be surprised, therefore, if
today, in celebrating the victory of the struggle
for liberation, in celebrating Independence, we
experience at the same time, from all levels,
negative reactions against the Church, missionaries,
and against evangelization. . . .

In terms of *Repentance:* Can we continue with a
theory and praxis of two planes and two missions?
. . . The new situation causes us to think of the
presence of the Church in terms of a liberating
ferment. . . . The time of power, alliance and
privilege has passed. The hour of the Church in
the midst of the people, as leaven in dough, has
arrived. This presence of a liberating ferment
necessarily implies a break with all oppressive
and alienating situations; it implies opting for
the exploited; it implies a political commitment
for all the People of God. . . .

In terms of *Reconciliation:* A Church ferment
which liberates us from all types of slavery particularly that which is born from the sin of
idolatry, cannot accept within itself situations
causing or generating oppression. . . . Therefore
we have arrived at a theology of the mission of
the Church on two planes: the plane of evangelization and the plane of animation (IDOC 1976:4).

In theological terms, we maintain that the break from the
"old order" and the move to the "new order" is, in fact, a
critical exercise within the church affirming the necessity for
an interplay between its nature as a social reality and as a
religious reality. That means that the church must participate
fully in the social and political reality of life, in order to
contribute to the achievement of liberation. In this way, the
church as an institution is brought into a concrete relationship
with the state, and the people remain the central focus of
interest and responsibility of church and state.

In conclusion, we must also refer to a report, dated February
9, 1976, on a visit to Mozambique by two World Council of
Churches staff members. They are Dr. Baldwin Sjollema, director
of the Programme to Combat Racism, and Dr. Lukas Vischer, director of the Faith and Order Secretariat. This visit took

place between December 12-17, 1975. Both staff members report
favorably on the relationship between church and state in Mozambique:

> *Dr. Lukas Vischer:* In fact, however, there is no
> evidence of systematic measures against the Church.
> Though critical of the churches, especially the
> Roman Catholic Church and the groups considered
> as "sects", the government does not seem to wish
> to eliminate the churches from the life of society.
> This assurance was been given formally to the
> Roman Catholic Church and in more indirect ways
> to the other churches as well (WCC 1976a).

> *Dr. Baldwin Sjollema:* There is no evidence of
> church persecution. There is a feeling of un-
> certainty as to what the Government wants the re-
> lationship to be between itself and the churches.
> It is not even sure that a coherent policy has
> already been worked out, and the churches are
> anxious to get into conversations with the au-
> thorities concerning these matters. Such a
> meeting was planned to take place early in 1976
> (ibid.).

These two conclusions are also confirmed in an interview with
the Tanzania Catholic Secretariat's Information Service, by the
Roman Catholic Archbishop José Maria dos Santos of Maputo,
Mozambique. He denied categorically that there was any persecution of the church in Mozambique.

NAMIBIA, ZIMBABWE, SOUTH AFRICA

Namibia, Zimbabwe, and South Africa introduce us to quite a
different setting from that presented by Angola and Mozambique.
These three countries have a neo-colonial social, political, and
economic organization which is generated by a system of racism
which is justified by means of pseudo-christian principles.
These principles are found not to be Christian when examined
critically and on the basis of sound theological reasoning that
recognizes the existence of a universal human principle. Instead, they are found to be reflections of the cultural dynamics
of the system of racism. These dynamics have become the religious reality of the majority of the white people living in
this setting. They seem to find the Christian imperatives of
the New Testament too demanding, and cannot acknowledge them
to be more congruent with the universal human principle of life
as expressed in such sound socio-political tenets as freedom,
justice, and fraternity. The empirical form insists that human
beings have been created in such a way that they strive to have

the meaning of those socio-political tenets demonstrated within
concrete contexts of human experience; and when such contexts
are found to be diametrically opposed to the possibilities of
human creative efforts aimed to demonstrate the meaning of these
socio-political tenets, the obtaining contexts of concrete human
experiences are rejected. For such incongruencies represent
contraditions of the essential universal human principle of life.

Namibia, Zimbabwe, and South Africa vividly bring to the fore
the challenging responsibility which human beings are charged
with, namely, what is the context of life, and how is life to
be made possible in its constant reality of philosophical and
empirical forms? When one, therefore, considers the question of
the church in these three countries, one realizes that Christianity has been proposed and imposed universally there, as the
means by which life can be made possible. Christianity itself
is presented as the constant reality of the philosophical form
of life, yet the complementary constant reality of the empirical
form of life is lacking because the concrete human experiences
are diametrically opposed to Christianity. As a result, there
is a chain of contradictions which present the illusion that the
effort to achieve the universal human principle of life results
in a dilemma which supersedes human comprehension. Those responsible for creating the contradictions expect that the response should be: let live because what supersedes human comprehension leaves one powerless.

Consequently, the question of the state of the church in
Nambibia, Zimbabwe, and South Africa hinges on the challenge to
interpret the meaning of the following: life, Christianity,
concrete human experiences, and the possibility of human creative efforts to realize the universal human principle of life.
Engagements in that challenge lead to the realization or
achievement of a balance in the universal human principle of
life, that is a balance between the constant reality of the
philosophical form of life and the constant reality of the
empirical form of life, which is a balance between the socio-
political tenets of life and the concrete contexts of human
experiences.

We propose to examine some aspects of the church or church
life in Namibia, Zimbabwe, and South Africa, in order to demonstrate the tension in the magnitude of this challenge.

In this exercise, we consider ourselves to be attempting to
understand the existence of the church in these countries in its
nature as a social reality and as a religious reality. We will
do this by studying particular documents which were prepared by
representative church people as a reaction to the empirical or
socio-politico-economic contexts in which the church finds

itself as it attempts to express its nature as a social reality
and as a religious reality. These documents, we maintain, suggest a degree of distance which was taken by the people involved
in the life of the church *from* the church, in order to observe
and comment on its doings, whatever the strength of that degree
of distance might be as a satisfactory sign of objectivity.

NAMIBIA

The churches in Namibia are racially separate. Such separation was instituted by the churches themselves, on one hand,
and enforced by the white Afrikaner Nationalist Party of South
Africa, on the other hand. However, the majority of the population is black. This majority applies to the churches as well.
Our presentation of the setting in Namibia is based on an IDOC
report prepared by Dr. W. B. DeVilliers and initially published
by the Christian Institute of South Africa in 1971 (IDOC 1973).

The *Dutch Reformed Church,* which is comprised of three
branches, is the church of the majority of the white population
of Dutch, German, Flemish, Polish, and French origin, generally
called the Afrikaners. The branches are: Nederduitse Gereformeerde Kerk, Gereformeerde Kerk, and Nederduitsch Hervormde
Kerk,

> . . . whose political loyalty, these days, lies not
> so much with the governing Nationalist Party in
> South Africa any more as with the completely reac-
> tionary, far-right and outspokenly racist Herstigte
> Nasionale Party (HNP) of Dr. Albert Hertzog
> (DeVilliers 1973:81).

Taken as one church, it is said of these three branches in relation to the white Afrikaner Nationalist Party government:

> . . . this Calvinist-inspired church happens, on
> scripturally devised grounds of its own, to agree
> all too heartily with present government policy
> and forms the main spiritual and moral bulwark of
> the theory and practice of apartheid or "separate
> development" (ibid.).

It is no surprise that there should be such agreement with
government policy. It is reported that:

> Ever since 1857--long before the Nationalist
> Party with its policy of apartheid came into
> power--this church already decided to split up
> into a white "mother church" and various non-
> white, ethnically differentiated "daughter

churches" . . . at least nine new daughter
churches envisioned, an ecclesiastical ideal
which serves to give great spiritual power
to the elbow of the authorities in their
obeisance before the idol of apartheid theology (DeVilliers 1973:82).

The particular branch referred to here is the Nederduitse Gereformeerde Kerk.

This church is engaged in missionary work among black people
in Namibia, mostly among people of mixed racial origin. It is
satisfied that the system of racism is in agreement with the
Scriptures, and that it may engage in its missionary work with
a clear conscience: the pseudo-christian principles form its
grounds for justification in its mission. This church distin-
guishes clearly between black people of mixed racial origin and
the indigenous black population. It is not perturbed by the
totally abject context of human experiences imposed by the government on the indigenous black people, for example, through
the migratory labor system. But it does find itself perturbed
by the existence of this labor system among the black people of
mixed racial origin. The effects which the migratory labor
system has on black people are untold, but regarding black
people of mixed racial origin:

This means, in effect, that hundreds of married
men are at present accommodated in so-called
"single quarters"--the nearest place at which
their wives and families can stay behind being
Upington in the Cape (South Africa) . . . the
NGK has a quite considerable problem on its
hands: alcoholism, prostitution, broken homes,
bereft wives and children, etc. (DeVilliers
1973:82).

If the Dutch Reformed Church is satisfied with the nature of
social relations and religious organization described above, we
may conclude that the engagement in that challenge which leads
to the realization of the universal human principle of life is
outside the scope of its concerns. The tension in the magnitude
of the challenge, in this case, is discernible in: (a) the
concept of the church which is maintained here, (b) the dif-
ferentiation between the church as social reality and as
religious reality.

It is a concept of the church which is limited to the Pauline
view of mission, where the baptism of the individual--and individual conversion--gain pre-eminence. On these grounds of
justification, no cognizance is taken of the demands of

repentance and reconciliation, for these are not taken as pre-requisites for God's grace. Are we not supposed to be recon-ciled with our neighbor before we can ask for forgiveness, and is not such forgiveness possible only when we have repented? And when we are reconciled with our neighbor and are forgiven, is that not an experience in which we must meet God's grace? This is the context in which the theophanic and epiphanic presence as realities illuminate the interpretation of the meaning of life. Such is the essence of the church which black people in southern Africa are seeking for in the church.

In its experience as a social reality, the Dutch Reformed Church has precluded any possibility for the experience of the theophanic and epiphanic presence because its form as social reality, wherein people meet and interact, is based on the pseudo-christian principle which places the achievement of the universal human principle of life in abeyance or appropriates it, greedily or exclusively, for white people. Thus we find that black people are denied participation in the principle of life as it exists in its constant reality of philosophical and empirical forms for the white people in southern Africa. That is, black people are denied freedom, justice and fraternity. Black people are denied the right to exercise their creative efforts to have the meaning of freedom, justice and fraternity demonstrated within the concrete contexts of their human ex-periences. This denial deprives them of the experiences of the theophanic and epiphanic presence and its realities which illu-minate the interpretations of the meaning of life. Therefore, their strife for liberation is an effort to make real the cen-trality of the christological imperative of life, which can only be realized through the experience of the theophanic and epi-phanic presence. Through this presence, the church as religious reality comes into being relevantly, in a liturgical form: community.

The responsibility of the church as social reality is to facilitate the possibilities of human creative efforts to par-ticipate in bringing into being its nature as religious reality. When that is achieved, true liberation exists. And true lib-eration takes its form in freedom, justice and fraternity. Therefore, the conflict between black and white in Namibia is a conflict in which whites suppress black people's efforts to break down barriers and transform the concrete contexts of human experiences which contradict the essential universal human principle of life--also christologically identifiable as liberation.

In terms of the extent to which the church as an institution fails to commit itself to this task of liberation, there is a deep contradiction between its nature as social reality and as

religious reality. This seems to result from its view on
mission: this view has given pre-eminence to the Pauline view
of mission, instead of striking a balance between it and that of
Jesus of Nazareth, which identifies the concrete context of
liberation mission as the concrete condition of the neighbor
(Isaiah 58:6-7; Luke 4:18).

If Christ has become man and man is in bondage or imprisoned,
then Christ is in bondage and imprisoned. The imperative of
the mission of liberation is, therefore, a christological demand. This demand can be achieved by the church as social
reality and as religious reality when the church takes up the
challenge to interpret life, Christianity, concrete human experiences, and the possibilities of human creative efforts to
experience the theophanic and epiphanic presence and its realities which constitute the universal human principle of life.
When the church takes up that challenge, then it is participating in its teaching calling, namely, the theological hermeneutical exercise, which is the nexus of its nature as social
reality and as religious reality.

Our comment on the Dutch Reformed Church in Namibia, we
maintain, applies to all the white churches in Namibia--and to
those in South Africa. The foregoing comment, therefore,
equally applies to the church in southern Africa where liberation has still to take place and where missionary structures
of the church are still retained. Before we touch on anything
else about Namibia, we must turn to the other churches.

The *Lutheran Churches* exist on the same racially separate
model as the Dutch Reformed Churches. Here is their history:

> In 1960 the various congregations of the white
> German community joined forces and became an ex-
> clusively identifiable church, the German Evan-
> gelical Lutheran Church (DELK), whereas the
> non-white converts of the early missionaries
> and their descendants got their "own" church,
> the Evangelical Lutheran Church in SWA (Rhenish
> Mission Church; ELK), the latter becoming con-
> stitutionally independent in 1957. Thus,
> although along different paths, the South
> African Dutch Reformed Church and the South
> West African Lutheran Church seem to have
> attained the same end-result: a church
> clearly and cleanly divided along racialistic
> or skin-deep lines. . . . (DeVilliers 1973:83).

However, the Lutheran Church was implanted in Namibia in 1844
by two Rhenish Mission missionaries, Kleinschmidt and Hahn. At

their arrival, they also worked among whites, although indica-
tions are clear that they did not consider their work among the
whites as missionary work in comparison to their work among the
black people. It is said that:

> The early missionaries were saddled almost over-
> night with the spiritual care of also the German
> garrison and colonists--white German soldiers,
> farmers and businessmen . . . as missionaries to
> the natives, on the other hand, and as spiritual
> shepherd or pastor to the growing white German
> community on the other. . . . Thus it came about,
> through the practical exigencies of the time,
> that the ministerial and missionary activities
> of the German-based church drifted organizationally
> apart; most unfortunately also, on both sides of
> the strict dividing line between white and non-
> white (DeVilliers 1973:83).

The Rhenish Mission practice was sometimes that a white
missionary would serve black and white people, but in a kind
of double-shift function. Hence, the missionary, it is clear,
became a mediator between two racial communities, instead of
the church serving this function. This is probably one reason
why the churches seem to have abandoned the mediatorship of
Jesus. It was easy for that to happen because their view on
mission was not that of neighborliness, where Jesus is the
mediator and reconciler, but more the Pauline view, based on
baptism and individual conversion. This led to justification
of the individual and not justification of the liberated community: a crucial difference, it seems, to be kept in mind.

The pastors of the white German Lutheran church (DELK =
Deutsche evangelische Lutherische Kirche) would claim that
this church opposes the oppressive policy of the racist apartheid system of the South African Afrikaner Nationalist Party
because they are openly critical of that policy. The fact is,
these pastors are sent from Germany on assigned terms. Therefore, they are never effective nor do they have an impact on
that system because they can be deported easily, especially
when the members of the congregation clamor for moderation,
since, as whites, these members are obviously part of the
racist system; that is why they are in this part of the world
in the first place.

It is, therefore, no surprise, if our theological context of
analysis is correct, that the christological centrality of
liberation, as expressed in Isaiah 58:6-7 and Luke 4:18, shifted
from within the church to the Liberation Movement and the voices
of individual Christians. The human creative efforts aimed at

demonstrating the meaning of freedom, justice and fraternity,
and leading to the theophanic and epiphanic presence and its
christological reality, may now be said to be largely the preoccupation of individuals and not of the church as an institution. This is the point where there is a manifest contradiction
between the nature of the church as a social reality and its
nature as a religious reality.

There is also the *ELK*, which is said to be active among all
the black people of Namibia in the southern part of the country.
It is the African section of the original Lutheran Mission
Church in Namibia, started by the Rhenish Mission. This church
cooperates closely with the other black Lutheran Church, ELOK
(the Evangelical Lutheran Ovambokavango Church), which began as
a mission church of the Finnish Lutheran Church in 1870, with
Hahn as the pioneering missionary.

Because white people in Namibia have no conscience for the
effects of their oppressive system on black people there, these
two churches embarked on a different form of joint action to
demonstrate their abhorrence to the racist apartheid system.
They decided to adopt the biblical prophetic approach of con-
fronting the powers of evil head-on rather than make pronouncements from platforms whose loudspeakers cannot penetrate the
steel confines of evil "sanctuaries." They addressed a letter
to the leader of the Afrikaner Nationalist Party in South
Africa, pointing out that the captivity of black people in
Namibia under the racist system was a total violation of the
United Nations Human Rights Charter (*vide* Appendix I). The two
leaders of these churches, Bishop Leonard Auala (ELOK) and Rev.
Paulus Gowaseb (ELK), were also able to secure a conference
with the Afrikaner Nationalist Party leadership to Pretoria,
where they emphasized, in no uncertain terms, their abhorrence
for the racial system and its total rejection--in God's name and
as leaders of the two black Lutheran churches in Namibia.

Bishop Auala took his stand for the executing of this biblical prophetic task on Ezekiel 3:16-17 (NEB): "Son of man, I
have appointed you as sentry to the House of Israel. Whenever
you hear a word from me, warn them in my name."

These two black Lutheran churches reveal the peculiar functioning of the separation between church and state within the
racist apartheid system. Their existence as separate churches--
not by choice but mainly because their white Christian brethren
found them too black "as Ham's offspring"--leads the government
to maintain that they understand the hallowed nature of the
system of race separation, for they prove that that system is
applicable and proper. Church and state separation is applied
to them by forbidding them to suggest anything to the South

African government, and yet the government can enforce structures on their churches, forcing new directions in the mission
of the church, because they serve the oppressed. For example,
first, the permit system, which restricts the movement of church
members from one part of the country to the other, is always
forcibly applied when these two churches want to hold joint worship services. These churches regard this as a deliberate way
of making eventual union between the two churches impossible.
Second,

> Thus, for instance, political pressure has already
> been brought to bear upon the Paulinum [the ELK's
> theological training center at Otjimbingwe, which
> is shared by the ELOK] whereby it has been made
> difficult for Ovambo students to gain access, whilst
> there is already talk that the government intends to
> establish a separate training center for the benefit
> of the ELOK in Ovamboland. This is seen as a clear
> indication that the government's ultimate aims are
> at variance with the churches' striving towards
> unity (DeVilliers 1973:85).

In our view, the Anglical Church (Episcopal Church), however
much antagonism may exist between it and the white Afrikaner
Nationalist government in South Africa, is still a representation of liberalism. For example, this church is spoken of as
"a [multi-racial] church" (IDOC 1973:87), when, in fact, race
separation is applied universally in Namibia. The church is
the community of believers, who experience life together in the
same concrete context of everyday life. Black people and white
people do not share a concrete everyday life context; therefore,
even if they belong to denominations with the same name, they
cannot yet claim to be one church--and multiracial at that. The
spirit of liberalism has, therefore, clouded the issues that
matter for the Anglican Church, and their approach in creative
efforts aimed at demonstrating the meaning of freedom, justice,
and fraternity as a church institution in southern Africa cannot be promising.

There must be true relationships between black people and
white people in Namibia before the Anglican Church can claim to
be multiracial. For example, describing relations among members
in the Anglican Church, DeVilliers says: "Although there is a
pronounced difference in the attitudes of white and non-white
church members, there is nevertheless a remarkable tolerance towards each other" (1973:87). This tolerance is a direct consequence of the presence of white people for whose comfort the
racist apartheid system is perpetuated. Therefore, the concrete
everyday life context of Anglican Church black and white church
members is not the same. The voice of liberalism, at least in

southern Africa, is prone to speak of multiracialism even when
concrete contexts of human experiences attest differently. Until the white members in the Anglican Church also take up the
challenge of interpreting, for example, the impeded possibilities of human creative efforts which must lead to the achievement of the universal human principle of life, they are not yet
engaged in demonstrating the meaning of freedom, justice, and
fraternity. This is not possible because

> The majority of the white members appear to be com-
> pletely apolitical in their attitude to the country
> as such and the church in particular . . .
>
> Whatever political frustrations they may suffer, these
> definitely do not find expression in the church's
> stand, whereas the non-white members insist on political
> action and look up to the church to act as a mouth-piece
> of their frustrations (DeVilliers 1973:87).

In the light of that and the evidence that individual out-
spoken leaders of the Anglican Church are deported, it may be
concluded that the Anglican Church also still occupies a foreign
status in Namibia. All this and the loud voice of liberalism in
the Anglican Church form the nexus with other suggestions that
the churches are caught up in the glitter and glamor of the
system of racism imposed in Namibia and South Africa. That is
the social reality which the churches have substituted for their
true nature as a social reality in which the church must be
striving to demonstrate the meaning of those socio-political
tenets of freedom, justice, and fraternity; and from there find
connection with its nature as a religious reality, by taking up
the challenge of the theological hermeneutical exercise.
Through this exercise, the church will be enabled to pinpoint
the theophanic and epiphanic presence which forms the make-up
of its christological character, namely, liberation within the
concrete contexts of human experiences.

The *Roman Catholic Church* in Namibia also claims to be multiracial. In our view, the Roman Catholic Church falls roughly in
the same position as the Anglican Church on this question of the
theological hermeneutical exercise and christology or liberation. We support this view on the ground of this church's
claim to be multiracial, which inevitably tinges it with lib-
eralism--and human relations have always been hypocritical in
a context of liberalism. The following description of the Roman
Catholic Church expresses its "middle of the road" position:

> The Catholics also do not have to cope with such a
> pronounced form of chauvinism among their white
> members . . . with the result that they can pride

themselves on a fully "integrated" church in which
the members of various races tolerate each other
with good grace while the authorities leave them
relatively at peace--far more so than is the case
with the RCC in the Republic of South Africa itself today (DeVilliers 1973:88).

There are also the Oruano Church and the African Methodist
Episcopal Church, which are exclusively Namibian originated.
These churches, it appears, are not yet involved in the strife
for liberation. They also seem to be caught up in the glitter
and glamor of the system of racism imposed in Namibia, for it
is said of the Oruano Church:

Although the origin of this church was, therefore,
almost purely politically and anti-government inspired, it has suffered very little interference
from the side of the authorities--probably because
the government regards the activities of this openly
separatist church as strengthening its own separatist
hand (ibid.).

ZIMBABWE

Although there are attempts to adopt modern thinking towards
the responsibility of the church in Zimbabwe, on the whole, the
church is still organized on a missionary pattern. In this
pattern, the missionaries are largely involved in educational
programs, and carry on medical work, mostly in the rural areas.
In relation to the governing powers, the church has less influence in the urban areas, which is where the government is
evolved and managed from. Rural communities have no influence
on the government. Therefore, because the church is also
largely active among rural communities, it also comes to be kept
at more than arm's length from the center of government influence.

The missionary Christian church began in Zimbabwe around the
last decade of the 19th century. There was apparently at that
time a scramble and a real attempt at Christian occupation. The
Dutch Reformed Church is said to have entered Zimbabwe in 1890,
the period of the Pioneer Column (Kendall 1972:33). They became
one of the largest churches in Zimbabwe. The Roman Catholic
Church arrived next. Their missionaries later on were Jesuits,
Swiss Bethlehem Fathers, and Carmelites from Ireland. The
Anglican Church entered Zimbabwe also around 1890, coming from
South Africa. They anchored themselves in Mashonaland and
Matabeleland. In 1892 the Methodists also arrived from South
Africa to establish themselves in Salisbury, and in Bulawayo in
1895. The following churches came to Zimbabwe as part of the

colonial movement from South Africa, still in the last decade of
the 19th century: The American Board, the Salvation Army, the
Seventh Day Adventists, the South African General Mission,
American Methodists, the Presbyterian Church, the Church of
Christ.   Early in the 20th century the Church of Sweden anchored
itself in the southern border of Zimbabwe.   Therefore, the
history of the missionary Christian church presence in Zimbabwe
is entering its 87th year.

These churches have, ever since their presence in Zimbabwe,
been engaged in the following activities: education institutions, medical work, church building, evangelization, mission
organizational expansion, and industrial training of the African
people.   We may conclude that the large degree of involvement by
the churches in educational work and medical work, as contrasted
with the level of government involvement in these kinds of work,
leaves the church presently as a powerful institution.

The first move out of the missionary pattern began with the
event of church cooperation.   The Christian conference was the
first contact point among missionary leaders.   Their main em-
phases was on "regular conferences for fellowship and consultation on aspects of faith."   In 1965 the Christian Council of
Rhodesia was formed.   The Roman Catholic Church was no party to
this, although its representatives attend the Council meetings.
The Council comprises 17 members and six associate members.

We chart the course of development of the church in Zimbabwe
in this way because we want to demonstrate that, in our view,
the western or missionary or foreign grip on the church is still
strong, although the black population are the majority Christian
membership.   In other words, the place of black people has been
insignificant in the history of the church in its institutional
development in Zimbabwe.

But 1965 was a turning point in the history of Zimbabwe; in
that year the whites declared Unilateral Independence (UDI).   In
this respect, 1965 was the year when the key of the portals of
hell was almost turned to lock out any hope for God's grace to
the oppressed black population, and the key of hell taken down
to South Africa to be dumped in the bottomless oceans.   But the
glimmers of God's saving grace still shone and the silhouette of
the evildoers was portrayed against a background of reawakened
African nationalism, although the political leadership had already been imprisoned by the colonial or neo-colonial rulers.
In terms of the missionary Christian history of Zimbabwe, 1965
was a turning point because God willed that the Unilateral Declaration of Independence crisis form a large part of their
agenda of the churches.   In this regard, it has been commented
as follows on the preoccupations of the Christian Council after
its formation in 1965:

. . . the Christian Council has been in existence
during a period of national crisis and therefore
it has been inordinately caught up in national
questions, forced to make pronouncements and de-
cisions on controversial national issues. It has
consequently been subject to much criticism and
some bodies, such as the Salvation Army, have
withdrawn from membership. Some churches, such
as the Dutch Reformed Church have not become
members (1972).

Apart from the formation of the Christian Council in 1965,
therefore, white Christians had also to decide whether or not
the white-controlled churches in Zimbabwe would choose God's
side, and as Christian churches, face their legitimate task of
speaking in unison with the suffering, imprisoned, hated, and
starved black majority population of Zimbabwe.

Because of the turning point in the history of Zimbabwe on
all fronts, we hear that:

A more recent form of co-operation has been the
regular meetings of Church leaders, or Heads of
Churches, which brings the Roman Catholic and
Protestant Churches together, particularly for
co-operation of approaches to government and
consultation on policies (Kendall 1972).

After the churches had been cast in a new light due to the
1965 developments, events began to set the agenda for the
churches. Maybe because the long-suppressed mission of Jesus
of Nazareth was beginning to become apparent, it was a threat
to the totally oppressive neo-colonial government establishment;
it was beginning to lift the mantle of authority of the church
hierarchy, in order to rend it and clothe the naked, sell part
of it so as to feed the hungry, and give the rest of it to
those who had long been involved in and committed to the course
of liberation as a symbol of justification and authority. Thus
the significance of the turning point in the history of Zimbabwe
in 1965 is that the christological context of the theophanic and
epiphanic presence, subsistent in the creative efforts of liberation, began to widen. This meant that the imbalance between
the nature of the church as social reality and as religious,
evident in the contradictions between the constant reality of
the socio-political and empirical forms of the universal principle of life, became crushing, and the black majority who had
been bearing and suffering its burdens were beginning to find
it all unbearable.

The 1965 developments in the history of Zimbabwe had finally
revealed that the problem of Zimbabwe was not that of the

difference between the "civilized" and the "uncivilized", but a
naked truth of racism--white racism against the indigenous black
population of Zimbabwe. This racism had reached its vicious
maturity when non-recognition of the humanity of black people,
as its overt program, was a thing of the past, but the extermination of human hopes by all kinds of hypocritical maneuver-
ings was its determined goal. Thank God the consultation of
the churches in 1965 saw this clearly, and hence the telling
nature of some aspects of the Report of the 1965 Consulation:

> The Consultation was prompted by the recognition
> that human relations in Rhodesia have reached a
> point of acute tension and even crisis, in which
> the Christian Churches are deeply implicated and
> for which they may not disown responsibility.

> Many of the social evils in Rhodesia at the present
> time stem from long established attitudes and prac-
> tices of the white section of the community. All
> the reports reflect the paralysing influence of the
> Land Apportionment Act. Many of the provisions are
> an offence to human dignity.

> The only hope of real peace, just civil order, and
> good human relations lies in a new Constitution
> and a new deal acceptable to all sections of the
> community.

> The problems of human relations affect and are af-
> fected by the country's economy, which is on that
> account a proper object for Christian concern.

> It calls for a solution to the political problem
> which may win the assent of the country as a whole.

> It was agreed that the churches should speak out
> fearlessly and clearly, but there is no similar
> clarity and unanimity when it comes to the actual
> content of what should be said.

> In order to change an unjust situation, we agree
> that a non-violent course of action is always pre-
> ferable to a violent one (Kendall 1972:35).

However, this final clause from the quotation suggests convin-
cingly that the churches were still not committed to a particular choice of course of action. Maybe they should have polled
the suffering masses, for we are told:

> It should also be noted that the majority of Af-
> rican leaders have been trained in schools under

the auspices of the churches, and in the churches.
The present generation of African leaders have
learned their principles in the institutions of
the Christian Church. It is from Christian doctrines that Africans have learned of human rights
and the brotherhood of man (1972:36).

African opposition to the UDI neo-colonial occupation of
Zimbabwe intensified, so that when 1969 dawned and the UDI
Constitution had been drawn up, the churches had gone on record
as opposing it. Such opposition did not necessarily mean opposition to the maintenance of white racism in Zimbabwe, but only
opposition to the form and structures in which white racism had
to be maintained. This view is based on our interpretation of
the document "Rhodesia: Joint Pastoral Letter on the New Constitution," which was issued before the referendum of June 20,
1969. We have not had occasion to examine the summaries of the
opposition expressed by the other churches in these titles:
"Rhodesia--the Moral Issue--the Catholic Pastoral Letters" and
"Church and State in Rhodesia 1969-1971." But, what was the
principal reason for the Catholic Bishops' objection to the
Constitution? They say:

> The spirit of justice and fraternal charity which is
> at the heart of all our Divine Lord's teaching finds
> no place in the document. His command to do unto
> others as we would have them do unto us (Matt. 7,12)
> is outlawed in these Proposals which have clearly
> been drafted not with the purpose of achieving the
> common good, but with the deliberate intent of en-
> suring the permanent domination of one section of
> the population over the other, in such a way that
> practices of racial discrimination shall be inten-
> sified and the unwarranted privileges of one group
> consolidated at the expense of the other (BCC
> 1970:81).

> It is not by Proposals such as these that the tra-
> ditional understanding and friendship between races
> can be retained and the future of Rhodesia assured.
> Only even-handed justice and conduct enlightened by
> Christian charity can give this or any other country
> real hope of stability, progress and peace, or en-
> able it to establish lasting concord with other
> nations (ibid.:83).

In "Rhodesia: Joint Pastoral Letter on the New Constitution,"
the voice of liberalism seems to drown the senses for equality,
justice, and freedom, without any regard for race privilege.
For we read:

> We have brought to bear on our examination of the
> text of the Proposals our considerable experience
> of Rhodesian life and our knowledge of all its
> people. We have remembered the non-African mi-
> nority who have contributed so greatly to the
> country's development and whose interests, like
> those of any other group, must at all times be
> protected from undue interference. We have
> thought no less of the majority, the African
> people, of whom we have a particular knowledge,
> whose well-being as the weaker group we are in
> a special way privileged to enjoy (ibid.:80-81).

This continued attempt to distinguish between black people and
white people in terms of material achievement has been the standard of justice and the code of human rights in southern Africa.
Because of this, white people there have been led to develop
racist relations with black people. When the truth about human
nature and the naked truth of the gospel of Jesus of Nazareth
exposed their hypocrisy, they adopted and applied the principle
of "trusteeship" or "guardianship", whose history is described
as follows:

> The word "trusteeship" or "guardianship", to name
> the proper spirit in which Whites should govern
> non-Whites, has come into fashion through the
> Treaty of Versailles.

> When the victorious Allies, instead of annexing the
> German Colonies in the good old conquering way,
> agreed to administer them as Mandates under the
> supervision of the League of Nations, they solemnly
> laid down that the backward peoples in these colo-
> nies are a "sacred trust of civilization." Thus
> declared to the world that the chief aim and duty
> of the Mandatory Powers should be the promotion of
> the welfare of the indigenous inhabitants (Hoernle
> 1945:57).

It may be argued that only the colonial rulers employed that
principle of trusteeship or guardianship and not the churches.
But we hear that the technique of domination by white people in
southern Africa also determined human relations in the church.
It is said:

> Even the Christian Churches have to bow to the
> demand for social distance, though they do it
> with different degrees of consistency and thor-
> oughness. The Dutch Reformed Church, in its
> various branches, is most thorough of all. That

race differences have been established by God and
must, therefore, be treated as fundamental in the
organization of race relations is one of the
corner-stones of its version of Christian theology.
It has organized its non-European ministers, who
in spite of their spiritual office are not accepted as social equals by their White fellow-
ministers, let alone by the White laity (ibid.:36).

Although particular attention is paid to the Dutch Reformed
Church here, evidence will prove that other denominations are
also culpable.

Despite the nuances we have drawn above, which remain the
nerve and fiber of the white oppressive systems in southern
Africa, it is evident to us from the Pastoral Letter that after
the 1969 UDI Constitution the churches had come to realize that
what was at stake for the church in Zimbabwe was the problem of
the nature of the church as social reality *versus* the nature of
the church as religious reality. That is, that the constant
reality of the empirical form of the universal human principle
of life was colliding with the constant reality of the philosophical form of that principle.

The main handicap to the churches, generally, was, therefore,
theological. They were trapped in the maze of ambivalent directions proposed in Martin Luther's Reformation theology on
the doctrine of the kingdom of the two realms. Consequently,
the churches approached the reality of suffering and imprisonment and starvation in Zimbabwe as a matter of church and state.
If they had approached it as a matter of creative efforts for
liberation *versus* neo-colonial oppression, they might have
realized that the difference between them and the UDI government
was actually not that between the "Christian" and "unchristian",
respectively, but simply a difference between power zones, based
on racism.

However, the Pastoral Letter openly raised the reality of the
violation of human rights, for they (i.e., the bishops) judged
that: "In virtue of such powers [as granted the UDI government
by the Constitution], discriminatory executive and administrative acts would be excluded from the Declaration of Human
Rights" (BCC 1970:81). They expressed the inequities most
emphatically when they observed:

We are most seriously concerned at the limitations
which in terms of the Proposals could be imposed on
the rights of freedom of expression. This could
mean that the voice of the people could be silenced
by government decree, the teaching mission of the

Church gravely impeded and the means of communication perverted into becoming the brainwashing
instruments of any dictatorial regime (1970:82).

The Pastoral Letter does also witness to a contradition of
theological nature which would be institutionalized if the 1969
Constitution were passed. Such institutionalization would have
been affirmed by the majority of whites, since African voting
power was virtually non-existent by the terms of the Constitution; therefore, passage of the Constitution would have represented open white affirmation of racism. The Pastoral Letter
thus declares:

> The new Constitutional Proposals with their sepa-
> rate rolls and constituencies to be determined
> solely on the basis of race are therefore wholly
> unacceptable to us, as are also the proposed pro-
> visions for Land Tenure, which are obviously in-
> tended to render difficult any real unification
> of the nation. . . .

> The divisive and disruptive elements contained in
> these Proposals are not only irreconcilable with
> the Christian spirit of brotherhood and with the
> civil duty of promoting national unity, they are
> calculated to destroy every possibility of
> achieving the common good. . . . They offer a
> superficial but completely illusory hope of se-
> curity for the future, and can only breed hatred
> and violence. If they should be implemented in
> a new Constitution, it will be extremely diffi-
> cult for us effectively to counsel moderation to
> a people who have been patient for so long under
> discriminatory laws and are now presented with
> such extreme provocation (BCC 1970:82,83).

This presentation on Zimbabwe reveals that the dynamics of
the human condition there revolves around three forces, namely:
(a) the UDI government demanding total voiced support from all
the white people in institutionalizing a program of racism
similar to that presently imposed and maintained by white people
in South Africa; (b) disagreement over the terms of imposition
and enforcement between the UDI government institution and the
hierarchy of the institution of the church, thus leading to what
is traditionally termed a church and state confrontation; (c)
the creative effort for liberation by the majority oppressed
black people, who wield neither power in the hierarchy of the
institutionalized church nor in the UDI government. Therefore,
the place of the church in Zimbabwe and the theological significance of the creative efforts of the Liberation Movement

forces against white minority rule in Zimbabwe will become clearer when the situation in Zimbabwe is seen in relation to developments and theological engagements in Mozambique, Angola, Namibia, and South Africa.

SOUTH AFRICA

In order to understand why the majority of white people in South Africa continue to support the violent racist apartheid system in South Africa we need to remember that the "political theology" of the Afrikaner churches shows that they have as their task the favorable interpretation of this oppressive system. Also, we need to take stock of the fact that only the Dutch Reformed Church, to which the majority of white people in South Africa belong, is permitted by the government to engage in "political theology," while the other churches suffer persecution for similar engagements. Dr. Manas Buthelezi (now Bishop Buthelezi) unmasks this sometimes overlooked fact when he comments on the Landman Report:

> What I want to say is that here is a theological document drawn by responsible members of their respective church, which directly or indirectly lends support or establishes a theological basis for a contentious political theory of Separate Development. This is a clear example of a "political theology". By this I mean that the N.G.K. theological fathers conducted their theological research in the context of the existing social and political realities. In other words they took seriously the questions posed by the political phenomenon of Separate Development as they searched, according to their lights, for the answer as well as for the implications of the Gospel to those social and political questions. . . . The fact that I am not happy with the social and political implications of their theological findings is beside the point for the purposes of the principle I am trying to establish. The principle is that what is permissible for the N.G.K. to do should be permissible for other church as well (Buthelezi 2/75:3).

The Landman Report resulted from the findings of a Study Commission of the Dutch Reformed Church which lasted four years, and was presented to the DRC Synod in 1975.

The privilege which Dr. Buthelezi is contesting here is exclusive to the Afrikaner churches, and denied all of the following other churches also existing in South Africa: Anglican Church, Lutheran Church, Presbyterian Church, Methodist Church,

Congregational Church, Roman Catholic Church, and more impor-
tantly, the Independent African Churches. There is also the
Apostolic Faith Mission Church.

But that privilege of "free interpretation" or of "political
theology" is again a privilege of the white clergy only in the
Dutch Reformed Churches. Consequently, in 1976 the clerics of
the black sections of these churches opened their mouths,
wanting their voice of political theological interpretation of
the South African situation heard. There were seven of them;
they signed a statement after massacres of black people by the
government police and other forces beginning in June 1976.
These clerics begin their statement by admitting that they had
been silent for too long:

> We, the ministers of the NG Sendingkerk, are pain-
> fully aware of the fact that we have been silent
> for too long about the situation in South Africa.
> Events of the past weeks however, make it impera-
> tive for us to speak at this stage. We reject in
> the strongest possible terms the sinful structures
> of apartheid which make it possible that people can
> be detained without trial and be robbed of their
> personal freedom by wilful Government action which
> deliberately bypasses the processes of law (*Cape
> Times*, August 18, 1976).

Further in this statement, the violence caused by the apartheid
system is rightly pointed to as the event that will "call forth
counter-violence in whatever form." Consequently, these clerics
put the blame for the violence meted out on black people where
it belongs:

> We call upon the White community to realize that
> the sin of Apartheid can apparently be justified
> only through violence and wilful authoritarian
> acts from the side of the Government they have
> voted for and are keeping in power (ibid.).

Bishop Manas Buthelezi's comments (1975) speak to vital
points, namely: (a) the cooperation of the Dutch Reformed
Churches with government apartheid policy by refusing to worship
with black people; (b) the Dutch Reformed Churches' claim that
there is support for the apartheid system in the Bible; (c) the
fact that Dutch Reformed Church theological interpretations are
limited to the social reality provided by the apartheid system.
The fact of cooperation between the Dutch Reformed Churches and
the government has already been pointed out. Regarding their
claim that there is support for the apartheid system in the
Bible, Bishop Buthelezi says:

It should be clear to the N.G.K. as well as to
those of its members who hold high political
office that other theologians have also searched
the Scriptures in good faith and come up with
theological findings with different social and
political implications. The case in point is
A Message to the People of South Africa [issued
in 1969 by the South African Council of Churches]
(1975:3).

His view is that Dutch Reformed Church theological interpretations represent an engagement in "political theology" which is
equatable with "the theology of Separate Development endorsed
by the Landman Commission." That theology contrasts with "the
theology of racial fellowship espoused by the *Message to the
People of South Africa* and supported by many churches as well
as groups like the Christian Institute" (Buthelezi 1975:3,4).

In our view, efforts made by persons and churches other than
the Dutch Reformed Church or members of it must be considered
to be an engagement in the formulation of a new concept of the
church in South Africa. The resultant tension in the con-
trasting creative efforts of each side is properly identified
here, when Bishop Buthelezi observes:

Political stakes in these two opposing theologies have worked in favour of the Dutch Reformed Church simply because the political
party in power has found this theology con-
tributory to its viability as a party. On the
other hand those who have publicly advocated
the theology of racial fellowship as amplified
through concrete models in the SPROCAS [Study
Project on Christianity in Apartheid Society]
literature, have in varying degrees become
victims of Government action and, hence, religious persecution. I say that they were persecuted for their faith simply because the
stand they took derived from a theological
position opposite to that of the Dutch Reformed
Church (1975:4).

This must be a clear indication to us that the churches in South
Africa might succeed in the creative efforts of liberation after
they have succeeded in cutting off the Dutch Reformed Church--
white Afrikaner Nationalist Party Government nexus. Presently,
black church people and their pastors are still committed to
pushing the white controlled institutionalized church to its
farthest possible limits to have this Dutch Reformed Church--
government alliance severed. They believe that this can be

done if the institutionalized churches can be moved to recognize
their potential as a united force that can bring about liberation and a "new order" of a reconciled South Africa peacefully.
In a review of the book of interviews with a number of black
pastors in South Africa on the task of the church in the creative effort of liberation now in progress in South Africa, it
is asserted that:

> A characteristic of the book is the unanimity
> among the clergymen that the Church in South
> Africa was about the only remaining institution
> with potential power to bring about peaceful
> change in the racially-torn country. At the
> same time, the ministers express grave concern
> for the churches to be losing the "golden op-
> portunity" of taking the lead in shaping the
> future of South Africa (*EcuNews Bulletin*
> 1975:1).

A ready question comes: How can there still be such false hope
in the church as an institution when the church had all these
centuries and decades to seize that "golden opportunity" and
execute its task? Bishop Peter Buthelezi of the Roman Catholic
Church answers as follows:

> The bishop says by tradition, the Catholic
> Church had never practiced apartheid. He says
> there was no serious Black-White tension with-
> in the Catholic Church. He says the Catholic
> Church could show the way to race reconciliation
> in South Africa (*EcuNews Bulletin* 1975:3).

The churches as institutions have not moved far in taking
this initiative, but white people and the government in South
Africa are now aware that black pastors have found a link with
the black masses through Black Theology and Black Consciousness:
the former being the black masses' contribution to this end.
The strength of this link between Black Theology and Black
Consciousness became clearer when Professor Meiring, author of
Stemme Uit die Swart Kerk ("Voices out of the Black Church")
interviewed the black pastors on Black Theology; it is reported:

> One of the exponents of Black Theology, Dr.
> Manas Buthelezi (now Bishop), who was once
> under a Government banning order, was among
> those ministers who speaks in favour of Black
> Theology in *Stemme uit die Swart Kerk*. In
> reply to a question whether Black Theology
> was only concerned with the freeing of the
> churches of South Africa from Western

orientation, or whether is also included "phys-
ical liberation", Dr. Buthelezi says: "Yes,
Black Theology has a message to both" (*EcuNews
Bulletin* 1973:3).

This link now striven for by black pastors and the black masses
demonstrates how the christological context of the church widens
from its traditional context of the institutionalized church to
the context of the oppressed people, and takes the form of liberation in its theophanic and epiphanic presence. Also, this
link demonstrates that the theological hermeneutical exercise
necessary for achieving the theophanic and epiphanic presence
is not an exclusive prerogative of the institutionalized church;
it is embedded in all dynamics in the human condition whose pre-
amble is the mission of Jesus, which gives neighborliness--and
thus community--priority over a Pauline view on mission, which
makes baptism a prerequisite for salvation and faith a prerequisite for justification to participate in the creative effort
of liberation.

The widening of the christological base, we maintain, is
attested to when Makhathini says, on the occasion of the Consultation of the Missiological Institute at the Lutheran Theological College (September 12-21, 1972), that he

> can only give some clues about the style of
> witness characteristic of the Christian life
> in the world both for the church as such and
> for the individual member of the church
> (Makhathini 1973:8).

As he spells out these clues, he illustrates further the widening of the christological context emanating from Jesus'
mission:

(a) *Realism:* A Christian is one who takes history
seriously. He regards the actual from day-to-day
existence of the world realistically, as a way of
acknowledging and honouring God's own presence
and action in the real world in which men live
and fight and love and work and move and die. . . .

(b) *Inconsistency:* . . . a Christian cannot be put
into a neat pigeon-hole. . . . He knows no institution, no ideology, no nation, no form of
government, no society, that can heal the broken-
ness or prevail against the power of evil and
death except the church of Christ. Though the
Christian takes his stand and speaks out specifically, he does so not as the servant of some

race or class or political system or ideology
but as expression of his freedom from just such
idols. Black Theology then cannot be a racist
theology nor can it be a Black man's ideology.
It can and is only a black man's freedom in expressing his faith in Jesus Christ who is the
Good News. . . .

(c) *Radicalism:* The Christian life is inherently
and consistently radical . . . Black Theology
affirms this (Makhathini 1973:8,9).

Our view would be that Black Theology in South Africa has
become one definite means by which black people are committed
to that theological hermeneutical exercise which demonstrates
that liberation embraces a wider christological context than
one which is confined to the institutionalized church. This
wider context also makes the nature of the church both as a
social reality and as a religious reality practicable. That
preoccupation inevitably leads to the formulation of a new concept of the church. This, in our view, seems to be confirmed
when Makhathini submits:

Our way of understanding the Gospel has to be demonstrated and the demonstration has to be clearer
and more honest than ever before . . . Black Theology aims at reinterpreting the Gospel. By this
is meant that the old concepts must be understood
in a new way and must have new applications (1973:
15).

Also, the engagement in the theological hermeneutical exercise,
aiming to demonstrate that the church is truly present when its
nature as social reality balances its nature as religious reality, is an effort to make real Bonhoeffer's proposed concept of
the church, where he demands:

The church is the church only when it exists for
others. To make a start, it should give away all
its property to those in need. The clergy must
live on the free-will offerings of their congregations, or possibly engage in some secular
calling. The church must share the secular problems of ordinary human life, not dominating, but
helping and serving. It must tell men of every
calling that it means to live in Christ, to exist
for others. In particular, our own church will
have to take the field against vices of *hubris*,
power-worship, envy, and humbug, as the roots of
all evil (Bonhoeffer 1971:382f).

But what are the terms of this wider concept of the church
for South Africa? John W. de Gruchy attempts an answer in his
comments on "The Identity of the Church in South Africa":

> . . . but what kind of an inventory would we de-
> sign for the Church in South Africa? Certainly,
> if the Church is going to speak against racism,
> economic discrimination, migratory labour, and
> on behalf of God's justice and righteousness so
> that his glory can be revealed in South Africa,
> then it will have to order its life with a fresh
> integrity based upon the Gospel. . . . The
> proper use of the marks of the Church is to set
> them free from tradition and enable them to be-
> come once again available for God's use in calling
> the Church to discover and express its identity
> in South Africa today (Gruchy 1974:50).

Now what about Black Consciousness, the complementary force
in the theological hermeneutical exercise, which illustrates how
the creative effort for liberation leads to a widening of the
christological context? The force with which Black Consciousness engages in the theological hermeneutical exercise is discernible from the following definitional characterizations (by
Hubert Bucher), and its link with Black Theology is also ex-
plicit here:

> A key word for grasping the aim of South African
> Black Theology is the term "Black Consciousness",
> indeed one of the contributors says that the first
> is "the extension" of the latter. . . .

> As everybody knows, the situation is completely
> different in South Africa. South Africa's Blacks
> cannot put the hope for regaining their self-
> respect in the day when the Whites will have
> left the country. They realize that this would
> be a futile hope . . . Instead, Black Conscious-
> ness tells the South African Blacks to take pride
> in their blackness and to consciously manifest
> it. . . . Therefore the "unadulterated quin-
> tessence" of Black Consciousness is "the rea-
> lization by the black man of the need to rally
> together with his brothers around the cause of
> their oppression--the blackness of their skin--
> and to operate as a group in order to rid them-
> selves of the shackles that bind them to per-
> petual servitude. . . . The black man in South
> Africa, says Black Consciousness, must engage
> himself in a quest for true humanity. . . . In

this connection a large room is given to the
praise of the alleged "law of solidarity" which
was formerly operative in the African society.
And the demand appears that the black man in
South Africa must rebuild the "man-centred culture" of the past. . . . The Church in this
man-centred African culture must insist on the
wholeness of the redeemed person's life in
Christ, because "life in its social, economic
and political setting is our only place to
rendez-vous with God . . . poverty is a state
of displacement from this place of rendez-vous
with God as he comes to distribute gifts to
this children . . . men must be equipped with
the tools to overcome their alienation from
the wholeness of life" (Bucher 1973:330-334).

In fact, it is in the language in which Black Consciousness
articulates the theological hermeneutical exercise that our
view that Black Theology and Black Consciousness complement
each other in the creative effort of liberation becomes clear.
It is through this exercise, we want to emphasize, that the
christological context widens, and thereby makes possible the
theophanic and epiphanic presence. The reality of the theophanic and epiphanic presence is animated by expressions such
as "life in its social, economic and political setting is our
only place of rendez-vous with God," and "poverty is a state of
displacement from this place of rendez-vous with God as he comes
to distribute gifts to his children."

Still in the attempt to illustrate the complementary, if not
inseparable, relationship between Black Theology and Black Consciousness in South Africa, let us turn to how a black South
African explains the christological character of Black Consciousness, as a force in the creative effort of liberation, and
thereby affirms its centrality in the church:

Black Consciousness as has already been implied, is
borne out of the black man's experience of life in
this country. It is a response to an experience of
deep hurt, constant humiliation, sustained dehuman-
ization and forced self-denial. This is the point
at which the black man's being can never be shared
by the privileged and those in power. . . . It is
this experience which makes it hard for the black
man to hear the gospel proclaimed by the best in-
tentioned white preacher. Black Consciousness is
a response to the Gospel preached by the Church.
It is the black man seeking to respond to the Gospel.
This is the black man at the foot of the Cross

repenting, claiming forgiveness and trying to
accept as a child of God. . . . What I am saying
is, thanks to the Church, the black man has been
awakened (*Journal of Theology for Southern Africa*
1973:19).

Essays on Black Theology is the publication which presents
the body of theological thought on liberation whose undergird-
ings are Black Theology and Black Consciousness. Because both
of these creative efforts emanate from the dynamics of the
current socio-political-religious concrete context of the black
experience in South Africa, they cause alarm and consternation,
in the church as well as--obviously--in white Nationalist Party
government circles. Consequently, *Essays on Black Theology* was
banned together with some of the contributors in it (It has subsequently been reissued in London under a different title,
edited by Basil Moore). But the message of these essays has
found perceptive ears among certain white theologians, for example, Professor David J. Bosch, who reviewed the essays. One
or two of his assessments are worth considering, especially
since they contribute to our contention that Black Theology
and Black Consciousness, together, represent an engagement in
creative efforts of theological hermeneutical exercise which is
necessary for illuminating the assertion that the context of
liberation is a theophanic and epiphanic presence which represents a widened christological context. Thus Professor Bosch
assesses:

The majority of the contributors to this volume
speak decidely as Christians and Christian theologians. They confess openly a vital attachment
to historical Christianity. . . .

One of the most important messages in this book,
on the part of almost all contributors, is the
virtually messianic message of the self-discovery
of the black man, the discovery that in the past
the black man had always looked at himself in terms
of the definitions of the white man. The white man
and his values had been the norm of everything,
yes, even to the extent of his describing the black
and brown man as a "non-white." But that time has
now irrevocably passed (Bosch 1972:3-4).

We must now take a closer look at the impact that Black Theology and Black Consciousness had, and still have, on attempts
being made to formulate a new concept of the church. This concept must be a balance of the nature of the church as social
reality and the church as religious reality. That is, the
church must be equally eager to assert itself as the center for

worship, baptism and the administering of the holy communion as it is committed to the transformation of oppressive structures, be these of a sociological or political or economic nature. In this preoccupation of formulating a new concept of the church, there are voices from within the church as well as from outside it. It is an attempt aimed at realizing a church which has the marks of the liberation context, where the theophanic and epiphanic presence is the animating force of the christological imperative of the church.

The preoccupation in the formulation of this new concept of the church focuses on human relations, both inside the church and between the church and suffering oppressed and dying black masses in South Africa.

For the first kind of voices, we turn to a manifesto which was presented by five Roman Catholic Reverend Fathers to the Roman Catholic hierarchy in 1970. They demand as follows:

> We are primarily concerned with the well being of our Church. How long must we plead for its Africanisation in Southern Africa? No less an authority than the Supreme Pontiff has endorsed this urgent matter. Addressing the African Bishops on his recent visit in Uganda, the Pope said: "You can give the Church the precious and original contribution of negritude which she needs particularly". . . .

> The Black clergy have realised that aping Europe is not the answer to Africa's religious needs. Bishops and priests have expressed the need for Africanisation in Southern Africa. . . .

> The main object of every missionary or pastoral activity is to serve the people of God, irrespective of colour, creed, place or sex. Therefore, the White clergy must do this whenever a Black priest is not available. But alas! power corrupts. The Government's policy of restricting free entry of Whites into our townships has much to recommend it.

> The Catholics pretend to condemn Apartheid. And yet, in practice, they cherish it. The Church practised segregation in her seminaries, convent, hospitals, schools, monasteries, associations and churches long before the present Government legislated against social integration. The bishops, priests and religious, are divided on the question of apartheid.

We know from reliable sources that a number of
bishops and priests are sympathetic towards the
policy. Quite rightly, of course, they condemn
some aspects of its implementation, particularly
those which bring suffering and injustices. . . .

We ask the Hierarchy to expedite Africanisation.
Why should our townships be dominated by the
White clergy and African priests be dumped in
the bush, in non-viable parishes?

We loathe the unwarranted, self-appointed sur-
veillance of the White priests over their Black
colleagues.

We deplore the tripe that some missionaries write
about Africans. . . . Finally we would like to
reassure readers that we are sincere men who wish
to put things right in the Church. Please do not
misunderstand us. We have in the past presented
to the Hierarchy resolutions that were passed in
July, 1966, but to no effect. . . . We would be
hypocrites if we pretended to be contented with
the *status quo*. . . . (AFFER 1970:175-177).

This manifesto reflects the objectives of Black Theology and
Black Consciousness, and is one example of the whirlwinds of
mission which will continue to blow in the churches in southern
Africa until the churches are no longer subservient to the state
because white people want to continue to oppress black people,
and when the churches have made a commitment to participate in
the creative efforts of the theological hermeneutical exercise,
in the wider christological context of the human community,
where the theophanic and epiphanic presence prevails.

This manifesto appears to have had impact on the Roman
Catholic Church. Hubert Bucher observes the following about
the Roman Catholic Church since Black Theology and Black Consciousness came to prevail:

The Catholic Church in South Africa too can no
longer afford believing that it has managed to
escape the discontent among thinking Africans
with the way in which the churches are handling
the problems raised by South Africa's apartheid
policy. Ever since a group of Catholic priests
shocked the South African bishops' conference
by publishing a manifesto in one of the country's
leading dailies in January 1970, there have been
frequent eruptions of the same sentiments which

were expressed in that manifesto: the alleged
slowness of the Church in handing over key posts
to Africans and her alleged lack of taking a
decisive stance against the country's discriminatory social set up at grassroots level
(Bucher 1973:329-330).

To what extent is Bishop Manas Buthelezi's call upon the
church to change consistent with the christological purpose of
liberation which Black Theology and Black Consciousness have
identified? Following are some of his demands for change. We
will add comments to them as an attempt to determine to what
extent they are consistent with that purpose of liberation:

To some people "change" and "church" seem to be
two irreconcilable concepts.   The church as an
institution stands in sharp contrast to the
transitoriness of the things of this world.
While permanence and continuity describe the
character of the church, to them, it is to
worldly things that "change" relates. . . .

It is the wrong notion of what the church stands
for that causes many people here in South Africa
to find it difficult to see the church as an instrument of social change and social progress.
To them that is Social Gospel. This poses the
problem of the solidarity of the Church with
the mass of people among whom it ministers.
The issue at stake is whether the bridge between the church to the world or whether this
mission presupposes an already existing solidarity between the two (Buthelezi 1973:4).

Here the purpose of the church is clearly identified as the fulfillment of the universal human principle of life, which we proposed when we introduced this study, insofar as that principle
relates to the socio-political tenets of freedom, justice, and
fraternity which must never be contradicted in the concrete
context of human experiences. For such contradiction causes
an imbalance between the nature of the church as social reality
and its nature as religious reality.

Therefore, when we speak of change in the church,
it is not just a question of change in church
structures--even though that is also included--but
also change in the role of the church in the South
African society. The church does not exist for
itself but for ministering to South Africa. Therefore what is of primary importance is not just

structural change within the church but how the
church projects itself as a catalyst in changing
the thinking and behaviour of South Africa's
politicians, economists as well as all citizens
(Buthelezi 1973:4-5).

Here Bishop Buthelezi indicates, in our view, that the context
of the church is its community of the people committed to liberation, and not the community of those elected through faith
in the justificatory dispensation of baptism.   Therefore, together, Black Theology and Black Consciousness are legitimate
instruments to be employed for the theological hermeneutical
exercise with which the church must be always preoccupied, if
it is to interpret the liberation context properly.

Gustaf Wingren has made the observation that the
salvation event which is the content of the message of the church took place outside the religious
centre of Jerusalem.   It took place in the world,
in the sphere of the "secular".   Not an apostle
but a stranger, Simon of Cyrene, under compulsion,
carried the cross of Christ; a criminal at Jesus'
side and not a disciple received the promise of
the kingdom. . . .

From the beginning the church is part of God's
transforming social process in the world.   Is
there anything more transforming than the power
of the Gospel to the lives and destinies of the
peoples of the world?   When Christ sent his disciples to make disciples of all nations he was in
effect prescribing that the church should be an
instrument of change in the historical destinies
of those nations (Buthelezi 1973:4).

The bishop, we maintain, demonstrates here that the call and
demand for change in the church in South Africa is consistent
with the historical development and experience of the church.
This also evidences that the christological context of the
churches does widen when the liberation of God's creation is at
stake.   There is also indication here that the liberating nature
of Jesus' mission is of a prophetic eschatological significance.
That is, salvation is fulfilled or happens in the lived history
of God's people, and not after death.   The context for this
happening is the theophanic and epiphanic presence which God's
people experience in liberation when the christological imperative remains alive in the community of the church.

The irony of all this is that Christianity in
South Africa has a white image.   This is in spite

of the fact that almost all the major multiracial churches are over-whelmingly black.
"What the churches in South Africa are thinking"
is very often identical to "what white people in
South Africa are thinking". The voice of the
black man has not yet been heard in the church
in any significant manner. Added to this is
the fact that the white man has discredited
himself as the protector of Christian values;
the situation becomes very desperate indeed. . . .

There must, therefore, be change in the church
in order to reflect a changed situation, namely,
the white man's turning against that which pro-
motes Christian love and justice. The church
must release its potential by promoting the
reflection of its black constituency in both
its structure and proclamation. The church
must cease to be sectarian in order to reflect
the whole of the people of God. It must cease
to be a satellite of white power politics in
order to become a forum of communion for the
whole people of God (Buthelezi 1973:5,6).

We notice here an identification of deep contradictions in human
relations between black and white people in the church community
in South Africa. It is the state of these relations which ne-
cessitates change in the church. Such change is imperative because the church as social reality must be prepared to align
with its nature as religious reality within the concrete context
of human experiences. Through the creative liberation efforts
of Black Theology and Black Consciousness, the church as religious reality must change, and such change will be evident from
the christological happening outside the institutional church,
identifiable as liberation--for there the theophanic and epiphanic presence will prevail if it is true liberation.

This is the time of crisis: the crisis of
Christian discipleship. South Africa urgently
needs the Gospel of liberation: a Gospel that
will liberate the whites from the bondage in-
herent in the South African way of life--a way
of life that chokes brotherhood and fellowship
between black and white. This is the Gospel
which will liberate the white man into realization of the fact that he is nothing but a
fellow human being in relation to the black
man, and a Gospel which will liberate the
black man into realization of the fact that
he is nothing less than a human being . . .

The last three years have been characterised by
the evolution of Black Consciousness in South
Africa. This in turn called for the need to
relate the Christian faith to the experience
of the black man (Buthelezi 1973:6).

The bishop here sounds the voice of prophecy which culminates
in liberation. At the same time, the act of obedience as a
response to the moment of prophecy is submitted here. This,
in turn, creates the necessary tension for repentance and reconciliation. This tension is inevitable because once prophecy
and liberation have become the praxis and vision, respectively,
of the oppressed, the prerequisite for the theophanic and epiphanic presence have been met. Without such presence the broad
community of the church--*laos*, the people--cannot be in fellowship.

Once change has been achieved in the South African situation
of oppression, how much more liberating can be the following
agonizing words of suffering, repentance and reconciliation?

As a black Christian I have in anguish come to
the conclusion that the white man, through his
political and social governmental institutions,
no longer serves the promotion of God's love between black and white but is really doing his
best to kill and frustrate it. This spiritual
vandalism on the part of the white man is no
longer a theoretical possibility that Christians
suffer just for the sake of promoting love and
good will between black and white. At the end
of it all South Africa will have a unique distinction of producing martyrs who suffered
simply because they were trying to promote
good will between the races.

God demands that the white man must repent from
the political, economic and social sins he has
committed over the last three centuries. If the
white man will be saved at all, the English and
Afrikaners of this country must say in unison
mea culpa, mea culpa, mea maxima culpa (Buthelezi
1973:7).

CONCLUSION

We do not consider this study to be a definitive theological
statement of black theological analysis, or human liberation, in
southern Africa. Therefore, we invite the reader to join in
reflecting upon this undertaking as an attempt to identify the

concomitant factors which are responsible for the oppressive history of black people in southern Africa; and, to consider our
theological statement here as our own attempt to present a theological outline whereby we indicate some theological imperatives
for human liberation.

   The depth of our joint reflection and theological formulation,
we maintain, must be commensurate with the character of the
events of oppression and those of the effort of liberation as
time wears on.   That is, the more we gain insight into where the
history of oppression in southern Africa leads, the more we must
become committed to a theological rigor that bear historical
significance to the claim that God is present in all creative
efforts at human liberation.   Already, just before we go to
print, this challenge is placed before us by the following reports, which are example of the rising and unchanging tide of
the inhuman and oppressive events in the history of black people
in southern Africa; the first appears under the headline "Church
leaders in Namibia say torture is common":

(a) From Our Own Correspondent Johannesburg, May 27

   The leaders of the four main black churches in
   Namibia (South-West Africa), whose membership
   comprises more than two thirds of the territory's
   population, said in a statement today that torture appeared to have become standard practice
   in the interrogation of detainees by the defence
   and police forces.

   The statement said that particularly in the
   populous northern part of the territory, where
   South African forces are fighting a low-intensity
   war against the nationalist South-West Africa
   People's Organization (Swapo), the use of torture had reached "horrifying proportions".

   It said the methods of torture included beating
   with rifle butts, electric shock, burning with
   cigarette ends, being hung up by arms or legs,
   deprivation of sleep and long periods of solitary
   confinement.

   The statement was signed by leaders of the
   Evangelical Lutheran Ovambo-Kavango Church,
   the Evangelical Lutheran Church, the Roman
   Catholic Church diocese in Windhoek, and the
   Anglican Church diocese of Damaraland.

   The allegations were swiftly denied by Brigadier
   H. V. Verster, the divisional commissioner of

police in Namibia. It was a tactic of "leftist
organizations", he said, to accuse the authorities of inhuman acts.

These are not the first such allegations against
the authorities, but as the whole of northern
Namibia is a military zone and out of bounds to
unauthorized personnel, it has been impossible
to check the allegations.

The statement said the church leaders could not
remain silent about "this deplorable state of
affairs" and if pressed would produce evidence
in court (*The Times*, London, May 28, 1977).

(b) During that first week-end I had an extraordinary experience: an Afrikaner reporter from
Die Vaderland telephoned and asked whether I
would go with him to the Dutch Reformed Church
in Braamfontein, where services are conducted
in English. I was intrigued, of course, not
having been to such a service before, and
knowing full well that, at the time I left
the country, no black would have been allowed
through the doors of such a church. . . .
During tea I was asked to say a few words,
which in itself was unprecedented. I told
the people how I abhorred apartheid, that I
had been to prison for my opposition to apartheid, had been banned, and was as surprised as
they were to be together with them in one
church. . . .

"Johannesburg is not complete if you have not
seen Santon. It is the in-place for rich whites
with money to burn," said my companion. . . .
As I sat in the crowded train which took me back
to my sister's home I could not help comparing
the small houses which the train flew past, with
the immense wealth which was so evident in the
white suburbs like Santon. . . . Blacks and
whites, of course, live in different areas.
Blacks cannot buy or own homes in white-designated
suburbs. . . . But blacks still don't have the
vote. Banning notices are still issued. Arrests
and detentions still take place. Allegations of
torture continue to leak out, and detainees still
mysteriously fall out of windows of the John
Vorster police complex. . . .

What is clear is that some radical change must
take place soon. The Afrikaners to whom I spoke
were the first to ask: "How long will many
blacks go on extending the hand of friendship
to the whites?". . . . But is there still time
for them to grasp the hand of black friendship,
which surprisingly is still there? Or has the
black community become so impatient and embit-
tered that it is too late? I may be wrong, but
my feeling--after enjoying the confidence of the
many blacks I met--is that most of them earnestly
want neither violent revolution nor solutions
based on foreign ideologies. What they want,
among other things, are better and cheaper houses,
more and better-paid jobs, and to be treated and
respected like ordinary human beings. Whether
whites can meet these simple requirements, only
time will tell (Morrison 1977).[1]

(c) The basic humiliations remain unchanged. The
Immorality Act, the Mixed Marriages Act, resident
and educational segregation, the pass laws and
the whole apparatus of racial discrimination;
and it is here that the South African Government
will have to give some evidence of a change of
heart before it can expect its friends in the
West to stand firm against the prevailing tide
of world opinion (Chalfort 1977).

Because the white oppressors of black people in southern
Africa have, in the view of most students of southern African
affairs, had so much direct or indirect support from western
(white) countries based on economic interests and ideological
reasons (such as anti-communism), it may be a fair assessment
to charge that unless Christians in the western countries
awake to the oppression of black people in southern Africa,
black people there will be inclined to look less and less upon
these Christians as brothers and sisters in Christ's name.
Western Christians are responsible to their governments; and
their governments represent them in the support they give to
the white oppressors in southern Africa. If that is not so,
then Christians in western countries must now break their
silence and exert pressure on their governments to withdraw
all support to the inhumanity which white people in southern
Africa continue to perpetrate against black people there for
the sake of furthering white racism.

Unless Christians in western countries campaign actively
against white racist oppression in southern Africa--as 19th
century Christians in the West and elsewhere campaigned for

the abolition of slavery--it will be concluded that they are
themselves, as whites, racist; and, therefore, haters of black
people. The longer Christians in western countries remain
silent, the greater grows their culpability (because of the
economic gains of their governments from white exploitation
and oppression of black people in South Africa) in the continued
suffering of black people in southern Africa, simply because
black people, out of human conscience, refuse to cooperate with
white racism in the deprivation of their own God-given inalien-
able rights to lead a human life as God's creation.

---

[1]Morrison left South Africa seventeen years ago to escape
arrest and detention. In 1956 he was the youngest of 156
accused, during the famous "Treason" Trial which lasted four
years, of wanting to overthrow the State. All were acquitted.
As an active member of the Congress Movement he later spent
nearly two years in prison for defying the apartheid laws. Mr.
Morrison says: "When I got the telephone call from my sister
and brother-in-law in South Africa, to say that my mother had
cancer of the stomach and was not expected to live long, I decided to apply to the authorities to return for a month to
Johannesburg so that I could be with her. . . . In the meantime, I had taken out British citizenship and as a consequence
had forgone any citizenship rights in South Africa. . . . This
account of my return home would be incomplete if I did not
record that during my visit my mother died. But I was with
her at the end, and that alone made the trip worthwhile". Mr.
Lionel Morrison is Black. (*The Sunday Telegraph* May 29, 1977).

Response #1

An Anonymous South African

It is a real pleasure to respond to a paper like the one that Mr. Leeuw presented. His comprehensive paper shows the tremendous grasp he has of the sub-continent. This is obvious throughout his paper. There are some very telling statements he makes, e.g. ". . . evangelism and church growth . . . and the future of the church in southern Africa must take place within the dynamics of the existing revolutionary stage of the black and white experience there"; ". . . this church's incorporation into the white dominated structures in South Africa has made it appear to be supping with the devil, but, guardedly with a long spoon . . ."; ". . . the church has no choice but to participate in change . . ." (quotation from Buthelezi 1975).

The church of this century in southern Africa is facing a critical time indeed. This can only mean one thing, i.e. the church has to act radically, biblically, decisively, and immediately. This may be very costly because the church has contributed to and participated directly or indirectly in the situation that urgently needs to be reversed.

Admittedly, the church is a gathering of frail human beings which is as divine as it is dust; as spiritual as it is physical; as eschatological as it is sociological. Its human side will not find it easy to face the implications of change in this "crisis situation" because of the lengths to which it has gone in supporting the "old steady state," so that the prospects of being replaced by the "new steady state" may give a horrifying feeling. But fortunately the church knows what repentance and reconciliation are all about. The step taken by the missionaries in Lesotho is needed in southern Africa generally:

> . . . we [the missionaries] decided in 1898 to
> trust them (nationals) entirely, and to take
> them into our councils on terms of equality
> with ourselves . . . Our decision . . . seemed
> rash . . . but very wise . . . and has pre-
> vented Ethiopianism from making any headway
> in (Lesotho) . . . and from harming . . .
> churches.

The church will have to trust and hope that disaster will be
forestalled in southern Africa, as it was in Lesotho.

Unfortunately, most Christians live under paralyzing fear,
which obviously cannot coexist with *trust*. There is first the
fear of being overwhelmed by such a great majority of black;
second, the fear of retaliation after going so far with oppressive discrimination. Their conclusion may be based on a
wrong criterion, as blacks may not necessarily react the way
whites would react. But this fear is at the root of the hard-
ening attitude on the part of the white.

All the segments of the church in southern Africa are right
in the middle of the struggle at different levels and in different ways and degrees of involvement.

1.   The segment responsible for the policy of apartheid. Mr.
Leeuw points out how this was done as far back as 1857. This
segment has freedom as Bishop Manas Buthelezi points out, to do
"political theology," while others do not.

2.   The segment calling for change. It is not in the majority, but it is there. Among this segment there are those who
have not taken the opportunity that does exist in South Africa
to demonstrate their commitment to the unity of the Body of
Christ. They have withheld power from blacks even where they
should have given it to them long ago, in their own churches.
The Methodist Church appointed its first black pastor in an
all-white church only this year.

3.   There is the Romans 13 segment. To them the "powers that
be are ordained of God," and we should not meddle in politics.
Even Christ did not seek to overthrow the Roman Empire; the disciples came out of prison (e.g. Peter) and went on *preaching*, not
politicking. While this may be true, it is well known that to
these people, the powers that be are just those placed in power
by their vote; to many of them, Romans 13 does not really apply
in Mozambique as fervently as it does in Rhodesia or South
Africa. Also, they forget that the Roman empire never claimed
to be Christian. In southern Africa oppression is carried out
by extremely pious Christians, who are engaged in all the

oppression in the name of Christ.   To me, the true counterparts
of southern African "Christian" regimes would be the religious
leaders of Christ's day, say, the Pharisees.

It is only fair to accept the concept of "the powers that be"
in a completely unbiased fashion if the church truly represents
the Kingdom of God here; and more so if our priority number one
is to see that Kingdom preached effectively, and established,
unhindered, here on earth.   To the church, the "new steady
state" must be as ordained of God as the "old steady state."
The church can hardly afford to be "bedfellows of the oppressive
structures," as Mr. Leeuw put it so well.   It ceases to be the
"salt", the "light", and the alternative society that it is
supposed to be.

Black leaders who are skeptical of any church controlled from
overseas or by any foreign power, cannot be blamed.   The "long
spoon" type of fellowship with the South African controlled
church is particularly understandable.   When the South African
white mentality will not let blacks head up their black work in
black townships, they certainly cannot do better in countries
adjoining South Africa.

The mentality I am talking about has enslaved both white and
black people.   Thanks to Black Consciousness that is rapidly
liberating the black man from this dehumanizing mentality, and
restoring the dignity given to him as a man created in the image
of God, it could very well be that the liberated black man is
going to be Christ's instrument in the future to liberate and
humanize his white brother.   Anyone who has to live with a
loaded gun, keep it under his pillows at night . . . every night,
and keep extra hosepipes inside the house, every night, is certainly not free.   He needs to be liberated.   How long could
anyone endure that kind of life?   And yet this is the kind of
life many of our white brothers are putting up with, and will
do so as long as the overwhelming black majority is there.   An
insecurity of this magnitude can never be permanent.

I strongly believe that the situation in southern Africa
needs both Paul's emphasis and Christ's emphasis.   Somehow, I
seem to sense a measure of tension between "the Pauline conception which hinges on baptism and Jesus' mission, which focuses on the neighbor or the community."   I am not sure that I
see the difference between Paul and Jesus as sharply in the
Bible as it seems to come through in Mr. Leeuw's paper.   I know
that in my country people have tended to polarize a great deal
in this area, thus creating an either-or situation.   Yet it
seems to me that this is not fully justified because the same
Jesus who focused on the significance of the "neighbor" is the
one who said so emphatically to Nicodemus that "except a man be

born again, he cannot see the Kingdom of God" (John 3:3). And it
is Paul who says, "in Christ there is neither Jew nor Gentile"
(Gal. 3:28), and that the middle wall of partition between Jew
and Gentile has been broken down (Eph. 2:14).

Instead of seeing a tension here, I see the need of bringing
the two conceptions together and holding them in proper relation
if our contribution is to be well-balanced. In fact, I see the
Pauline emphasis (which is Christ's emphasis) providing the only
firm basis for the "new order" and a compassionate care for the
oppressed. This is part of our calling. Christ does not only
comment the so-called "Good Samaritan," but deals with the moral
condition of the Samaritan woman. God's people have had a twofold mandate from Genesis 2: the cultural mandate and the
evangelistic mandate. After justice has been achieved, the world
will still be in dire need of the unique message that only the
church can give. Professor David Bosch says, "The world is un-
aware that it needs to be saved from certain types of alienation
that are deeper, more intimate than sociolocial and political
alienations" (Bosch 1975:176). The message of the church is
both, "Be reconciled to God" (2 Cor. 5:20), and "be reconciled
to your brother" (Matt. 5:24); and it is both, "Where are you?"
(Gen. 3:9) and "Where is Abel your brother?" (Gen. 4:9).

It is this twofold mandate that compels groups like Africa
Enterprise to be fully committed to the two-way reconciliation:
the vertical and the horizontal. Time may not be on our side in
southern Africa, but the role of such a ministry is vital. The
interracial, interdenominational nature of this team is a model
of what the Body of Christ should look like in southern Africa.
The way it operates in integrated situations further shows its
commitment to reconciling people. The team seeks to present the
gospel to the entire spectrum of the peoples of southern Africa,
with special emphasis on intellectual circles where the gospel
has lost its credibility; the leadership as a whole, via Con-
gresses etc.; sustained thrusts into cities to touch every segment of the people and using a multi-directional strategy em-
bracing our twofold mandate.

We can only hope that efforts of God's people will be rewarded
in southern Africa and that even in this eleventh hour God will
overrule, and that disaster will be averted. If that does not
happen, we can only trust that God will give us sufficient grace
to face the situation with him who said,

All authority in heaven and on earth has been given to
me. Go therefore and make disciples of all nations,
baptizing them in the name of the Father and of the Son
and of the Holy Spirit, teaching them to observe all
that I have commanded you; and lo, *I am with you* always, to the end of the age (Matt. 28:18-20).

Response #2

Norman E. Thomas

Mr. Leeuw has made a commendable attempt at introducing simultaneously the complexities of the liberation struggle in southern Africa and categories from European theology to interpret
them. In these comments, therefore, I shall analyze several of
the key terms, their meaning and usage both in this paper and in
other related contexts.

LIBERATION

The term "liberation" has been given rightly as the principal
concept for interpreting the church and its mission in southern
Africa today. The author has elaborated both its political and
theological connotations.

What is "true liberation"? Mr. Leeuw in his section on
Namibia calls it "the essential universal human principle of
life," that man has been created for freedom, justice and
fraternity but is often in bondage and imprisonment. Christ
came as Man both to share in human bondage and imprisonment, and
to proclaim release to the captives and to set at liberty those
who are oppressed (Luke 4:18). That is, according to Leeuw, his
"christological demand." As men and women struggle for freedom,
justice and fraternity, they experience the presence of God in
Christ. That is the meaning of his "theophanic and epiphanic
presence."

Does a change of political systems as has happened in
Mozambique by itself constitute "liberation"? Mr. Leeuw seems
to imply this in asserting that in Mozambique liberation has

happened. Others will find confusing this narrowing of the use
of the term.

Is liberation an event or a continuous state of being? The
writer seemed to imply the latter in his words, "Liberation is
only possible where there is continued revolution or change."

I found Tom Leeuw's discussion of the "new order" in Mozambique pregnant with meaning in the context of liberation. We
believe that God is actively at work. He works not only through
the gathered congregation of faith to bring freedom, justice and
fraternity, but also through the revolutionary struggles of a
people to achieve these ends. Therefore, we who desire to live
actively with God will experience his presence not just in the
church building but also in the "concrete reality of neighborliness."

In Mozambique, a nation undergoing radical social change,
this implies being open to experience the living presence of
Christ amid these changes. When Christians join in proclaiming
release to the captive and in setting at liberty those who are
oppressed they walk with Christ and experience his presence. No
rigid separation of church and state is possible. Instead, to
walk with Christ involves active participation in politics by
individual Christians and a dynamic working relationship between
church and state.

Tension remains, however, in Mozambique as in every country
in which the state seeks to influence and transform every segment of society. Those who emphasize the church as the instrument of God's present transforming power seek to expand its
institutional ministries not only through worship but through
social service. In doind so they evoke a sense of competition
between church and state which leads to conflict between them.
Those, on the other hand, who emphasize God's living presence in
all of society may so narrow the specific program of the gathered church that it appears to be concerned merely for worship,
pastoral care and institutional maintenance.

THE CHURCH AS SOCIAL AND RELIGIOUS REALITY

Do the terms "social" and "religious" reality as used by Mr.
Leeuw denote ideal norms for the church or its real objective
situation?

In interpreting the objective situation of the German
Lutheran Church in Namibia, the author appears to give the
second meaning. Pastors on contract from Germany are openly
critical of the apartheid system whereas the resident members
of their congregations are accepting it. Leeuw concludes: "This

is the point where there is a manifest contradiction between the
nature of the church as a social reality and its nature as a
religious reality."

In other sections the author uses these terms to refer to
what he feels ought to be. The church as social reality ought to
be open to change, to be revolutionary. As a religious reality
it ought to perceive God's presence in the history of liberation.

The problem of varying usage of these terms in the paper
would have been reduced, I believe, if the author had utilized
them in interpreting the Afrikaner churches of South Africa.
They too have a perception of God's presence in their Afrikaner
history of liberation. Theirs, however, is a radically different understanding of liberation from that of black Christians.
Can it be said that Afrikaner Christians also suffer from a conflict between the social and religious realities in their
churches? I believe so.

POLITICAL THEOLOGY

This term is coming into increasing usage today among Christians who understand theology as *praxis*--as an ongoing process
of combining action and reflection upon it. Theology thereby
involves not just thinking but doing, as Jesus said. "Not
every one who says to me 'Lord, Lord,' shall enter the kingdom
of heaven, but he who does the will of my father who is in
heaven" (Matt. 7:21).

I wish that Mr. Leeuw had used this term in reference to
various Christian responses to the political situation in
southern Africa. He uses the term only in describing the Dutch
Reformed Church's religious sanction of apartheid. But the
religious critics of that system also engage in "political theology." The South African Council of Churches' "A Message to
the People of South Africa" in 1968 was a profound theological
critique of the apartheid system, as were the subsequent writ-
ings of black theologians. In Zimbabwe, the speeches of Bishop
A. T. Muzorewa, President of the African National Council, can
best be described as "political theology."

THE CHURCH IN ZIMBABWE

The response by Christians to the liberation struggle in
Zimbabwe (Rhodesia) differs significantly from that in South
Africa. In common with Stark and Morton in their analysis of
the church and southern Africa, Mr. Leeuw gives insufficient
weight to this fact.

In 1965, the Rhodesian Prime Minister, Ian Smith, claimed that
his Unilateral Declaration of Independence (UDI) from Great

Britain was a blow struck "to preserve Christian civilization."
Most church leaders within the country condemmed both the act
and the fraudulent attempt to give a religious sanction to it.
In doing so they continued in their role of being the voice of
the oppressed African minority rather than of the privileged
white minority in that country. The preponderance of Africans
over Europeans (as the white settlers are called) in Zimbabwe
has grown in the past fifteen years from a 16 to 1 to a 25 to
1 ratio. The churches, both in membership and in leadership in
African education, have for the most part mirrored the national
population profile.

One important development in recent years has been the rapid
advancement of Africans to leadership in the mainline denominations formerly known as "mission churches." By 1974, Africans
headed the Methodist, United Methodist, United Church of Christ,
United Congregational and Evangelical Lutheran Churches. These
major denominations have almost total African membership and African principals and headmasters today for their schools. Since
1974, the larger Roman Catholic and Anglican churches have ele-
vated Africans to the episcopacy, recognizing that their membership is preponderantly African although many parishes are still
dependent upon the financial support of European members and
upon expatriate personnel. In denominations with separate
branches for black and white members (e.g. Dutch/African Reformed and Baptists), African leaders are increasingly out-
spoken. The profile of Zimbabwean churches would not be
complete without mention of the large and growing African independent churches which today comprise approximately 25% of
the Christian community in that country.

These facts lead me to question Mr. Leeuw's judgments that
"the place of black people has been insignificant in the history
of the church in its institutional development in Zimbabwe" and
that "on the whole, the church is still organized on a missionary pattern."

The church has played a very significant role in the growth
of Zimbabwean nationalism. Rev. Ndabaningi Sithole, the first
Congregational minister to be university trained, became a nationalist leader in 1960 upon his return to his country. He describes in his book, *African Nationalism,* the contribution of
the Christian church in broadening the outlook of many Africans,
discouraging tribal hatred, and providing educational opportunities. He concludes: "The present enlightened African political leadership would be next to impossible but for the Christian Church that spread literacy to many parts of Africa" (1970:
94).

There has been a long history of political protest by churchmen in southern Rhodesia against political injustice and white
minority rule.

Prophetic criticism by missionaries against white racism
reached high points in the 1920s and 1960s. Rev. John White
and Fr. A. S. Cripps led the Southern Rhodesia Missionary Conference in active opposition to repressive laws in the 1920s.
The tide of protest then ebbed until church leaders championed
the cause of African nationalism in the decade after 1959 as its
leaders were denied elementary human rights. Prominent among
them were the Honorable Garfield Todd (former Prime Minister and
missionary of the Church of Christ of New Zealand), United
Methodist Bishop Ralph Dodge (deported in 1964 when President
of the newly-formed Christian Council of Rhodesia), Anglican
Bishop Kenneth Skelton (who succeeded Dodge as CCR President),
and Catholic Bishop Donal Lamont of Umtali.

The vein of religious protest against racism by African
churchmen is equally rich and deep. T. O. Ranger in *The African Voice in Southern Rhodesia* (1970) documents the active
involvement by African churchmen of both mission and independent
churches during the 1898-1930 period. Leaders of mass political
movements, beginning with the African National Council in 1957,
were invariably graduates of missionary schools. In December
1971, nationalist leaders turned to churchmen as symbols of
national unity. Bishop A. T. Muzorewa became President of the
United African National Council and two other clergy executive
officers.

During the 1960s two religious newspapers became the political voice of the voiceless, following the banning of the *African Daily News* in 1964--the Catholic weekly *Motto* ("Fire")
and the United Methodist monthly *Umbowo* ("Witness"). Both
newspapers were subsequently banned in the turbulent 1970s by
the Smith regime. They provide abundant evidence of the
churches' condemnation of U.D.I. in 1965, although their most
impressive act of opposition to the state was but one in a
long series of church protests.

These comments, however, are minor amendments to a solid and
profound analysis of liberation and the churches of southern
Africa.

In closing, we should note other important themes for the
church in southern Africa which are present through eclipsed
by the central one of liberation in Mr. Leeuw's presentation.

EVANGELISM AND CHURCH GROWTH

In many communities vigorous church growth is taking place as indigenous church leadership emerges.

In Zimbabwe, the early disruptions of the civil war were a stimulus to evangelism. The "keeps" in which African villagers are being forced to live behind barbed wire become the churches' growth points. Lacking church buildings, Christians began to worship in their homes. Men and young people increasingly took leadership in what had often in the past been considered a "women's church." The church today proclaims a gospel of salvation and liberation. Prayers of confession and new professions of faith are followed by prayers for "the boys in the forest" (the freedom fighters). In these communities, the church has become the people's church and is often self-supporting for the first time. Meanwhile, churches are growing rapidly, both among those fleeing to town from the war zones and those seeking a sustaining faith and fellowship amid the stresses of urban life.

AFRICAN INDEPENDENT CHURCHES

From many points of view the African Independent Church movement is unprecedented in size and scope in the history of Christian missions. Of the more than 6,000 movements already identified, over half are found in South Africa alone! Surely this is one of the most dramatic developments in the history of Christianity in southern Africa.

Since 1882, large-scale secessions have taken place from almost all churches and missions in South Africa, as African leaders ought to escape from patterns of racial segregation and to have a fuller opportunity to exercise their own leadership. At first, the South African government favored repression of these movements fearing that religious revolt would lead to movements of political rebellion.

Later movements of the Zionist type emphasized the expression of an authentic African spirituality while affirming the apostolic *kerygma*. Today, they provide a channel of Christian creativity in the African setting--a place to feel at home.

Of particular interest in connection with Mr. Leeuw's paper is their relationship to the liberation struggle. In 1961, Bishop Sundkler reported that

broadly speaking, the politically awake and active, if subscribing still to 'Christianity' at all, are found in other Churches, and not among "the Native Separatists". The Separatists go out of their way to state that they take no part in politics (1961:305).

The concern for legal recognition by the South African government, as well as the strong desire of many groups to acquire
land, may have also contributed to their political quietism.

The absence of any data concerning their involvement in the
South African liberation struggle would indicate that Bishop
Sunkler's findings remain true today. The situation may change
in the future, however, both as independent church members become better educated, and as more Africans become personally
involved in the liberation struggle. Recent evidence of growing
contacts between independent churches and African nationalist
leaders of Zimbabwe would seem to support this prognosis.

PART II

The Church
in Eastern Africa

The Church in Eastern Africa

Negash Kebede

In the last few years the western Christian press has been fo-
cusing attention on the development and growth of the church in
Africa. Suddenly the tone has changed from a paternalistic
concern to one of listening and observing new and strange happenings in the church. However, some of the literature and
especially statistical data are conflicting. Having come from
Ethiopia, I often had to compare what I read with the facts I
know from experience. For example, the membership of the Ethiopian Orthodox Church was given to be 14,000,000 by one source
(Coxill and Grubb 1968:11), while another one gave 6,000,000
members for the same period (Barrett 1968:284). The region of
eastern Africa which has been suggested for my analysis includes the countries of Burundi, Ethiopia, Kenya, Malawi,
Rwanda, Somalia, Sudan, Tanzania, and Uganda. Statistics available for this region for the year 1968 put the number of foreign
missionaries at about 3400 and the total number of major denominations at about 110 (Coxill and Grubb 1968:61-95). Unreliable
statistics coupled with an enormous number of denominations to
sort out reveal the difficulty one encounters when conducting
any type of reasonably organized study. To get around one of
the problems we notice one factor which is common to the local
churches of almost all the denominations: they are all alike
in that they have all gone through the same stages in their
development process. In this connection an in-depth study of
a particular church might be desired in order to generalize
and make application to other churches. Unfortunately, where
the culture and background of the churches in different nations
differ a lot, a survey type of analysis is to be preferred. In
this paper there will undoubtedly be a reflection from my

experience with the Meserete Kristos Church in Ethiopia and my close association with the Eastern Mennonite Board of Missions, which has been working in partnership with the Meserete Kristos Church during the last twenty years.

SOME BACKGROUND FACTS

Christianity has a long history in eastern Africa. Today we find Catholic, Orthodox, and Protestant Christians. Since our discussion will not include the Catholic and Orthodox groups, "the church in eastern Africa" will refer to the Protestant and related bodies. The majority of the Protestant churches are the result of western missionary activities during the last 150 years. Therefore any worthwhile discussion of these churches is impossible without reference to the missions from the West. Because of the constant contact with missionaries, the Protestant churches have not suffered isolation from the rest of Christendom. At the same time this has had both negative and positive consequences. Most of the Protestant groups have been targets of acculturation. On the other hand much can be learned from examples like the Ethiopian Orthodox Church, which has the longest history of any in this region and has developed its own liturgy, church organization, and administration.

Let us examine what the churches in eastern Africa have in common the process of their development. All of them have passed or are passing through one of the following stages.

1. The period of mission independence

A mission sponsored by a board or Christian organization in Europe or North America is sent to Africa. Its members suddenly find themselves in a new situation. They find out that they are the most important, the most educated and respected people in the area. They begin to assume key roles in the small church composed of mostly mission personnel. It is not uncommon to see an individual missionary simultaneously playing the role of a pastor, teacher, evangelist, technician, etc. This is the period where many adherents are directly won by the missionary to his particular denomination. Many mission experts agree this period has been the era of the pioneer missionaries and such a situation should not exist at the present time. Others disagree because they feel the national churches are not yet able to send pioneer missionaries.

2. The period of the young church

The goal of a mission being the establishing of churches, the mission soon takes initiative to organize its adherents into a body of believers having explicitly defined goals. This results

in the formation of committees and councils and the sharing of
the responsibility the missionary was holding with the local
people. Until now, the adherents have lived individual lives
whose success or failure is measured only by the individual's
quality of moral and spiritual integrity in conformity with
the standard set in the Bible. Now they begin to see that
being a Christian goes beyond the holiness of an individual.
Suddenly it dawns upon them that the Christian life is not to
be measured by subjective feelings alone. It is a life of
interaction with the whole community. This community needs to
grow and influence others. It needs leaders, which in turn
means the sharing of power to achieve this goal. The sum total
of the effects of the second stage is more self awareness for
the local people and maybe a little bit of uncertainty and am-
biguity in the meaning of the whole process for the mission.

3. The period of dissent

A young church has actually been born during the second stage.
It is young in every sense of the word. It is totally dependent
on the mission for resources, vision, authority, and ideas.
Nevertheless it is growing. During this process, it is the
common experience of the majority of the churches for tension
to exist between different groups in the young church. The
mission might have its "loyal" members. There are others who
might be looked upon as hostile groups or disturbers. Sometimes
these could be real enemies of the church and real disturbers,
but often they are people who see things in the local context
and want change accordingly. Furthermore, tension could be the
result of differences on matters of theology, church administration, or a power struggle between emerging leaders. If
tension builds too much, it could result in a breakaway as in
the example of the independent churches. Usually the conflict
stays inside, greatly hampering the rapid growth of the church.

4. The period of independence of the local church

The use of the word "independence" here does not refer to the
throwing away of the yoke of oppression as in the political
sense. Here it is used in the sense of determining that a
church is capable of self-governing, self-preserving, and
self-propagating. If a church is capable of fulfilling these
goals through the use of local resources and without its people
losing their identity, then it is an independent church. This
demands the ability to express the life of the church through
one's own culture and the discerning of what elements in the
culture are in harmony with the Word of God. In short, independence means self-reliance of the church. It may seem at
times that such an aspiration has an overtone of pride and
narrow nationalism. There could be cases where such an

accusation is valid. But the real goal of independence is the
survival of the church in spite of shifts and changes in the
world. In a world where kingdoms rise and fall and where power
changes hands often, the church in eastern Africa cannot afford
to be totally dependent on the churches abroad. Whatever
changes are going to occur in the future, the church must be
able to stand on its own now. Many of the churches in eastern
Africa would like to believe that they are in stage four. But
I believe it is a gradual process and there are many subtle
aspects of it which make it impossible to know whether it has
been achieved or not. There are also dangers to be avoided in
advocating independence. Independence to me does not mean a
complete stopping of fellowship and relationship with mission
agencies, as the advocates of moratorium would like us to believe. If the church is truly universal, fellowship must be
possible by the working together of Christians from different
nations without serious conflicts or domination of one by
another.

THE CHURCH TODAY

In Africa the present has a short duration. Dynamic changes
are constantly taking place. We will look at some major areas
of the churches' life in the recent past.

1. Church growth and evangelism

I have not found up-to-date and accurate statistics which gives
the total number of denominations and their membership in
eastern Africa. Such facts seem to be scattered here and
there. The following rather antiquated figures may help to
compare the situation almost a decade ago with the present
(Coxill and Grubb 1968:61-95):

Country	Population (in thousands)	No. of Churches or Missions	1962 Membership	1968 Membership
Burundi	2,600	7	32,857	226,194
Ethiopia	22,000	26	164,767	227,125
Kenya	9,000	22	748,107	788,070
Malawi	4,000	12	393,402	634,914
Rwanda	3,000	6	3,736	170,645
Somalia	2,300	3	30	140
Sudan	14,000	7	87,190	166,000
Tanzania	10,000	19	537,708	1,034,588
Territory of Afars & Issas	70	0	0	0
Uganda	7,100	7	835,721	1,520,969
	74,000	109	2,803,518	4,768,645

It is evident that the above figures do not say the whole truth even for the period 1962-1968. The value and use of statistics is not popular in Africa. Perhaps that is one factor which contributes to the problem of gathering information. We must also note that significant changes have taken place since then. There are no missions or recognized church bodies in Somalia today. In the Sudan the church is concentrated in the South. Civil war between the South and the government was being waged until 1972. Now churches are being reconstructed. The main defect of the above table is its failure to include figures for the independent churches. In Kenya alone by 1971 there were 180 independent churches (Lamont 1971:11). The independent churches are growing and stimulating growth in the traditional mission churches. Other sources reveal that the independent churches are growing at an incredible rate. The following gives a picture of the expansion of these churches in the whole of Africa for the period 1960-1970 (Lamont 1971:11).

	1960	1970
Nations Involved	33	34
Ethnic groups involved	260	330
Denominations (Distinct bodies)	4,000	5,300
Adherents	6,000,000	10,000,000
Annual increase in adherents		
a) Natural population increase	132,000	250,000
b) Increase by conversion	168,000	250,000
Total annual increase	300,000	500,000

It was pointed out earlier that in the development of the churches, a possible reason for the emergence of the independent groups was the creative tension existing between the mission churches and certain dissatisfied elements within them. But in most cases it has been initiated by individuals who felt God's call through supernatural means such as dreams and visions. In any case the emergence of an independent group should not surprise us. The nineteenth century witnessed the scramble for Africa by European powers. On the other hand the long list of the different mission denominations existing in eastern Africa cannot but lead one to believe that there was also a spiritual scramble for Africa. The question mission denominations seemed to ask was not "Who is on the Lord's side?" but rather "Who is on my side?" No wonder then we find moving and perhaps shocking words like the following:

The Independent Churches are the closest we have come to making Christianity our own. The bishop here is also the local carpenter. To you it may seem a queer

mixture. To us it is right. . . . The streets
of Africa are fast becoming their witness
points. Politics is a major factor in church
independency. God understands it. Beyond the
schisms one can sense the emergence of a genuinely indigenous renewal of Christianity. . . .
The slums of Africa have found a religious
identity. The imperialism of the missionary
societies has come to an end. . . . Elitist
missionary education was subversion of our
tribal communal solidarity. Welcome to our
huts! Dear God come in! . . . Concentration
on missions enables churches in Europe and
America to overlook injustice on their own
door-step. Back to your own land! There has
been a failure of love in missionary churches.
Christianity in Africa cannot afford to be
stiff, old-fashioned, unchanging. Divisions
of Western Christendom have been propagated a
thousand times in Africa. Drums, holy words,
communal sharing, life seen as a whole and un-
inhibited joyous expressions of faith have
always been ours. They jump and run with joy
trembling the earth with their feet. There
is life to be found in the soil of Africa
(Kinuthia 1973).

The mission churches are not expected to agree with all that
has been said. They are simply asked to understand and to stop
their hostility because these movements are only revivals from
within the church. They break away when they are denied com-
fortable accommodation inside the church. In Ethiopia there
were no independent churches as such, but there were similar
movements. To those inside, it seemed like a movement stirred
by fanatics and immature young people. However, observers from
outside did not fail to note that this was also a part of the
revival of the church. A summary of happenings in Ethiopia is
given in the following:

In 1964 a further, unconnected, revival movement
began among the students around Addis Ababa, which
soon involved large numbers at the university and
colleges in the capital. In 1966 the students
(formerly members of the Orthodox and Protestant
churches) formed an independent church, the God's
All Time Association, also known by the Amharic
name "Yesemaye Berhan" (Light of Heaven), which
lays its emphasis on healing, exorcism, glossolalia
and evangelism. Similar groups exist throughout
Ethiopia and in 1967 were seeking government recognition as independent Association (Barrett 1968:31).

The impact of such movements on the church is something I have experienced. Ten years ago our church in Ethiopia (Meserete Kristos Church) was struggling to exist with only 200 members. Since the revival, we have witnessed the steady growth of the church. Today the Meserete Kristos Church has over 2000 members. Other churches in Ethiopia are also going through the same changes.

Those who seek revival tend to be propelled by emotions. The mission churches emphasize theological depth, teaching and religious form. There seems to be a coming together of these elements. This has contributed to the rapid growth of the church.

As far as evangelism is concerned, the church's strategy can best be described by the famous saying "The Church can go no farther till it goes deeper." The opposite has proved fruitless. The church is no more interested in covering a geographical area by the process of proselytizing and reproducing churches. The only motive for evangelism is renewal of life. I remember an incident in Addis Ababa two years ago. After a young man had witnessed to a person who apparently had a real spiritual hunger, the man sought advice as to which church to attend. The reply was something unexpected: "Do not go to our church because it has no life." In other instances I have known people who felt the call for the work of evangelism, quit their job and began preaching. There was no guarantee of support by a board or a church.

As for plans and strategies, there are none compared to standards in the West. The few boards and planning committees often are bogged down with bureaucracy and are not very effective. In spite of lack of planning the gospel is reaching to every ethnic entity in eastern Africa. However, I must admit that the Moslem communities continue to be a real challenge to the church. This is evident from the statistics cited in the tabulation at the beginning of this sub-section. Efforts by missions and churches to enter the Territory of Afars and Issas have not been successful.

Evangelism is one field where the local church and outside mission agencies can show cooperation. The church is zealous but is not taking advantage of scientific planning. Missions are welcome to use their skill in this field. Although the days of the pioneer missionary are over, missions are continuing to work behind the scenes with the local church. There are also indirect ways the missionary can help in evangelism. The technician who fixes the public address system for the church is participating in the work of evangelism. Another important role an outside agency can play is in assisting the church in the

production of Christian literature and other materials for
communicating the gospel message.

2. The internal life of the church

Missions used the "healing, teaching and preaching" method to
propagate the gospel. As a result in many countries the highest
literacy rates are found in church communities. Furthermore,
one of the institutions churches have inherited from the missions is schools. This has been a blessing for the church.
Although expensive to run, it is a means of teaching the gospel
to the younger generation. The church continues to suffer from
lack of education for its leaders. In the past individuals have
been sent abroad for education. Some churches also have attempted to open Bible schools on their own locations. Both have
proved to be very costly ventures. Here is also an area where
outside agencies and the church can cooperate in the sharing of
resources and creative ideas.

Another aspect of the internal life of the church is that it
must not be a replica of the mission which created it. It must
be relevant to the situation in which it exists. In the artic-
ulation of its faith, customs and traditions which are not
damaging to its faith are to be appreciated and practised. Not
very long ago, in Ethiopia and other parts of eastern Africa
congregations used to be heard echoing western tunes. Today
they have learned to worship and sing in the tunes of their own
tradition. As a result the church has been flooded by literally
hundreds and thousands of songs on inspiration.

The secret of the growth of the church during the past years
is due to the simplicity in form and organizational structure.
At the same time this structure and form is more strict when it
comes to adhering to biblical standards. The danger is that it
is slowly moving toward being a large institutional body. In
an institutional church professional leaders are hired. The
importance of hierarchy is emphasized. This results in many
members aspiring to positions in this hierarchy, not for service
they can render but for honor and publicity they can gain.
Power struggles and rivalry between leaders are created. The
situation does not allow the participation of the average member
in church life. The average person is lost as a passive lis-
tener. From experience the alternative to this is a "lay
church." Even though it has its own defects, I have seen it
avoid some of the problems mentioned previously. The leaders
are not paid for their services. The idea of hierarchy is
played down so that a power struggle is avoided.

The stage at which the churches are today in eastern Africa
is comparable to the stage which scholars label the stage of a

sect. This idea is articulated in an article by John W. Eby entitled "The Institutionalization of The Church" (Eby 1976). Although the comparison he makes is between a sect and a church, in my experience I have found the same to be true between a "lay church" and other, institutional churches. I have selected the comparisons which I think were true in some of the churches I have known in eastern Africa.

Lay Church	*Institutional Church*
At cultural periphery of community	At cultural center of community
Renunciation of or indifference to prevailing culture and social organization	Acceptance of prevailing political and economic order
Self-centered religion based on personal experience	Culture-centered religion based on affirming of citizenship in an existing community
Strict standards for membership	Few requirements for membership or laxity in implementing stated membership requirements
Social community excluding unworthy members	Social institution embracing all who are socially compatible
Many religious services regardless of interference with other aspects of life	Regular services at stated intervals
Adhering to strict biblical standards such as tithing	Acceptance of general cultural standards as practical definition of religious obligations
Unspecialized unprofessional part-time ministry	Specialized, professional ministry
A high degree of congregational participation in services and administration	Delegation of responsibility to a small percentage of the members
Fervor and positive action in worship	Restraint and passive listening

As long as the congregation is composed of people, it can
never be perfect. What we can do is to choose an administrative
structure which can allow the Spirit of God to work.

The institutionalized church is accused of lack of vitality
of life and keeping its members dormant. On the other hand a
lay church can also be locked in the letter of the law in trying
to measure up to the spiritual standards of biblical times.
Nevertheless I would say because of its vitality of life and
simplicity the lay church model would fit for the situation in
Africa. Here is where mission agencies need to be careful. The
right attitude of any mission is described by Paul's testimony:
"And unto the Jews I became as a Jew that I might gain the
Jews; . . . To them without law, as without law that I might
gain them that are without law" (1 Cor. 9:20). Those missions
which have adopted this view have had a harmonious relationship
with their partner churches in eastern Africa.

3. The Church's total service to the world

What we refer to as the world is the social environment in which
the church finds itself. As regards service rendered to the
world, first we have service simply by presence. The world is
watching. There are ample opportunities to influence by living.

Secondly, in many countries of eastern Africa civil servants,
high ranking government officials, and even some heads had their
roots in the church. People with church background are known
for their honesty, integrity, and duty consciousness. Though
now, in most cases, they seem to have abandoned the church,
there is still that remnant of the church in them which makes
them favor the truth. Thus indirectly the church is helping in
the building of the nations by teaching them to do justice.

Thirdly, it is through the church and mission agencies that
the biggest achievements have been made in the fields of education and medicine. Church and mission school students are
often known for their high academic and moral standards. In
some countries the number of hospitals and clinics run by the
missions and churches is comparable to that of the state.

Finally, during times of natural disaster like the drought
and ensuing famine the church was there to help. In Ethiopia,
the different mission and church groups formed the CRDA (Christian Relief and Development Association) during the time of the
drought and famine. All aid from church-related organizations
was channeled to the famine-stricken areas through this organization. Another example is the work in Kenya. Although Kenya
and Somalia were not always the best of friends, in 1974 the
National Christian Council of Kenya (NCCK) sent food to Somalia
to help the people who were faced with natural catastrophe.

The significance of the church's involvement in this way is that its aid is without any strings attached. It used to be that education, medicine, and other aid to the needy were used as a bait to attract people to the gospel. That would be concentrating evangelism only on the poor, sick, and illiterate. Today service is rendered without even a hidden motive to convert the people. The church has learned that it is only the love of Christ which can attract people. With this understanding, churches are extending their program to agricultural and other forms of development which improve the life of the unfortunate ones in the world. The work of the NCCK is a good example to cite here. Its program includes education, urban development, relief and rehabilitation, rural development such as village polytechnic, home industries, etc. (NCCK 1974).

Despite the above successful aspects, the church must continue to penetrate more into the world and change it. We must remember, however, that the church is never in charge of things. We cannot have things our way. The greatest challenge for the church is its relationship with the state. It is difficult to know when to speak against injustice and when it is proper to keep quiet. The whole issue regarding repressive regimes is something to which an answer has not been found. Quiet pietism and submissiveness are definitely not the way of Christ. It also does not seem the duty of the church to force all things to be right. When it discovers a way between these two extremes, the church will have added another important dimension to its ministry.

CONCLUSION: THE FUTURE OF THE CHURCH

We have discussed many encouraging aspects of the church in eastern Africa. A recent statement in a brochure issued by the Eastern Mennonite Board of Missions reads that in Kenya alone, there are 10,000 adult baptisms a week. It is believed that Kenya today is more than 70% Christian. Other sources estimate that by A.D. 2000 there will be 350 million Christians in Africa. Then Africa will become a "Christian continent." Personally I am praying that the latter will not happen. The Lord is not interested in attaching his name to masses of people but rather he is looking to individuals who are willing to carry his cross.

The present situation is that of prevailing optimism. But what is the future of the church community? Politically, the situation in eastern Africa is very tenuous. There will be inevitable changes. How will these changes affect us? New ideologies are being introduced. The days when the church was the only body concerned with the salvation of souls and the physical welfare of people are over. Rival philosophies which at the

surface look similar to that of the church are emerging. The
church now is being pushed to a corner where it appears that it
has nothing different to offer except the promise of salvation
in heaven. The Bible tells us that we have been placed in
heavenly places. Has the church forgotten that? Especially in
these days of revolution and scientific socialism the big task
of the church is to demonstrate to the world that its precepts
go much beyond a set of moral codes which often are viewed as
inhibiting the individual from positive action. It is necessary,
therefore, to restate the infallible doctrines of Christ in contemporary language and show that Christianity is also concerned
with the life to be lived here and now.

We may ask what churches outside, especially the churches of
the western world, have to contribute in the shaping of the future of the church in eastern Africa. First, they must believe
in the church triumphant. We hear of persecutions and socialism,
communism or other philosophies taking over. It is true that
the church as an institution may cease to exist in many countries. But the real church against which the powers of hell
cannot prevail will continue to conquer. This belief by
churches abroad will strengthen the solidarity of the church
universal. Second, the church in any part of the world should
not identify itself with a secular system. If the church is
triumphant it must be able to exist under any system.

The universality of the church is also important. I am surprised to find in songs about the church and the reign of Christ
such as the following lines ("Jesus Shall Reign," by Isaac
Watts):

> From North to South the princes meet
> To pay their homage at His feet;
> While Western empires own their Lord
> And savage tribes attend his word.

As long as the above mentality remains in the minds of Christians in the West, the church will be vulnerable to attack by
other forces which try to find loopholes. Our song should
change to the words found in the Revelation of John (Rev. 5:9):

> Worthy art thou to take the scroll and to open its seals
> For thou wast slain and by thy blood didst ransom
>   men for God
> From every tribe and tongue and people and nation
> And hast made them a kingdom and priests for our God
> And they shall reign on earth.

Response #1

Vincent J. Donovan

Having spent seventeen years in Tanzania, East Africa, working with the Catholic Church, and for more than ten years in close collaboration with the Lutheran Church (Missouri Synod) there, I appreciate the analysis of the church in East Africa made by Ato Negash Kebede, beginning with the work of the pioneer missionaries, up to his thoughts on the future of the church in that area. I would like to follow the same division of stages he made in the life of the church, and address my remarks accordingly.

PERIOD OF MISSION INDEPENDENCE

The author rightly points out that missionaries sent from Europe and North America to Africa found themselves in an entirely new situation, as the most respected, important and educated people in the area to which they were sent; and, I think it should be added, as part of the colonial structure that had come to Africa. Being the most respected members in the area was one side of the coin. The other side was decidedly negative. It was the culture shock we went through. It took no time at all to realize that we were forever destined to walk as strangers in a strange land. That should have been a salvific lesson for us. I am not sure that it always was. Looking back on it now, I think I can say that I and missionaries like me, of different denominations, were rather well prepared theologically and scripturally, but we were not prepared culturally for the task given us. We had no idea of the richness and importance of the cultures to which we were being sent. Most of us, Catholic and Protestant, had come in a real way as a response to the call of Doctor Livingstone to help make the Africans "gentlemen, civilized and Christian," presumably in that order.

I think the author should have included the methods of the
apostolate, used at that time, in his appraisal of the mission
period of the church in East Africa, since those methods have
left their mark on the church there. Starting with the apostolate to the slaves, buying slaves, freeing them, Christian-
izing them, settling them as Christian families on the huge
mission plantations; the failure of the apostolate to the slaves
and the turning to education, first with catechetical schools
where reading, writing, arithmetic and religion were taught,
into the blossoming of true academic schools of every level, the
birth of the school system in East Africa, leading up to the
time of independence of the East African countries, outside of
Ethiopia.

I say that these methods have left their mark on the church,
and I believe they have. The mission compound idea came from
these methods, the idea of a centripetal center towards which
everything should flow, the center of salvation drawing people
away from their life style and values, away from their very culture. The mission compound became a true foreign enclave. The
child-oriented and child-flavored mission was a result of these
methods; the "parents of tomorrow approach." The subservience
and dependence of the Christianized peoples was another effect,
an effect which did not begin to disappear until the arrival
of political independence. Religion considered as an academic
subject was another effect. Perhaps the most serious effect was
the questionable motivation for baptism created in first generation Christians. A price was being exacted from the people
for the freedom they would receive at the hands of the missionaries, first a freedom from slavery and later a freedom from
ignorance, and that price was the acceptance of Christianity.
The basic premise was that no child would emerge from Standard
Four or Standard Eight of the mission school without being a
Christian; and the premise was essentially correct.

The author mentions that this mission period was a time when
many adherents were won by the missionary to his particular denomination. That is true, and it would also be true to say that
the mission period was one of a total lack of ecumenism. The
scandal of the hatred and division among the Christian churches
scarred the Christians of the mission period. Almost in the
very first generation of Christianity in Uganda, there was open
warfare between Protestants and Catholics.

I mentioned that in comparison to the cultural preparation of
the missionaries, the theological and scriptural preparation
they received was satisfactory. However, even here there was
room for much thought and improvement. The gospel in our hands
had become an acculturated gospel, grown over with layers and
layers of white, western, European and American interpretation

and tradition. It required a great deal of time and effort and courage to peel away these accretions, to come again to the naked kernel of the gospel message. But most missionaries did not have time even to try to make such an effort. So involved were we in the social apostolate that we scarcely had time to take a look in depth at this gospel we were preaching. Indeed, except for Sunday ministry, it is questionable whether we even devoted a major portion of our time to the preaching of the gospel. In a survey taken up by the Catholic Church in the early sixties, it was found that 90% of the instruction given to new Christians in East Africa (Tanganyika, Kenya, and Uganda) was being given by catechists and evangelists, not by missionaries. These catechists and evangelists, by and large, were ignorant (that is, not trained in the teaching of religion), and they were passing on their ignorance to others. The edifice of the church was resting on that rather shaky foundation.

The purpose of mission was not at all clear in the minds of missionaries during that initial period. And the leaders of the sending churches did not dispel that lack of clarity. We have the extraordinary statement of a man sent from Rome to a gathering of Catholic bishops in Dar es Salaam, in 1928. He was Monsignor Hinsley, Apostolic Visitor to East Africa, and he told the bishops: "Where it is impossible for you to carry on both the immediate task of evangelization and your educational work, neglect your churches in order to perfect your schools" (Moffet 1958). Whether there is in existence and in print a similar exhortation to Protestant missionaries matters little. The effect was the same. Missionaries of every denomination spent their lives acquiring, building up, supplying and teaching in schools of every description. It is no exaggeration to say that the school became *the* missionary method of East Africa. In 1970 when Tanzania by one swift move completely took over the mission schools, the government robbed the missionaries of their main apostolic method and rendered the advice of that apostolic visitor of 1928 hollow indeed. Missionaries, by that time, by and large had lost their nerve, their sense of direction and their purpose.

We had intended to establish churches in Africa. We ended up establishing missions.

THE PERIOD OF THE YOUNG CHURCH

I like very much the author's pointing out that as the young church begins to become a reality, there is an awakening to the fact that Christianity and the church involves much more than a gathering of individuals, but is essentially a life of interraction with community. Missionaries came from cultures which stressed individuality as an important value, and were sent to

cultures where community was a reality. I think what actually
happened was that the local church began to take on the flesh
and blood of the culture in which Christianity was planted, in
which community was an essential element. This throws light on
the gospel which we had brought to these people, a gospel which
we had unknowingly riddled with individuality. The people's
reaction to the gospel serves as a corrective to our understanding of the gospel. Perhaps the gospel will be fully known
only when it has been preached to all the nations of the world.
The author rightly points out that the goal of mission is the
establishment of churches. As with the gospel, so with the
church, we can be more than a little culture blind. We can
conceive only of that form of church with which we are familiar
in our own culture. And so, in establishing church, we establish in a predetermined way that form which we know. We can
become involved in preaching the church and not Christ. The
author, later on in the paper, discusses at length and with
understanding the phenomenal rise of the independent churches in
East Africa. I believe the difficulty arises in the beginning,
in our understanding of the church we are commissioned to establish. We sometimes conceive of the form and structure of the
church almost as if it were part of the gospel message we are
bringing to a people. I would think it is more the *response* to
the gospel message, on the part of a people of a particular culture accepting the gospel. And that people have a form and
structure already built into their lives and in their culture.
I think they have a right to accept the unchanging, supracultural gospel, and to respond to it, from their own cultural
stance. And their response will be the church, as they are,
where they are. Paul Tillich says that beyond everything else,
the church is simply and primarily a group of people who express
a new reality by which they have been grasped (1964).

PERIOD OF DISSENT

The author's view of the period of dissent is interesting and
highly accurate. The dependence of the young church insofar as
authority, resources, vision, and ideas go is a reality. The
sending church, or mission, expects only gratitude for this continuing dependence, but more often than not, a kind of bitter-
ness builds up, and a tension arises between the mission and the
church. The mission is thinking of the continually rising
spiral that threatens the very expansion of the church. The
local church is thinking of the lack of freedom it has in the
area of authority and vision simply because of its indebtedness
in the line of resources. The tension is a known fact in every
church.

Once again here, I think, the difficulty arises because the
church should not have been born in the second period, when the

period of the mission was finished, but in the very first period
of mission, with church itself, and not mission, as the goal of
the first period. Mission should have been a transient, mobile
reality in that period, on its way to becoming something else,
namely church, not itself the end of the line. And local church,
when it did come into existence in that first period should have
been independent from the start, as far as resources, authority,
and ideas go. The mission should have stayed in existence only
as a counseling, guiding factor, not as an authoritative, con-
trolling, supplying source.

PERIOD OF INDEPENDENCY OF THE LOCAL CHURCH

The author paints a clear and simple picture of the ideal of
a self-governing, self-sustaining, self-propagating church,
which he calls a self-reliant church. It is certainly a goal to
be aimed at, but as the author points out, it is not easily
achieved. There is much discussion these days, and much effort,
regarding the achievement of independence and maturity of the
young churches, but one has to wonder at the sincerity of many
of these programs, instituted nearly one hundred years after the
missionaries first arrived in East Africa. If independence and
maturity of the local church had been a goal from the beginning,
it surely would not have taken one hundred years to achieve that
goal. A church one hundred years old is not all that young.
The maturing of the church, or the bringing of the young church
to independence, has to be one process, begun on the day the
missionaries first come among a people with the gospel.

I think the author does not go deeply enough into *culture* in
discussing the nature of self-reliance in a church. I believe
it involves more than just discerning which elements of a culture are in harmony with the Word of God. I believe a culture
is the proper field for the preaching of the gospel, and the
coming to birth of the church. The gospel which is outside and
above every culture, must be preached to all the nations and
cultures of the world. When the gospel comes to any culture,
something in that culture must live and something must die.
When Christ comes to a culture, he comes not only to fulfill it,
but to prophesy against it. But it is up to the people of any
culture, it is their affair to judge, in the light of the gospel, what must live and what must die. It is not the affair of
the missionary, except in a guiding and consultative capacity.
His domain is the gospel. His task is not to lure the people
away from their life and their culture, in a centripetal movement towards the mission, to the center where salvation resides,
but to go out to the people where they live, in the midst of
their culture, and to surprise them out there in their darkness
with the light of Christ. The movement of Christianity will always be a centrifugal movement, away from Jerusalem and Samaria,

outwards towards the nations and cultures of the world. And the
people out there, as they are and where they are, if they accept
that light of Christ and respond to it, *are* the church, in the
midst of their culture. A culture comprises many things: a way
of thinking and philosophizing, a way of relating to other humans
and of distributing and using the goods of the earth, a way of
praying and relating to God, a way of structuring life and relating to it. All these things, if touched by the gospel become
the very texture and fabric of church life. They become the theology, and morality, and asceticism, and liturgy, and religious
and social life of the local church. They are eminently and
primarily the affair of the people of a Christianized culture.
They are not the affair of the missionary. His affair is the
gospel. All these things are involved in the concept of a self-
governing, self-sustaining, self-propagating, self-reliant
church. And they in no way militate against the universality or
catholicity of the church. It is only by evangelizing or discipling *panta ta ethne*, or all the ethnic, social, cultural nations
of the world, that we can arrive at a universal brotherhood or
fellowship of believers, instead of a culture-blind religion
based on a single, western, cultural version of Christianity.

THE CHURCH TODAY

The author has quoted a remarkable statement of a member of an
independent church which I think throws light on some of the
points I have mentioned.

*Founding of missions rather than churches, culture threatening
missions:* "The imperialism of the missionary societies has come
to an end . . . Elitist missionary education was subversion of
our tribal community solidarity."

*Interpretation of Christianity belongs to the people of the
culture:* "The Independent Churches are the closest we have come
in Africa to making Christianity our own . . . one can sense the
emergence of a genuinely indigenous renewal of Christianity."

Lack of ecumenism: "Divisions of Western Christendom have
been propagated a thousand times in Africa."

As the author states, the growth of the church in Africa is
phenomenal. And the leadership of all the churches has become
indigenous. Since independence, most of the bishops, presidents
and leaders of the churches are Africans. Another thing which
came with independence was ecumenism. Tanzania, for example, has
made great strides since 1961. There is now a common Bible in
Kiswahili for Protestants and Catholics. There have been numerous cases of exchange of pulpit and seminary rostrum in the
last few years, between Catholics and Lutherans. Today there is

a common training center in Scripture, church history and related subjects for Lutheran and Catholic evangelists and catechists. And there is still a vast field for evangelism among
the Nilo-Hamitic nomadic tribes of East Africa who have been
scarcely touched by the gospel.

THE FUTURE OF THE CHURCH

Africa may well become a Christian continent. I would disagree with the author on this point. He seems not to want this
to happen. With less than 18% of the world Christian, we badly
need the Christian witness of Africa in a darkening world: the
light to the Gentiles held up as hope to a world desperately in
need of hope. And unlike the author I do not see this hope
coming merely from "individuals who are willing to carry his
cross," but from communities and nations dedicated to the task
of bringing the kingdom of God.

Much thought and prayer will have to be undertaken in Africa
so that we may come to a better understanding of the church's
role in true human development. Glib, facile answers will be
no solution to the terrible problems facing us. To use development as an inducement to Christianity is, as the author
states, a perversion of the gospel. But the thought of development without the gospel is just as bad. Nazism will stand
forever as the indictment of progress for its own sake. And
the whole area of the church's relationship with politics and
political systems is a delicate and difficult one. The agony
of Africa is not over.

Response #2

Byrum Makokha

The East African zone assigned to Mr. Kebede for this symposium is indeed wide and varied in many ways. Yet Mr. Kebede was to address himself to it within a very limited time at his disposal. It is in this light that I think even though most of his data are based on Ethiopia, his own country, he has responsibly taken into account the current situation as it obtains in that part of Africa. Therefore, I sincerely congratulate him for a job well done.

In my response I shall use the term "church" for the church universal and "churches" to designate denominations. Also toward the end two other terms, "modality" and "sodality", will be mentioned; the former for institutionalized churches and the latter to signify agencies, whether or not they are denominational in structure and function.[1]

With only one exception, as will soon be mentioned, I do agree with Mr. Kebede on most points in his paper. While dealing strictly with the data presented in the paper, my response will include my reflection of *indigeneity, independence and church statistics, evangelism, the relevance of the church to the socio-politico-economic currents in East Africa,* and *the role of the church in America.*

INDIGENEITY

The presenter is right in the observation that such church-related terms as "national" and "selfhood" tend to be vaguely understood in many quarters, Christian or otherwise. Most

people have so glibly focused on the famous Nevian three-fold
selfhood that they never go beneath the surface to discover what
really constitutes the true selfhood of the church. Practical
experience and the insights derived from cross-cultural studies
astound us with the fact that a church can qualify in the three
selfs and yet be just as foreign to its cultural milieu as it
was under mission control. So few individuals ever realize that
a church is born indigenous; it is not age that produces one,
as Tippett correctly reminds us (Winter 1970:24). The questions
to be asked are, for example: How direct is the relationship
between God in Christ and the people the church is ministering
to or among? Is the gospel being communicated through the local
cultural forms or is it channeled through another culture?
These questions are very relevant to the churches in eastern
Africa, formerly missionary controlled and/or directed.

In point of fact, besides the relevance of these two questions the church in East Africa is faced with another struggle.
For instance, as Mr. Kebede points out, the general world scene
in that region continues to change. So the churches in struggling to become themselves are further challenged to relate to
the socio-politico-economic changes taking place, thus being
caught up in a double adjustment process.

Mr. Kebede at one point refers to a kind of isolationist independency. The possibility for both misconstruction and mis-
application of such independency is crucial. Every church,
whatever its size, is validated in the Body of Christ on the
basis of its faith in him, works of service in his name, and
openness to fellowship and service with all without distinction.
Consequently, "nationality" or "indigeneity" of the church do
not inhere in "yellowness" or "blackness" or "chocolateness" or
"brownness" of the group designated as "church"; nor is it the
strangeness or the differentness of the language. It is rather
the localness of the background being reflected in the way the
church in a given place expresses its faith in and loyalty to
Christ, the Head. Therefore, whether or not one is a Morator-
iumist, I would like to think of "the church in Africa," "the
church in India," "the church in America"; *not* "the African
church," "the Indian church," "the American church," etc. The
implications, granted it is a semantic problem, are astounding.
Why do not the Scriptures speak of "the Hebrew church" instead
of "the church in Jerusalem," or "the Greek/Italian church" instead of "the church in Rome" and "the church in Greece," etc.?

We belong to one another in Christ. I believe that is why
some groups in the United States for example organize themselves
under the "Good Samaritan" programs to go to some part of Africa
where the church has gone autonomous to help the Christians
there, for instance with a building project. However, such

programs need to be purged and streamlined so that they are
properly and adequately channeled through the national administrative mechanism lest they should be mistaken for some
hidden interests. This of course means that the expatriate
missionaries serving under new relationships between the church
in Africa and the church in North America should do so strictly
under the direction and control of the national church, not as
agents of another outside body such as tends to frustrate the
much belated indigenization process. In fact it is this point
that has contributed to the advocacy of moratorium.

INDEPENDENCY AND CHURCH STATISTICS

Next, Mr. Kebede's point on statistics cannot be treated
lightly. While appreciating statistical data on the church in
Africa, for the start they provide in this needful area of information, much is left to be desired. Those collecting the
data usually do it so hurriedly that they sometimes come up
with anything at all; and those approached for the information
either inflate or deflate the figures according to what they
consider to be gained or not gained thereby. Besides, the
truest picture of church growth is by conversion versus re-
version, not by transferal or by biological addition. Most
statistics are not adequately refined to reflect this posture.

Dr. Barrett's data on independent church movements in Africa
are very helpful. To a good measure, as Mr. Kebede observes,
the rise of independent churches has stimulated the growth of
the established churches.

Needless to say, some of the churches in the movement are
breakaways from the established churches, not only because of
racial overtones as some people have misconstrued such occur-
rences. Some breakaways have come about under national leadership. For example the Church of Christ in Africa (CCA) by
Ajuoga resulted from his refusal to serve under Bishop Festus
Olang' before the latter became the Archbishop of Kenya. Also
the development of African Israel Church, Nineveh, was an outcome of a quarrel between two blood brothers in the Pentecostal
Church at Nyang'ori, western Kenya.

Of course some of the breakaways are caused by theological
wrangles emanating in the West. For instance the 1930's revival
in Uganda developed the *tukutenderesa* faction which could not be
contained in the Anglican Church in Kenya because of the
latter's long history of formal rigidity. There were excesses
in the faction, to be sure, yet the open confession pattern in
it was African enough and biblical enough for incorporation had
the church polity developed an indigenous outlook toward forms.
In other words, wherever people have not been allowed to be

themselves and lay involvement has been lacking, the force of
indigenous resurgence is not adequately resolved.

Another example of a western-originated church problem is
that of segmentation. To illustrate: in Malawi, before 1963,
the Church of Scotland serving in the north, the Dutch Reformed
in the center, and the Free Church of Scotland in the south
could not work together harmoniously. When autonomy was granted
in 1963 the three groups joined hands and have since worked together as the Church of Central Africa Presbyterian (CCAP) with
encouraging results.

EVANGELISTIC MANDATE

Mr. Kebede's paper deals next with evangelism and, I must
think, church growth. He seems to agree with the saying "The
Church can go no further till it goes deeper," as some quarters
tend to hold. To this I take exception. As I look at the
Church of Christ in retrospect I find that whenever the people
of God have tried to isolate themselves from the evangelistic
task on the pretext of depth first, the result has been continued ineffectiveness and diminution until they once again find
themselves in evangelism. Depth growth and outreach cannot be
separated from each other. To serve actively under the influence and direction of the Holy Spirit is to be challenged to
depth growth, and depth growth is never wedded to isolationism.
Both depth growth and outreach have to go together; indeed they
do.

One problem in eastern Africa is for evangelism to be understood as a mere presence, even where opportunities for discipling are evident. A case in point is the school situation
in Kenya. Whereas the Kenya government, though in control of
the schools, has left the door wide open for the churches to
evangelize in these institutions, much of what goes on is no
more than the presence syndrome. This is alarming when you consider the fact that 60% of the population in East Africa are
young people and children--the very groups that are clamored
for by divergent voices! Such voices are not only religious,
but also social, economic, and political.

SOCIO-POLITICO-ECONOMIC CURRENTS AND THE CHURCH

Since independence, African states have been open to various
political, social, and economic world ideologies hitherto carefully suppressed under the colonial rule. It is the young educated and/or quasi educated mind that has provided the fertile
ground for the ideologies. Yet at many points these ideologies
have damaged the ideals of the individuals and/or the societies
that have embraced them indiscriminately.

For instance at the turn of the 1960's as Tanzania (Tan-
ganyika-Zanzibar), Uganda, and Kenya became independent, there
was much excitement about the possibility of an East African
Federation as a step beyond the East African Community bequeathed to them as the East African Common Services by the
colonial governments. The signs were bright; especially in
the light of the fact that Zambia, Ethiopia, Somalia, Zaire,
Burundi, and Malawi had come to the point of indicating an
active interest in joining the community. But, regrettably,
because of the different social, political, and economic ideologies pursued by each of these countries' governments, the
community has moved farther and farther apart instead of closer
together.

The pertinent question therefore is: Can the church(es) in
East Africa, whose leadership is largely of primary school educational background supplemented by two or three years of Bible
School courses, address the message of Jesus Christ relevantly
to the issues invading the region's communities through their
respective governments' programs? The churches have scarcely
even developed strong Christian education programs. And those
who seem to understand segments of the multi-faceted issues are
far too few, usually trained outside the continent. Nonethe-
less, despite the dearth in church leadership of a high level,
so far the fact remains, as Mr. Kebede reminds us, that the
Church of Christ has been firmly rooted in Africa. That the
church has phenomenally increased in the past ten years or more
under extreme pressure from African nationalism on the continent
is proof enough of the rootage of the church in that soil.

Only the church is not penetrating the society enough. The
sense of mission is yet dormant; that is why there is still so
much financial dependency on outside sources for many programs,
specifically in the established churches. And herein lies the
shining example of the independent churches. They depend on
local resources. Hence spiritually and academically qualified
leadership, committed to Christ for the people, and a heightened
sense of selfless stewardship programs are sorely needed to save
the church in eastern Africa from wilderness wandering.

THE CHURCH IN AMERICA HAS A ROLE TO PLAY TOO

With all that has been expressed and implied the question
that might be raised is: Has the church in America any role
to play in Africa? The answer is an emphatic YES. Space would
not allow me to go into the expansion of this "yes", quite a
bit of which Mr. Kebede has covered in his presentation. But
to supplement him, the church in America can:

1. help the church in Africa develop higher level seminaries
on the continent with more comprehensive curricula on an

interdenominational basis, to equip especially the pastoral leadership of the church to relate to the African world, past and present;

2. foster open fraternal consultative programs between the church in America and the church in Africa through interdenominational agencies;

3. help the church in Africa establish properly equipped and adequately manned research and training centers for closer analyses of growth patterns, to encourage greater growth;

4. consultatively with the church in Africa, restructure the former or current church-missionary boards relationships in such a way that sodal relationships increasingly replace modal ones. That is to say instead of a missionary board-church relationship, it becomes a church agency in America relating directly to a church agency (its counterpart) in Africa. This would on the other hand diversify and strengthen the much needed responsible church leadership development, and on the other hand eliminate the current bureaucratic delays in communication that usually eventuate in the loss of golden outreach opportunities for Christ;

5. organize interdenominational sodalities to support outreach programs thought out and planned by the churches in Africa, especially in the area of transporation, audiovisual and communication aids of a technical nature, where and when such aids have been determined to be essential to the program, and since technical know-how is yet lacking in many churches in eastern Africa.

A question may be raised, Why should the church in America participate when the church in Africa wants to do its own thing? Or, For how long will the church in America continue to help the church in Africa?

The first question is already answered in the earlier part of this response. That is, we belong to each other, in the Body of Christ. We each are our brother's keeper. To the second one the answer is: For as long as Christ has not yet returned. The Scripture says, "When a man has been given much, much will be expected of him" (Luke 12:48, NEB). What we have, we do not have by accident; it is a gift from God, for everything good and just and right is from him; and he gives to us for a purpose, namely, to be used to his glory.

CONCLUSION

Practically all the East African countries have been under western rule and influence. As a result, societies that

traditionally did not have many distinctly separated socio-
economic classes (except the clan/tribal distinctions) have
become that much more segmented. Most governments for their
part, in the attempt to obtain international respectability,
pursue programs which at best meet the needs of higher and
middle class brackets, with only token benefits to the masses.

For a time the saying of our Lord Jesus Christ, on his way to
Jerusalem, that out of the stones by the wayside he could raise
those that could sing and shout Hosannah to the Son of God, dis-
turbed me; I could not understand it! Not that I know its
meaning now. But a look at his ministry tells us much. To the
common, the forgotten, the downtrodden, he addressed the gospel;
he called them to himself, and commissioned the disciples. And
in obedience and faith in their positive response, they (the
common people) turned the world upside down.

The masses are still with us, readier for the gospel than
ever before; the middle and higher classes are yet searching
for meaning in life when what was once thought to satisfy does
not. Mission has only begun, in creativity and fresh dedication!

---

[1]These terms have been proposed by Ralph D. Winter of the
School of World Mission, Fuller Theological Seminary (e.g.
Winter 1974).

PART III

The Church
in Central Africa

Problems of the Churches in Central Africa

Mutombo Mpanya

The question that this paper deals with is: What is the basic problem of Christian churches in central Africa? To us the answer seems to be dependency; which means that Christian churches in central Africa rely too much in every area on western Europe and North America. But defining the problem this way raises some questions.

First of all, central Africa is too big. According to the specification of the symposium it includes seven countries: Zambia, Zaire, Central African Empire, Congo, Gabon, Equatorial Guinea, Chad. In this paper we will limit ourselves to Zaire and use the Mennonite community as a case study, since Christian churches in central Africa have many traits in common--most were started as western missionary churches and all lived under colonial administration.

The *second* question has to do with the word "dependency" itself. It may mean that one puts the blame on the foreigners and avoids looking at local problems such as tribalism, jealousy, or polygamy. But these local problems are not typical to central Africa. Even the issue of polygamy could be a case of dependency if people take a stand only on the basis of what the missionaries told them. Dependency could also suggest that the solution is independence. This cannot be the case because we all know that nobody is independent. Furthermore, the churches in central Africa were born as a result of relations between western Christians and Africa; that link cannot be broken without the risk of isolation.

Third, this way of defining the problem is arbitrary. What
may be basic for one person may be secondary for another. However, to us the basic problem of Christian churches in central
Africa seems to be dependency. To illustrate this point, we
will look at five areas of church life: administrative structures, finances, personnel, programs, and theology.

ADMINISTRATIVE STRUCTURES

Most of the churches in Zaire are divided in regional conferences on the North American model. Each conference is sub-
divided in smaller sections. In general those sections send
representatives to a general assembly which elects the board
of the churches and the top officers who are responsible for
the central administration. Because people have to campaign
in order to be elected, there is much politicking and bribery.
Sometimes each ethnic group wants its people in top leadership
positions. Tension may exist between the local and central
church authorities or between local groups.

This kind of structure tends to be very expensive and costly
for local churches. These structures tend to emphasize voting,
while African tradition is inclined to reach consensus through
long discussion. However, these structures have helped to
create other groupings around which African people can work beside the traditional ethnic groupings. This is very important
at this time of African nationalism where people are trying to
transcend their tribal groups.

The solution, in broad terms, seems to be that churches need
to become decentralized; more responsibility should be given to
the local churches so that people can identify themselves more
with what is happening. People need to know that they are the
church and that the church is theirs, rather than something
imposed by an outside authority.

FINANCES

The Mennonite Church, for example, gets about 80% of its
finances from North America. Most of this money is spent at
the top level of administration and for traditional, institutional programs like hospitals, Bible schools, including salaries of missionaries who work in these areas. This financial
dependency raises a few problems.

The first problem in this area has to do with the relationship between top administrators and local pastors. Pastors
think that the administrators are there simply to have the money
that comes from North America. This money is not channeled to
the local congregations. Thus, people are struggling in the

church to get to the highest leadership positions because there they can receive a higher salary and good housing. The church has created social classes. The top administrators of the church form the wealthiest class; they have more money and own more private businesses than other church members.

The second problem is that of the relationship between the giver and the receiver, between North America and Africa. After a meeting with North American brothers, a church treasurer once said in a private conversation that he would not push anything that would upset missionaries because he is paid by the mission and does not want to lose his job. How can one be sure that these church leaders represent the interests of African Christians? Actually, they often represent their own personal interests or the interests of North American Christians who salary them. Psychologically, the giver has power over the recipient and can generally control the receiver.

The third problem is that this aid from North America is not going to continue forever. North American churches are considering the establishment of other mission fields in other parts of the world. Although the North American church has been sensitive to African feelings about these new fields, they still think rightly that they cannot spend all of their resources in one place. But Africans question why missionaries should start other missions while African churches are still in need.

In terms of solution, the churches in central Africa need to become self-supporting. Members tend to think that the only way for the church to be self-supporting is for the church to engage in business. They want to see the church start agricultural co-ops, small business loans, or cattle raising. Others claim that this may divert the church from its main functions, evangelization. They, therefore, propose helping individual Christians to become successful businessmen and good farmers who will make enough money to support the church.

Also, church members must be encouraged to give more of their resources to the church. If each national member gave two dollars, the church would have enough money for its annual budget.

Although these ideas may provide financial resources for local churches, one has to admit some important limitations. Church and business have different goals and need different organizations. It is quite difficult for the church to become a business and still remain the church. In the same way, it is difficult for a business to become a church and still remain a business.

Another limitation is that the local peoples' economic and cultural background does not help them to increase their giving. People are too poor. In general the annual income for the area is less than $70 a year. Most of the people are accustomed to the role of recipient in relating to the church rather than that of giver.

PERSONNEL

In the area of human resources or personnel, although church leaders are African, the church still depends heavily on North American missionaries. All of the professional positions in the church are held by missionaries: medical doctors, qualified mechanics, builders, and theologians.

The cost of maintaining a group of missionaries in Africa is high. It costs about $12,000 a year to maintain a young couple in Africa. Add to that figure medical expenses, lodging, and transportation, as well as overseas travel expenses. With that money one can train Africans who could do the same job and still remain in the country and be an asset to their own people. Some missionaries are sent to Africa not because they are needed but because they are available. And African leadership is then simply asked to invite them.

Sometimes it is difficult for expatriate personnel to work under African leadership. This is understandable because many missionaries have been in leadership positions themselves, whereas some of the African leaders have not had adequate experience in leadership roles.

However, there is a growing frustration of nationals in regards to the seeming inaccessibility of the management of their own churches to them as church leaders. Seemingly their destiny will always be in the hands of expatriates. There seems to be no African future.

The solution to this kind of problem is to train African leadership even if there are uncertainties as to where, when, and how such leadership can be trained and what the content of such training should include.

Whether training should take place abroad or at home depends on the kind of skills to be learned and resources available locally. Whether leadership training should be formal or informal again depends on the situation. Most Africans prefer formal training. During the colonial period people learned to recognize personal importance on the basis of a formal degree. Persons without formal degrees cannot be convinced that they should not seek such. What is important is the possession of skills that are needed rather than the degrees as such.

In other areas like mechanics, agriculture, and medicine,
on-the-job training has been used. Theoretically, this is a
good way to gain training and experience. Although it has
worked well in many cases, it takes too long for people to get
to the level of responsibility required. This frustrates both
the missionary and the African. Often missionaries claim that
they did not see anyone competent to learn a given position to
replace the missionary eventually. Africans say that missionaries simply do not want Africans to take over. I think the
truth is somewhere in between.

Another question is whether leadership should be trained in
evangelism techniques, in management and economics, in agriculture, or in health. Some churches have arranged their priorities in terms of evangelism and leadership training. This means
that these two foci are different. Leadership training relates
to equipping the church with qualified people at the head of
different church ministries, from evangelism to medical work
through agricultural extension programs. Evangelism means that
each one of those ministries has as its primary goal the
preaching of the gospel in an appropriate way. People are
being trained in the management of agricultural programs with
the idea that they will help the people in the village as part
of the gospel. The same thing can be said about education in
medical work.

Although it is possible to train leaders in a given field
with an evangelistic emphasis, the tendency has been to train
people only in evangelism. Churches have many pastors and
several Bible schools. However, qualified doctors, nurses,
or mechanics are few. This shows that the priorities of the
mission church were more oriented to converting people than to
helping the converted live a fuller life. The church still depends on expatriates.

PROGRAMS

The churches still continue to work mostly in programs left
by missionaries--school, hospitals, biblical institutions. The
problem with this orientation is that most of church effort,
personnel, and finances are channeled into these programs. And
yet one cannot be sure that they meet the needs of the people.
For example, the medical programs tend to be curative whereas
most of the diseases that people suffer from can be prevented
through public health and nutrition. The schools don't necessarily meet the needs of the country because of their emphasis
on book learning and office type work.

While churches are involved in public health, agricultural
and nutrition programs, these efforts are not as important as

the traditional programs. Then, too, the whole area of social
and political life is one which the church should speak or do
something about but doesn't often open itself to.

Many people, especially young people, migrate to the city in
central Africa. These cities are growing very fast, creating
problems of disintegration of traditional family life, unemployment, and urban poverty. Yet most of these people have
been once Christians in their life through missionary schools.
Churches can become a healing source in the urban life of
Africa. Certainly people talk in Africa of urban missions,
but again the emphasis is very small when one thinks in terms
of what people need.

Politics can be a challenge to the churches, although one
knows the danger of holding openly political attitudes. But
that is not an adequate rationale to justify the silence of
Christian churches in relating to political structures. In
terms of solution, the churches in central Africa should try to
relate to the broader and long-term concerns of African people
in central Africa.

Church programs should be redefined to meet the needs of
people. For example, with the breakdown of traditional structures, the church can present alternatives for some of the
structures. Through non-formal education programs the church
can help people to acquire the kinds of skills that are needed.
This doesn't mean that evangelism becomes a low priority; but
it is a way of making evangelism effective.

THEOLOGY

On the theological level, the problem is reflected in the
church's dependency on its inheritance from missions. The most
prevalent forms of theology and worship are those left by the
missionary. Consequently, theology today does not take into
account peoples' political, social, and cultural life. People
don't know how to relate their faith to their traditional
African background.

Often one hears stories of polygamy or witchcraft in the
churches, but leaders do not take time to observe how people
relate Christianity to their traditional African religions.

At the liturgical level, although several attempts are made
specifically among young people to use African traditional
music in worship, the church as a whole still looks at these
cases as marginal. Seemingly African traditional music does
not have the status of western hymns in liturgy.

The churches have given little importance to what African theologians have written about African theology. The Christian churches in central Africa should first give priority to finding how to relate not only to the traditional religious belief system, but to the traditional culture as a whole.

The church should look at the work of African scholars in theology and discover how this can be translated in terms of the life of the congregations. African theologians like Mbiti and Idowu should be read in order to see how their insights may be helpful in central Africa. Maybe the need felt by African scholars and intellectuals for an African theology is based on their own alienation from the western culture. Perhaps the common people are African enough with little need for identification through an African theology. On the other hand, there would appear to be some points of conflict between African culture and the gospel since no culture is completely compatible with the gospel. To such issues the church could address itself.

The churches should add to this task of relating Christianity to African culture a dialog with western Christianity. Such a dialog is necessary in order to avoid the danger of isolation. Dialog also facilitates mutually constructive criticisms and encourages feelings of universal Christian brotherhood and sisterhood.

This theological search needs a strong biblical basis. The churches should start this search for an African theology with strong biblical competence, scholarship, and commitment, commiting itself to a higher quality of biblical training.

CONCLUSION

From these illustrations one can conclude that the Christian church in central Africa is dependent on western churches. This dependency is very well felt at this time of African nationalism. However, the solution is not independence as it may be possible to think, but interdependence. The choice is between the relation of domination and a Christian brotherhood or sisterhood. Interdependence means that Christian churches in central Africa need "partners not patrons, brothers not benefactors." It means a relationship that should allow an authentic African Christianity to develop and reflect African life and thought without being mothered by its western influence.

Response #1

John E. Ross

The presentation by Mr. Mutombo-Mpanya is both interesting and stimulating. His exposition of the present situation and problems of the Mennonite Community of the Church of Christ of Zaire is forthright and clear. He evidences a genuine concern for the development of a truly autonomous indigenous Christian church in Zaire. He suggests means of unshackling the autonomous church from some bonds which limit its true autonomy.

The Church of Christ in Zaire is a cooperative body incorporating most sectional church groups inherited from the early mission enterprise of western church groups. During the pre-independence period, the western agencies were urging decentralization while centralizing the church in America. The program called for dispersal from centers or posts with their strength in institutions toward a village infiltration. When the African church came into its own it followed the pattern of the western church. Centralization became the goal with concurrent emphasis on central power, development of institutions and a vested authority at the head. Authority was, by constitutional act, placed in the hands of the ordained clergy. This authority has become the controller of properties, institutions, and the wealth of the church. It is parallel to the western church in this respect. There is a modicum of democratic procedure in church government which, at times, appears to be a token of response to the grass roots constituency of the Zaire church. Mr. Mutombo-Mpanya's statements of conditions in the Mennonite sector of the Church of Christ in Zaire are paralleled in many groups within the other affiliated churches in Zaire.

Some problems faced by the churches in Zaire are carried over from their heritage of mission in the past. The influences of Christianity, deeply rooted in western culture during the decades of the mission enterprise, are not easily shed. As the autonomous African church develops there will be modifications in forms of worship and interpretation of God's word are closely molded to African culture and understanding. The Kimbangui movement is one example. It is the unique church which has its origin in Zaire itself. Other evidences of change have been seen in recent years. Distinctly African songs of worship and praise are forerunners of the movement to develop the expression of their faith and beliefs in their own way. This is to be expected, honored, and encouraged.

However, some problems are outgrowths of efforts to develop an authentic and autonomous African Christian church and community. Sister churches in other lands hunger for news of the new church. In August of 1975 Canon Burgess Carr, secretary of the All Africa Conference of Churches, spoke to the delegates at the General Assembly of the Christian Churches (Disciples of Christ) in San Antonio, Texas. His message was basically a castigation of missions and missionaries of the past. It told nothing of importance that the African church is doing today. It sounded as if he were beating an old drum which needed both a new skin and a fresh rhythm. The delegates were anxious to hear what was being done by the newly autonomous church. They were disappointed. How much better it would have been if Canon Carr had told of the great things the African churches are doing now and closed with a statement saying "we know we are making some mistakes and we pray you will forgive us our errors as freely as we forgave yours when you were bringing the gospel of Christ to us."

It seems the time has come to refrain from blaming all our ills on others. The privilege of autonomy carries with it an obligation of responsibility, integrity, and devotion to the causes involved. Moving on to greater tasks and fulfilling its mission will do more to strengthen the African Christian church than recriminations. Errors will be made but mutual forgiveness will nourish the soil in which the seed of growth is planted.

Considerable concerns has been expressed about a number of practices followed by the leadership in the Church of Christ of Zaire. Among these are inner struggles for power by African leaders, the centralization of authority in a predominantly ecclesiastical hierarchy, the disparity of income between high level leadership and the constituency which supports it, and a lack of a cultural and political impact by the church on the evolving community and society which it attempts to serve. These problems are not peculiar to the African church. Struggles

for power and centralization of authority are common faults in
the western churches when overdone.

Some centralization is necessary to effective working together. However, when inbred structure and vested interest can
no longer communicate with or respond to the collective will of
its constituency, a subtle and insidious disintegration begins.
A government which is not responsive to the needs of its people
will decay and die. A business which gives no attention to the
requirements of the consumers will become bankrupt. A church
leadership which drives against the will of its corporate membership will be disenfranchised and the church lose its witness.
If the influence of materialism and humanism and more at work
in the church than the Holy Spirit, the church loses its witness
for Christ.

Several years ago Zairian church leaders began to say, "There
is no longer a need for missionaries. Africans can do the work
expatriate personnel have been doing. Since money will no
longer be necessary to pay the salaries of missionaries, it
should be sent to the African church to underwrite the work
being done by Africans." Some western agencies have listed the
names of Africans with those of expatriates serving as personnel
of the agencies in the African church. Does this mean those
agencies are paying the salaries of church leaders in Zaire
either directly or indirectly? If this is true, as suggested
by Mr. Mutombo-Mpanya, the question of a truly autonomous church
existing unfettered by western sources is challenged. When one
raises the specter of a leadership paid by sources outside the
indigenous constituency, it opens a Pandora's box of problems
of freedom and loyalty as well as disparity.

Mr. Mutombo-Mpanya states the average income of the people
in the Mennonite area of service is about $70 per year per per-
son. Pastors receive $40 per month or $480 per year. There is
marked disparity in this case. One can well imagine the feeling
of low-income laymen in this situation. If top church leadership are receiving salaries commensurately higher from outside
sources, a very real problem could develop. This poses another
serious question: Can and will the indigenous Christian lay
people of the church in Zaire pay the salaries of their own
leaders? Will the leadership of the church in Zaire accept
salaries which a truly autonomous Christian church can pay?
Canon Carr made international news when he urged a five year
moratorium on assistance from expatriate resources in money and
personnel. What would have been the result? Canon Carr was not
consistent when he asked for a half million dollars to establish
an ecumenical church center in Nairobi.

It is hoped no offense will be taken at a statement which may
need to be said. Too often some have thought it to be the sole

responsibility of the so-called "haves" to rehabilitate the
"have nots." There is a heavy responsibility for assisting all
peoples but it is a mutual task whether inside or outside of
the same community. Someone put it brutally in these words, "If
you want to live like the rest of the world lives and have what
the rest of the world has, you must work like the rest of the
world works." This is simple economics.

In some areas a mason will lay 70 concrete blocks a day compared to up to 500 blocks in other countries. There are instances in which workmen work a half day for a full day's pay.
These same employees walk off at mid-day carrying mortar belonging to their employers in order to work on personal jobs
during the rest of the day. Reports have been received that
some church leaders are absent from their areas of responsibility as much as six months out of the year. In all these
instances the church suffers. This is not a criticism but an
effort to suggest possible causes of some problems. There are
a large number of effective, conscientious, responsible, and
dedicated Christians serving in task in church-related programs
and projects as well as in government and business.

Recently a very dedicated and effective Christian educator
was chosen as Minister of Education in his own province. A very
capable Christian in serving the Zaire government in radio and
television communications. Conscientious and able young Christians are preparing themselves in the fields of education, the
ministry, medicine, and business. In the future these young
people will be contributing to the development of their own
nation. The hope for a truly autonomous and an effective
Christian witness will rest in their hands.

It is important that the church in Africa develop a position
in the political and cultural life in their own countries.
Western agencies and missionaries are expatriates and have no
political rights or privileges. This influence must come from
the indigenous church leaders and lay people. The course of
action must be founded on Christian principles and in the spirit
of Christian concern and love.

It would seem more desirable for western agencies to limit
support to specific programs in horticulture, education, church
development, evangelism, medical work, and many other fields of
service critically needed by the people. Funds sent for such
programs should be monitored to assure they are used as designated. Practices of "creaming off parts or all of designated
funds" and using them for other purposes in administration have
been common among some leaders. A direct accounting may be
offensive to some people but integrity and responsible administration are the only alternative which can replace it. Trust

is the reward of trustworthiness. The limiting of support to
specific programs and projects, rather than including salaries
and undesignated subsidies, will do much to insure the establishment of a truly indigenous and autonomous Christian church
in Africa. The leadership of the church would be encouraged to
respond to the lay constituency upon which they would depend.

There is an appreciable body of dedicated Christian lay
people in the African church. These are the viable witness of
the living Christ working in them and through them. They are
the hope of the church in its struggle to survive as a dynamic
and powerful force in a changing structure and world. The
Christians of the world must listen to God the Father, witness
to the saving grace which comes through Christ the Son, and
follow the will of the Holy Spirit. Then and only then will
the church be the church in all its glory and in his name. This
hardly seems human but at least it could be divine.

Response #2

Max Ward Randall

Mr. Mutombo-Mpanya is to be commended for having prepared a
meaningful case study of his own denomination in Zaire, and for
observations to be carefully noted, out of the Mennonite Church
development, that echo loudly missions problems, experiences,
and lessons of churches, both in Zaire and other African countries. One could wish he had looked at other churches in Zaire
as well as in other countries and that he might have given a
word concerning the relationship between the Mennonite Church
and the United Church of Christ in Zaire. Reflection on this
relationship between the Mennonite Church and other evangelical
churches to the United Church of Christ speaks to contemporary
challenges in other African states.

The Congo Protestant Council, formed in 1925, came out of the
Congo Continuation Committee created in 1911. Most mission
societies within the Congo belonged to it. The CPC was Africanized about 1960. In 1970, its structure was radically
changed, coming out of eight days of tense debate during which
time such concerns as patriotism, paternalism, politics, national unity and neo-colonialism were hotly discussed. The
result, in which 32 churches or missions voted in favor and 14
voted against, was that the CPC went out of existence and the
United Church of Christ in Zaire was created. "The new church
adopted a policy of neutrality with relation to all foreign
religious movements, notably the World Evangelical Alliance
and the World Council of Churches" (Kane 1971:365). In spite
of this decision, a representative of the All Africa Council of
Churches was there, and a few days later the general secretary
of the WCC visited Mr. Bokeleale, Chairman of the new United
Church of Christ.

Most Congo missions failed to become autonomous and to Afri-
canize until after 1965; some as late as 1972. Our own African
Christian Mission in Zaire did not become fully autonomous until
1972, "perhaps years too late." In Zambia where we were working,
not one mission within the country had Africanized until after
independence in October of 1964, and some mission societies are
still struggling with growing tensions as a result.

Many issues discussed by Mr. Mutombo-Mpanya, problems that
still plague the Mennonite Church in Zaire, were matters hotly
debated in March, 1970 when the Congo Protestant Council was
voted out of existence in favor of the United Church of Christ.
Such issues as patriotism, paternalism, politics, national
unity, neo-colonialism and others, are still points of explosive
concern, in spite of national political independence, and in
spite of claims of autonomy and indigeneity of every mission
society. Mr. Mutombo-Mpanya is relating present difficulties
of every mission-church relationship in that part of Africa
coming under our scrutiny.

The difficulty of being torn between a situation of dependence inherited from colonial times and the need for independence affirmed by African nationalism is not unique. Churches
in every country of our purview face the same problem.

George Upton (Hodges 1953:6-7) has described the missionary
with his mission society of colonial days who assumed financial
responsibility, treated his people like children, led them,
fought for them, and "unintentionally robbed them of those
practical processes which develop strong characters." Though
the period described is gone, its effects are still present and
very real. The transition from colonially oriented missions to
autonomous churches has not been easy. Colonial missionaries,
paying salaries, subsidizing all sorts of institutional work,
determining policy, defining theology, exercising discipline
and assuming leadership in every sphere, bred a stultifying
dependence difficult to overcome, even in face of the demands
of African nationalism.

The national churches have also inherited cumbersome church
structures from their founding mission. Too often the strong
central administration of the mission church of the colonial
era with its American missionary personnel in all areas of
control was inherited as one piece by the new autonomous church
after political independence, with the only difference being
that missionary-trained African personnel assumed the same
domineering oversight from superintendent down through all the
offices of the outdated administration of the colonial era. The
same gap exists between the central administration and local
congregations, and the new structure continues to be as costly

as the colonial, demanding the same subsidies from overseas as did the old, subsidies that are still absorbed at the level of administration, that never reach the areas of greatest need. Local leaders in numerous mission-church relationships in many African countries think that top administrators, in one way or another, absorb all subsidies that come from overseas.

"Many missionaries and their supporting societies can only think of the missions church in terms of a ministry paid by funds from overseas and supervised by the missionaries" (Randall 1970:90); this relationship between subsidy and control "has invaded the very organization and life of the church itself" (Allen 1965:102), and it is sadly true that African personnel, particularly at administration level will not agitate for any changes that might upset the missionary. Their salaries are paid by the mission, and to distrub the missionaries and the missions society could well cost them their job.

African churches must free themselves of this dependency on foreign support, but it is essential if the church is to gain maturity and autonomy. To accomplish this, members of every church must be taught the joy of giving.

Though the average African may earn comparatively few dollars in a given year, even though he may live and work in an urban area, he is not, within his own cultural context, absolutely poverty stricken. If he lives in the city he has his job and salary. If he lives in the rural area he has his gardens, cattle, a team of oxen and a plow, a few goats and several chickens. True, most African Christians are accustomed to the role of recipient in relating to the church rather than that of giver. The missionaries too often trained them that way, treating them like juveniles, but African Christians can and must be taught the blessings of stewardship, being encouraged to give, in cash if they now labor in a cash economy, or if not, then a bushel of maize, or peanuts, or a hundred pounds of cotton, or a goat, or a calf, or a dozen chickens. In a significant number of areas in Africa it is being done. A small denomination in Zambia, through the giving of its members, employs two full time evangelists. Churches of the same denomination in South Africa provide sufficient money to build one new church building within their fellowship every year.

Furthermore, what is to hinder men with a compulsion to preach from providing their own livelihood through a job, their own gardens, animal husbandry, trucking or some other kind of labor? This is not unlike the Apostle Paul who supported himself in Corinth by making tents (Acts 18:3). The suggestion that in all leadership training programs the curriculum should include other forms of trade for leaders in evangelism like

agriculture and animal husbandry is a good one. Such courses,
however, must be kept in perspective in relation to the priority
which must always focus upon discipling and church planting.
The history of Christian education is filled with examples of
Christian training schools and colleges where peripheral courses
became central, and Bible courses, evangelism and focus upon
church planting were crowded out. However, in the province of
self-support the African churches must exercise great courage
and faith. It will not be easy.

All church leadership should spring from the grass roots. We
have learned in Zambia that

> Churches must choose their own leaders. No movement
> could happen without strong indigenous leaders to
> break the path for others to follow. The church knows
> these trail blazers. They are the natural leaders.
> To bypass them would be to kill the movement. This
> indigenous leadership is a potent factor. The church
> must be theirs (Randall 1970:173).

Leaders who have a compulsion to preach the gospel that is
greater than any desire for a certificate or degree, can best
be trained, initially, through a decentralized training program.
The Assemblies of God in Central America learned that

> There is real advantage in having a decentralized
> training program. The school can then be carried
> to the districts and it is not necessary to depend
> entirely upon students coming to the central location.
> The nearer the training program can be kept to the
> source of workers, i.e., the local churches, the more
> effective it will be (Hodges 1953:57).

Maintaining numbers of American missionaries in Africa, in
the future, may involve more than the question of exorbitant
costs. What will American supporting societies do if, for political or other reasons, missionaries are refused the privilege
of remaining in the country? It is already happening in some
areas. The time may come when committed national Christians
must assume full responsibility for both nurturing existing
churches, filling leadership roles in social service institutions and in propagating the gospel to unreached peoples. They
will need continuing support from American churches. It is
possible that, with dedicated national leadership, more can
be accomplished than with the same number of missionaries at
ten times the cost.

It is naive for a former African expatriate to venture opinions regarding the strength of the political voice with which

the African church should speak, but this I would observe: an
African church still tied by subsidies and subtle kinds of missions control is vulnerable in the ferment of growing nationalism. It is suspect, and it cannot speak, but it must speak.
It must provide the Christian conscience for the newly developing African nations, which it can do only if it is free and
autonomous!

African churches must be encouraged, at the liturgical level,
in the use of African traditional music, the writing of African
hymns, the development of African worship forms, and the use of
African musical instruments. Houses of worship could well be
African in design and ornamentation.

Great courage must also be exercised by the societies and
the missionaries. It is alarming that the Mennonite Church,
with 30,000 members, and with African leadership, is still dependent on North American missionaries. Many African churches
in other countries are bound and gagged in the same way. Here
is a problem that should have been resolved long ago. Basil
Matthews wrote of 1900,

> The first weakness was the "Grandfatherliness" of
> the missionary, who was everywhere at the top in the
> church, the school, college, hospital and social work.
> At the end of the 19th century, most missionaries were
> sure that if left to themselves, the younger churches
> would go disastrously astray (1960:175-176).

What a commentary on the lack of faith the missionaries have
in their African brothers that the situation has so little
changed. A friend from Zaire has recounted with sadness that
associates within his mission still cling to the paternalism
described by Matthews. I know of two missions in Zambia where
continuing domineering mission control has brought dissension,
almost to the point of division between black and missionary
brethren.

Taylor and Lehmann wrote in 1961,

> Something startling is required to shift this pattern
> which is stamped so firmly on people's minds. That
> might be done if the church proceeded to make its Af-
> rican clergy the exact equivalent of their European
> counterparts in respect to the scope and the autonomy
> of their ministry (Taylor & Lehmann 1961:172).

I would go further.

The missionaries must concentrate upon leadership training,
by every possible means; by theological education by extension

where the missionaries take the training program to the indigenous, locally chosen church leaders where the latter live,
which is of major importance; by training institute and college
programs within the country; and by making it possible for recognized exceptional African leaders to gain additional training
overseas.

If the frustration of national Christians in regard to what
so far has been the inaccessibility of the spiritual and material oversight of their own churches is to be eliminated, the
missionaries must in fact joyously step aside, becoming servants
indeed, to freely give control of the national church to its own
indigenous leadership. Missionaries who cannot do this should
return to their homelands, and their societies and supporting
churches should insist upon it.

Orlando Costas has written,

For far too long, mission to the non-affluent world
has been characterized by the philosophy of "He who
pays the piper calls the tune." Budget and financial
priorities have been determined from the North. Mission policies have been largely established on the
basis of the criteria established by the sending
parties. . . . There are signs that point in the
direction of more subtle, indirect controls. This
may be seen even among the most advanced and progressive mission organizations. Even though they
may have handed over all administrative and strategic
control, their leaders always manage somehow to get
their way. And when, for any number of reasons, the
national church or organization refuses to go along
with their suggestions, they are penalized or threatened.

It is time that missionaries, missionary societies,
church bodies—denominational and congregational—
pastors and laymen in the North renounce the temp-
tation of power and domination by putting their
talents and resources at the disposition of the Church
in the non-affluent areas of the world *without any
strings attached* (Costas 1973:414).

One last word, and this, coming from the Apostle Paul, speaks
to the contemporary missionary, but it speaks also to the African Christian leader:

For though I am free from all men, I have made myself
a slave to all, that I might win the more. To the
Jews I became as a Jew, in order to win Jews; to those
under the Law I became as one under the Law—though not

being myself under the Law--that I might win those
under the Law. To those outside the Law I became
as one outside the Law--not being without Law to
God but under the Law of Christ--that I might win
those outside the Law. To the weak I became weak,
that I might win the weak. I have become all
things to all men that I might by all means save
some. I do it all for the sake of the gospel, that
I may share in its blessing (1 Cor. 9:19-23).

PART IV

The Church
in Western Africa

The Church
In West Africa

John S. Pobee

It is a measure of progress that I have been invited to con-
fine myself to West Africa rather than to Africa, an area of
11,000,000 square miles, i.e. 28,497,409 square kilometers. In
other words, we are concerned with the surface of the globe
straddling latitudes 5° South to 20° North and longitudes 15°
West to 15° East of the Prime Meridian, an area of about
2,074,404 square miles. It is a vast area with diversities
and differences of geography, vegetation, temperament, cultures,
politics, orientation, etc., and these even within one country.
One, therefore, approaches the study of this vast area with
great trepidation. One realizes you are concerned to know the
present state of affairs with regard to the church situation
in a vast area. But one also believes you know not whither
you go unless you know whence you came. So I have set myself
the crazy task of relating the past, the present, and the future
of a diverse institution in a vast area, and that, in 60 minutes. I see my task, therefore, as an attempt to cut a lady's
frock: it has to be short enough to make it attractive (yet
not obscene), long enough to contain a lot.

People in these parts often romanticize Africa, virtually
treating it as an anthropological curio and a museum piece.
That is often a figment of their own imagination, bearing no
relationship to the realities of today. West Africa has not
been cut off the rest of the world; through history new influences have been at work in West Africa. Three such influences
are outstanding. The first is *western culture and education*
which has been linked with the colonial history of the various
countries. One properly speaks of colonialism after the Berlin

Conference of 1885 (Ward 1967:48-78), organized by Chancellor
Bismarck, at which Africa was carved up between the European
powers. As it affected West Africa, the scores are as follows:

1. British Colonies:

Nigeria	(373,250 square miles)
Gold Coast, now Ghana	(91,843 square miles)
Sierra Leone	(27,925 square miles)
The Gambia	(3,978 square miles)

2. French Colonies:

Dahomey, now Republic of Benin	(43,629 square miles)
Togo (after World War I)	(36,000 square miles)
Ivory Coast	(123,166 square miles)
Guinea	(106,178 square miles)
Senegal	(80,695 square miles)
Mali	(460,617 square miles)
Mauritania	(416,216 square miles)
Niger	(494,980 square miles)
Upper Volta	(105,791 square miles)
Cameroun (after World War I)	(183,381 square miles)

3. German Colonies:

   Togoland (until World
     War I)
   Cameroons (until World
     War I)

4. Portuguese Colonies:

Guinea Bissau	(13,944 square miles)
Cape Verde	

5. Liberia[1]   (37,392 square miles)

This partition of West Africa has to some extent determined
the orientation, the cultures, etc. of respective West African
states, with the colonial power serving as the model for the
West African countries. Thus a bank-transfer of money from
Togoland to Ghana, which is just next-door, goes through Paris;
so too does a trunk-call! The long and short of this is that
Anglophone Africa hardly ever met Francophone Africa. In a
sense London is nearer Accra than Lome is to Accra. For Lome,
Paris is nearer than Accra. The result is that with the exception of the Eglise Evangélique du Togo which has a sister

church in the Evangelical Presbyterian Church of Ghana, which
likewise developed out of the Bremen Ewe Church, the churches
in various countries have not been much in touch. This awareness *inter alia* threw up the All Africa Conference of Churches
(AACC) to be a unifying factor for the churches of Africa. The
church's present problem is to relate to the churches next-door
in the neighboring countries of West Africa. Even the Anglicans
who have the Church of the Province of West Africa are plagued
by all sorts of uneasiness between sister churches in West
Africa. The partition has affected the sense of the oneness
of the church in West Africa. The problem of church union in
African countries is *inter alia* to stop individual denominations
looking more to mother churches in Europe and America than to
the church next-door in West Africa.

Again, in the scramble for Africa, the boundaries of West
African states were arbitrarily drawn by the colonialists and
at their convenience, with the result that sometimes coherent
ethnic groups have been split between two nations. For example,
the Nzima now belong to both the Ivory Coast and Ghana; the Ewe
belong to both Ghana and the Republic of Togo, with the result
that families are separated by the emigration regulations and
rules of two different countries and systems of government. No
wonder that again and again there are political tensions between
adjacent countries--friction between Nigeria and Benin, between
Benin and Togo, between Togo and Ghana, between Ghana and Ivory
Coast, between Senegal and Guinea, as well as friction between
groups in one country. Obviously this prescribes the role of
the church: to be a messenger of peace and reconciliation in
such situations, especially sometimes within the one nation in
which different ethnic groups are put together. It is this
situation that makes church union a vital and urgent issue:
the divisions of the church affect the credibility of the
church--how can the church be a minister of peace and reconciliation when it comes so hopelessly divided? The words of
the late President of Ghana, Kwame Nkrumah, the prince of African nationalism, to the Ghana Assembly of the International
Missionary Council held in Accra from December 28, 1957 to
January 8, 1958 are worthy of quotation and constitute a re-
proach to the church:

> How can there be good-will if Christians think more
> of their differences than of their whole-hearted de-
> votion to the God of all? Above all, how can the
> Christian message be spread effectively to the hope-
> ful and inquiring masses of Africa if it does not
> come to them rooted in charity "which is the bond
> of perfection"? (Orchard 1958:149).

This task involves not only the churches in West Africa but
also the churches of Europe and America. Part of the difficulty

is that the churches in West Africa find it difficult to move
ahead for fear that they will be out of communion with the so-
called Mother Churches in Europe and America. So *your* divisions
are now a drag on our reunion. Therefore, I urge churches in
America and Europe to take seriously the reunion of the Church.
To this we shall return later.

This impact of the western culture and education also means
that West African states with western technological civilization
superimposed and mixed with traditional culture live in a sort
of twilight zone between the traditional and the modern. West
African states are both "ancient and modern." This is bound to
affect the communication of the gospel. According to the United
Bible Societies, statistics prove that many of the growing population of the world will not learn to read: society is becoming audio-visual and post-literate. So far the churches have
proceeded on the printed word--translation, publication and
distribution of God's word. That has been the point of the
emphasis on the school as the handmaid of evangelism. That has
been good. But lots of our people are illiterate. So I wonder
if the time has not come for the churches in West Africa to
apply audio-visual techniques as well. Can the churches have
for example, Radio-TV stations of their own? I believe Liberia
with its heavy American influence is about the only exception.
Can you in Europe and America give both the stations and the
expertise? That is a role for the fraternal worker in our midst.
The church in West Africa cannot afford to do "business as
usual" in the face of the rapid social change resulting from
the impact of western culture and education. That would be a
sure way of reducing the church to an anachronistic irrelevance.

Let us for the meantime leave the first major influence and
turn to the second important factor, namely *Christianity and the
Church*. Some, particularly African nationalists and afrocrats,
have sometimes seen Christianity as another front of the colonial system. For example, Nkrumah once said:

> The stage opens with the appearance of missionaries and
> anthropologists, traders, concessionaires and adminis-
> trators. While the missionaries with "Christianity"
> implore the colonial subject to lay up "treasures in
> Heaven where neither moth nor rust doth corrupt," the
> traders, concessionaires acquire his mineral and land
> resources, destroy his arts, crafts and home industries
> (Nkrumah 1958:13).

That is not entirely true (Pobee 1975). The fortunes and goals
of the Christian church are not always identical or congruent
with those of western culture, even if the church came to West
Africa with the European and American stamp on it.

The church's influence goes beyond the church building. Nor should it be determined only in terms of the numbers of self-confessed members or attendance at the Eucharist. As a result of the church's twin main media of communication, namely the school and the hospital, many outside the church, even if they went through state schools, have had the Christian brush at work on them. This we term diffused Christianity, which to our mind is also a useful asset of the church. It means that there are many people in all walks of life who are neither against nor for the church. But it also means there has been and there still is a fund of goodwill towards the church and Christianity. And the church has been coasting on that capital of goodwill.

Apart from the church's involvement in education and hospitals, her record with regard to the iniquitous slave trade earned her the reputation of the defender of the defenceless and downtrodden. Initially the chiefs of Nigeria gave a welcome to the church because they could trust the church to defend them. Today the church shares her reputation as a liberator with the politicans who liberated African states politically from colonialism. But the church cannot rely too much on her past glory. It may be the church in West Africa needs a reminder that human memory is short, so that it begins to live with the present realities.

If the church has been an important factor in West African society, so too has *Islam*. This third important factor has been strongest in Francophone West Africa, i.e. Niger, Mali, Upper Volta, Senegal, Mauritania, Guinea. Figures are difficult to come by. But it is estimated that in each of these countries, at least 70% of the population are Muslim. In Anglophone Africa the Gambia, Sierra Leone, and Nigeria have sizeable numbers of Muslims (Trimingham 1959; Lewis 1966). Islam entered West Africa from the northern Sahara in Medieval times. There were even Islamic kingdoms like the Ghana, Mali, and Songhai empires. Islam presented West Africa with the Fulani *jihads* of the Futas Toro, Jalon, Masina, and Sokoto. West African Islam puts strong emphasis on the *Maliki* (law) as the basis of Islam. It is also connected with the rise of centralized states and was eventually fulfilled in theocratic rule. There is also emphasis on indigenous spirit-possession cults, e.g. the Hausa *bori*. The *Qadiriyya* (e.g. Senegal) and *Tijaniyya* (e.g. Northern Nigeria) are the two main *tariqas*. Now also, the Indian *Ahmadiyya* movement, with its strong missionary emphasis, is active in the area. They have schools and hospitals in Ghana, Nigeria, and Sierra Leone.

Islam has often offered stiff opposition to the Christian missionary onslaught, especially in the northern belt of West Africa. In 1833 the Church Missionary Society's efforts among

the Temne of Sierra Leone came to grief as a result of Muslim
opposition. Today the Gambia is about 85% Muslim. The result
is that the future of denominations other than the Roman Catholic is very precarious. One has been arguing in Anglican
circles that the Anglican mission to the Gambia be abandoned
and treated as a chaplaincy, through "worker-priests." The
Roman Catholics, who have had moderate successes, may continue
with the moral and financial support of the other denominations.
That situation calls for the union of the church. Further, in
some of these countries where Islam predominates, as in the
Gambia, the church has a siege mentality which needs revision.

    In addition to the three major factors of influence in West
African society, we may also add newer factors--Hinduism, Bud-
dhism, Guru movements, secularism (which has in part been in-
duced by western education itself), syncretism and materialism,
not to mention African traditional religion. All these threaten
the church. Thus the church lives in a pluralistic society and
must learn to live realistically in a pluralistic society. She
cannot claim a monopoly of the truth and must contend on eschatological tip-toe for the body, soul, and heart of *homo africanus*. In spite of the fund of goodwill for the church as a
result of her past achievements and services, complacency is
ruled out; that is a challenge, nay a threat, to the church.
The church's contribution then is alongside the contributions
of other ideologies and institutions. Besides, as more and more
African states declare for the welfare state and socialism, the
church can no longer rely on the school and the hospital as her
two important channels of communication because it is the government's proper function to provide social services and
amenities.

    The pluralism calls for an overhaul of the church's methods
and strategies, a development of new powers of resistance and
new resources of genuine vitality and relevance. One believes
that there are three possibilities before the church as she
faces the pluralism of West African society: (a) to seek a
synthesis of religions by addition, i.e. one adds the most important of all the important factors to create a new uniform
world faith in which everybody irrespective of background feels
at home. This approach is doomed to failure because religion
is "a living organism, animated by the faith of the believers
and expressing itself in forms and symbols which cannot simply
be transferred into a different setting" (Gensichen 1976:33);
(b) the church may seek a synthesis by reduction of all the
diverse religions to the lowest possible common denominator,
namely what seems to be common to all of them. This approach
is also unsatisfactory because it is rather abstract, satis-
fying no one's spiritual needs, or often arbitrarily fastens
on one religion which dictates the terms for others to conform

to; (c) the church may seek inter-faith dialog, which means a realistic engagement with the existing religions and institutions in their particularity, as well as meaningful religious co-existence. To our mind this third approach is the only viable and fruitful one.

There are at least three signs that the churches in West Africa are waking up to this. The first is the change of Departments of Divinity in African universities to Departments of Religious Studies, e.g. in the Universities of Ibadan (Nigeria) and Ghana (Legon and Cape Coast) (Zorn n.d.). Even the seminaries are now including more of comparative religion and philosophy and social studies in their curriculum. Such departments, committed to the scientific and comprehensive study of religions, are not only studying theology along the traditional lines but are also committed to a serious engagement with indigenous African religions and other world religions like Islam. It is hoped that the feedback from such institutions to the churches will be salutary, "equipping men and women to be equippers of the entire people of God" (Zorn n.d.ix). In the 1960's, churchmen were suspicious of such developments in theological education. They were anathema. Today they are proud of us. But there is a long way to go, especially in Sierra Leone, and Francophone Africa. But there are humble beginnings.

The second sign is the negotiations with a view to church union in Ghana and Nigeria. These have been disappointing or even collapsed, partly because prejudices die hard. But, at least, the mere fact of such discussions shows evidence of awareness of the need to have an authentic and effective mission of the church to the pluralistic society.

The third sign is the Islam in Africa Project established in 1960 as a channel for expressing the concerns and responsibilities of churches in Africa in their relationship with Muslims. That program reflects on the challenge of the large scale movements of peoples and ideas across communal and international frontiers, so as to bring the insight of faith and commitment to bear on shared ideals and common failings. And I am proud to say that in July 1977, the University of Ghana hosted a conference to discuss the challenges which face Christians and Muslims in Africa, the undefined and yet real forces which motivate and inspire committed people to engage in mutual sharing and exchange, and the unarticulated hidden spirit which makes people push aside their inherited reservations. Apart from this the Christian Councils of Ghana and Nigeria have departments concerned to hold dialog with Muslims.

The churches and theologians are, therefore, conscious of the need to take seriously the pluralism of our societies and to hold dialog with groups outside the church. But we have only just begun and there is a very long day ahead in which to react positively to the pluralism of society, seeing that there are several competing attractions. There is urgent need to get the children and youth for Christ, to provide training in leadership; youth halls and equipment for sports, farming, etc. are needed. The present methods of working through Scripture Union, Church Societies, and Child Evangelism need adapting and supporting with practical activities. Some of my Muslim friends are still very suspicious of Christian intentions. So we have to tread cautiously in this dialog, but with hope and faith in the guiding hand of God.

The church in West Africa has almost the whole spectrum of denominations. First we have both Roman Catholicism and the Greek Orthodox Church. But the latter tends to be the immigrants' church or the sojourners church: very few indigenous persons of West Africa belong to it. Then we have almost the whole range of Protestant churches, and the Independent African churches, e.g. Aladura Church of the Lord, Musama Disco Christo Church, Twelve Apostles, etc.

The story of the church in West Africa begins in the fifteenth century with the Roman Catholics. The prime mover was Prince Henry the Navigator of Portugal (1395-1460), who was at once a prince and prior of the religious Order of the Knights of Christ, an order founded in 1319 to fight off the Muslim Moors who had jeopardized Christian Europe. He initiated voyages into Africa to learn about West Africa beyond Cape Bojador, to open up trade relations, to ascertain the extent of the Muslim power, to find Prester John (the mythical Christian prince in Central Africa), and to evangelize the peoples of Africa and thus to undermine the Muslim influence in Africa south of the Sahara. Clearly human motives are often mixed: adventure, study, politics, trade, and evangelism came in one package. It would, therefore, not always be easy to isolate religious aims from other aims. Furthermore, Christianity came to West Africa in a crusade. That, of course, determined to some extent the presentation and aspect of the Christian mission in West Africa. It meant the church took a militant attitude to the cultures and religions she met in West Africa. Thus, for example, the early Roman Catholics pursued the policy of *requerimiento*, i.e. the demand for obedience to the gospel, the rejection of which meant hostilities. Or again to the present time all the historic churches by and large implemented the doctrine of the *tabula rasa*, i.e. the missionary doctrine that there is nothing in the non-Christian culture on which the Christian missionary can build and therefore, every aspect of the traditional non-Christian culture had to be destroyed before Christianity could be built up. Dialog was ruled out.

The *tabula rasa* has been most unsatisfactory. And the Africans were quick to protest. For example, Nii Akwaa Mensah II, *Nai Wulomo* (Chief Priest) of the Ga traditional area of Ghana once said:

> With the advent of Christianity and Western civilization we have been taught to disregard our way of living--a set-back to our culture and an opportunity to the imperialists and their agents. . . We have too much adopted the Christian way of life and if we could not force the imperialist to go bag and baggage from our God-given land (*Daily Graphic*, Accra, Dec. 12, 1950).[2]

One cannot help sympathizing with the *Nai Wulomo*. For the negative approach to the African cultures was bound to be counterproductive in the sense that it undermined anything like a real encounter between the Christian faith and African society. If you know not whence you come, you know not whither you go. The church has made an impact on African society. But its full impact has been dulled by the lack of real encounter with African society. The urgent task before the church in West Africa today is how to have a genuine encounter with *homo africanus* in order to find her own being and the meaning of her own existence. There is another danger, a very insidious one, resulting from the *tabula rasa:* it has led to a very eclectic and syncretistic type of Christianity. There is a "world-taken-for-granted," so to speak, taken in with the mother's milk, which surfaces in crises. In such crises the authentic Christian faith recedes into the background. And so, for example, childlessness often leads to men contracting second marriages.

There are signs that there is awareness that the *tabula rasa* approach has been unsatisfactory. This is the meaning and significance of the Independent Churches: they are an attempt to operate at the wavelength of *homo africanus* through worldview, non-conceptual media for theologizing (e.g. song and music), exorcism, etc. Even if one is unable to accept all their theology and practices, one cannot deny that at the very least they are an attempt to have an encounter with African culture, and the historic churches have something to learn from them: to evolve authentic African theology and authentic African worship. Another sign of this awareness is the emergence of African Theology. There is now the West African Association of Theological Institutions which *inter alia* seeks to promote a genuine encounter between Christianity and African society. Besides that, several works have appeared on the market, e.g. Vincent Mulago (1965), E. Bolaji Idowu (1965), K. A. Dickson and Paul Ellingworth (1969), H. Sawyerr (1968), E. Ilogu (1974), J. V. Taylor (1967), Mbiti (1976:164-168), Goreham (1975:233-236).

The emergence of the Independent Churches, the WAATI and
African Theology are healthy signs of an increasing awareness
of our self-identity and role and function as agents for the
renewal of the church. In the coming years the WAATI will need
the right ecumenical support, the *right* being determined by
right relationship between the donor and the recipient. Above
all, the emergence of WAATI and African Theology provides a
"Theological Fraternity" within which we are more and more able
to enter into an authentic and fruitful dialog with our counterparts in other countries.

In this exercise one is proud of the contribution of the Theological Education Fund, a service of the Commission on the
World Missions and Evangelism of the World Council of Churches.
Particularly in its Third Mandate the TEF has been a catalyst
in reform and renewal via contextualization, has helped create
"nerve centers" or "brain centers" of creativity in the third
world (TEF 1976). I know other agencies like the Arbeitsgeme-
inschaft für Weltmission (Germany), the United Church Board for
World Ministries (New York), have been financially supporting
the TEF with no strings whatever attached. That in itself is
a wonderful display of Christian sharing. I exhort you your-
selves to take stock of your own resources and see what you can
offer.

The first phase of the Christian mission in West Africa was
characterized·by the *padroado,* i.e. the highest possible recognition of the ecclesiastical and political sovereignty of the
King of Portugal over new dominions. By it the Pope held the
King of Portugal responsible for finding and supporting missionaries and bishoprics. This means that Christian faith and political ideology were next-door to each other and that the
church and the foreign power (later the colonial powers) were
inextricably involved in each other's business.[3] It is this
that led Nkrumah to his simplistic analysis of the church as
an agent of colonialism. But whether this is true or not, this
is not an uncommon allegation against the church in Africa. At
least such an allegation indicates that in some circles, at any
rate, the image of the church is that of a foreign institution
that seeks the enslavement of *homo africanus.*

Today the colonial era has given way to the age of independ-
dence. Ghana was the first (after Liberia) to become independent, in 1957, and the rest of West Africa followed in the
1960's. Today the church is faced with new political realities:
cultural self-consciousness (cf. the ideas of Negritude in
Senegal and African Personality in Ghana), national self-
consciousness, and economic self-consciousness (cf. Economic
Community of West African states). As the church seeks to relate to the peoples of West Africa, these areas will have to be

explored. It means structural changes in the form of the Christian mission. Is it any wonder that in Nigeria the Methodist
Church now has a patriarch instead of a president? Is it any
wonder that we are uneasy about the precise role of the foreign
worker in our midst? Is it any wonder that instead of calling
them missionaries we now call them fraternal workers? Is it
any wonder that one of the perennial problems in West Africa
is whether the national governments should be allowed to take
over the church schools and hospitals? Is it any wonder that
we are today talking of moratorium on missions? Max Warren is
absolutely right that

> it is a cardinal assumption of the Christian Mission
> that whatever the changes in the world the Gospel,
> God's good news for man, remains unchanged. Never-
> theless it calls for new interpretations as man's
> vocabulary of experience widens and deepens. To
> this exciting task of interpretation the Christian
> Mission is, I believe, of necessity being called
> (Warren 1976:119-120).

Until the nineteenth century the church's presence in West
Africa had not been much of a success, for diverse reasons:
first was the high mortality rate resulting from malaria, dys-
entery, yellow fever, etc. For example, out of the 70 missionaries sent out by the CMS between 1804 and 1824 to Sierra
Leone, only 27 survived. That problem was reversed or at least
normalized by the discovery of quinine in 1854, which went a
long way to improve the hazards to health by the little mosquito which along with others had earned for West Africa the
title "The White Man's Grave." This little detail is not without significance for the present study. For that reputation
created in Europeans, except the adventurers who were excep-
tionally tough characters, a disinclination towards settling
in West Africa. This fact gave the history of West Africa a
course different from that of East Africa. For with no desire
to settle, the involvement of settlers in economic structures,
leading to minority racist regimes could not become a serious
issue with which to contend in West Africa. This in part
accounts for the difference between the primary concerns of the
church in West Africa and those of the church in East and South
Africa. The latter is preoccupied with the issue of racism and
with that they talk Black Theology which is a type of liberation theology. We in West Africa are primarly concerned with
authenticity and therefore, with African Theology, the encounter
or dialogue between the Christian faith and African culture.
Yes--West Africa can be grateful to the little mosquito! No
wonder Sierra Leone may, according to the statute books, honor
her distinguished sons with the Order of the Mosquito. The
little mosquito has made all the difference to the history and
objectives of the church in West Africa.

The image of West Africa as the White Man's Grave even after
the discovery of quinine had yet another relevance and consequence for the history of the church in West Africa: from the
very beginning of the renewed mission in the nineteenth century,
one mission board after another sought to involve Africans in
the governance, mission, and financial arrangements of the
church. For example, the Rev. Mr. Henry Venn, Prebendary of
St. Paul's, London, and Secretary of CMS (1842-1872), initiated
the policy known as the Euthanasia of Mission, i.e. a self-
governing, self-supporting, and self-extending African church
(Ayandele 1966:175ff).[4] He sought a gradual evolution of the
churches in Asia and Africa towards becoming indigenous: the
mission field was to assume responsibility for the financial
care of their ministers; he sought to raise African pastors to
take charge of the church; and the church was to be self-
governing through councils and committees comprising a European
bishop, European and African missionaries and laymen. To that
end he created the Sierra Leone Native Pastorate which required
the support of pastors, churches and schools by native congregations through the "class pence" and the CMS as a mission body
withdrew from the hinterland in 1908, handing over their work
there to the SLNP.

Perhaps the policy of the Euthanasia of Mission was implemented too soon: they tried to run before they could walk, in
the sense that the infrastructures of a mission, i.e. sound
finances, an army of dedicated native missionaries, etc., had
not been set up before the vision was implemented. Some of the
missionaries too, being men of their time, could treat the Africans only as "infants". They were only timorous and mis-
guided. But by and large, it was not for lack of right vision
or for lack of trying or bad faith that an authentic African
church did not spring up earlier than the second half of the
twentieth century. Incidentally such attempts, which were not
peculiar to the CMS[5] make the recent discussion of moratorium
in mission sheer missing of the bus. The lesson for the church
in Africa today is that adequate preparation should be made for
even the good things. All too often the church trusts too much
to the Holy Ghost!

The second factor was the slave trade which was very lucra-
tive between the fifteenth and the eighteenth century. The
trade was such a great threat to the Roman Catholic efforts
that on May 29, 1537 Pope Paul III decreed excommunication for
any Catholic who indulged in that trade. Again on February 17,
1687 the Cardinals of the Sacred Congregation de Propaganda
Fide had to consider a complaint from the missionaries on the
coast that Christian merchants from Portugal were buying slaves
from "pagan" middlemen. Its wickedness and disastrous consequences for the church were too obvious to the church, even if

from time to time some individual churchmen upheld the slave trade.

The slave trade resulted in the coalition of the products of the Evangelical Revival of the eighteenth century and the humanitarian concerns in Europe, a coalition which was to change the fortunes of the church in the nineteenth century. The Evangelical Revival in Europe, typified by John Wesley and George Whitefield, stressed personal conversion and salvation by faith in the atoning death of Jesus Christ. They also preached atonement by good works of national life and charity towards the whole race of mankind, black as well as white. They also stressed the conveyance of the gospel to the spiritually less fortunate. In this their concern for the underdogs at home and abroad, they received active support from the humanitarians, men like William Wilberforce, Charles Grant, Henry Thornton, Zachary Morpley, James Steven, and Granville Sharpe. Specifically they advocated better government in India, better treatment of prisoners; and for Africa, the abolition of slavery. The movement towards the abolition of slavery received a great boost in the famous judgment of Lord Mansfield in 1772 that a slave was free immediately he set foot in England. Slavery was abolished in Britain in 1807.

Believing, as the coalition did, that the slave trade had been a great sin against God and Africa, for which atonement was to be made, the Evangelicals and humanitarians sought to make atonement by the conversion of Africa to Christianity and the introduction of education into that unfortunate continent. This led to the enunciation of the policy of "the Bible and the Plough," "the Bible" standing for education in the classical form; "the plough" referring to the efforts to teach the Africans to explore their own natural resources rather than to sell one another. That philosophy characterized the policies of the church. Education became the handmaid of evangelism. In Ghana, for example, the historic church's involvement in education was as follows for 1966:

	Primary & Middle Schools	Secondary Schools	Teacher Training
Roman Catholic	1,554	16	10
Methodist	1,131	5	6
Presbyterian	1,031	6	8
Anglican	370	2	2
Government	10,421	104	84

With that came modern scientific education which was born in the
womb of the church and not of the colonial administrators.   And
with that also, the church became "the guardian angel of African
nationalism" (Sithole 1959:55; Kimble 1963:151-167; Pobee 1976:
121-144).   The corollary of this is that where missions were de-
barred by the French and the British in the so-called Islamic
belt of northern West Africa, education and development were
poor.   This accounts for some of the tensions between Northern
Nigeria and Southern Nigeria.

"The plough" was aimed at replacing the iniquitous slave
trade with honest and honorable trade.   But it was also to contribute towards the evolution of self-supporting churches in
West Africa.   As early as the nineteenth century, the Roman
Catholics established Topo, a nine-mile stretch of agricultural
settlement near Badagry which reared cattle and produced coconuts and cassava.   In 1892 Topo's copra fetched ₺69.19s.   In
1897 the coconuts fetched ₺19.19s.   Today in Guinea Bissau the
Italian Roman Catholics have a very exemplary farm at Bafata.
In Ghana the Basel Mission established farms at Abokobi and
Aburi.   Today the Evangelical Presbyterian Church of Ghana has
farms at Chireponi.   However, the farming aspect of the strategy
lack the thrust and punch of their efforts in education.   That
was in part the result of a false theology which considered that
pursuit of such things was to follow Mammon.   The church in West
Africa should be more serious with "the plough" in order to
really identify with the aspirations of developing African
states as well as build the right infrastructures for a self-
supporting church.   I believe it is the area in which churches
and sound Christian men and women overseas, in Europe and
America, can make solid contributions in terms of personnel,
expertise, farm equipment, etc.   West Africa remains agricultural and had better develop the vast expanses of good soil to
produce food to feed itself.   Christians in Europe and America
have the responsibility to help us stand on our feet.   Today the
churches in Ghana, at any rate, are talking of going into
farming in a big way.

Classical education served its day.   African governments
which have declared for the welfare state are interested in
taking over even the church schools.   I myself can say "Laus
Deo" that we as a church have blazed a trail in the area of
education and taught the nations the lesson in charity and
responsibility for all in the society.   I would gladly give
them to the state because they have the resources for it, not
to mention that it is the proper function of the state to provide the social services.   Only let us ensure that the administration of these schools would at least be as good as what
the churches did.   Let us also ensure that religious education
is on the curriculum; but not primarily because we wish to use

the school as the handmaid of evangelism, but because education is concerned to develop man to enable him to cope competently with life in its diverse forms, of which religion is a veritable part. The church in West Africa needs to grow beyond the earlier philosophy of education as the handmaid of evangelism to education as a means of equipping man for life in its manifold forms.

Two things need to be done urgently: first the church must blaze another trail in establishing vocational institutions which are woefully lacking in West Africa. Too many people are in blind-alley jobs with no prospects. They went into them only because that was what was available when they left school. They, consequently, do not love the job, but go to work with a grudge against society and themselves. These should be the Church's concern: a vocational school can help them be self-fulfilled and realize themselves as men "in the image and likeness of God" and, therefore, with dignity. The second is that the education must be broad-based and relate to other disciplines.

Christian education in Africa needs an overhaul. The teacher-catechist sought to raise up literates who would serve as interpreters and other church functionaries. For its day that was revolutionary. Today we as a church do not appear to have the enterprising spirit of the first generation: we do not have good catechetical books and teachers of religion. We need to pay attention to the principles of design and curriculum review. We must try to reach the pre-school child and the non-school youth who at the moment appear to be forgotten. Sunday schools, women's groups, youth fellowships, Bible classes, etc., can be used to teach Christians to cope competently with their environment and to contribute to society positively. That too is liberation and self-fulfillment (Oduyoye 1976:190-200).

The third major obstacle to the advance of the church in its first phase was Islam. On that we have touched earlier. Only let us emphasize that in some West African countries such as Nigeria, we have to be on our guard against religious wars. That can only be counter-productive. It is in the last decade that we had the tragic civil war in Nigeria, which has as one of its ingredients the Christian-Muslim conflict. In Sierra Leone and the Gambia there is that tension. In Francophone Africa where Islam predominates the question is still asked whether Christianity will disappear just as it did in North Africa. Personally I think the church will survive in those parts because being conscious that she is in the minority, she is steadily evolving survival strategies. That is where the mission strategy of the White Fathers yields dividends because it tries to incarnate the gospel in the culture of the people so that it does not become an alien institution.

The fourth major obstacle was wars. Inter-tribal wars between the Asante and the Fante, between the Asante and the
Akwamu, etc., are too well-known to be recounted here (Ward
1958). Each war disrupted any achievements of the missionary.
Today such inter-tribal wars are virtually non-existent. But
the civil war of Nigeria, 1968-1970, as well as man's innate
bellicose tendency should warn against complacency and over-
confidence that it is no longer a problem. The church should
proclaim the dignity of every man and the universal brotherhood
of mankind.

The fifth major factor was the failure of the earliest missionaries to be sensitive to African culture. With the rise of
the concept of Christendom, there was a tendency to equate
Christianity with civilization and African culture with Boeotian
darkness and gross primitivity. The Africans for their part
were proud of their heritage. As Asantehene said to the Rev.
Mr. Picot, a Methodist missionary to the Gold Coast in the
nineteenth century,

> The Bible is not a book for us. God at the be-
> ginning gave the Bible to the White People, and
> another book to the Cramos (? Muhammedans), and
> fetish to us. . . We know God already. We will
> never embrace your religion, for it would make
> our people proud. It is your religion which has
> ruined the Fanti country, weakened their power
> and brought down the high man on a level with the
> low man (Findlay and Holdsworth 1922:175).

Obviously for the Asantehene, Christianity was a positive evil.
The Church and African society never really met or communicated.
In Nigeria King Jaja of Opobo resisted CMS efforts among the
Bonny because he regarded Christianity as a disturber of society
through preaching individualism to the well-knit communal
society, through undermining slavery, preaching egalitarianism
and disparaging *"juju"* (King Jaja himself was the priest of
Ikuba and therefore, a diehard protagonist of indigenous religion as the cement of society) (Ayandele 1966).

What was said earlier would confirm that African traditional
culture still holds its ground. That is the import of the
aspirations of the emerging African personality. That is the
import of the rise of the independent churches today. That is
the significance of the fact that many Christians in the historic churches still perform funeral rites, etc., which have
been declared evil by the churches. The traditional worldview
is still a "world-taken-for-granted" which surfaces in crises.
This may indicate a certain amount of selectivity among the
Africans: they welcome Christianity not only because they are

convinced about the message but also because of the benefits of
education and the hospital as well as the general respectability that accrues from association with the church. But it also
means that the church should not be complacent about numbers;
more important is that she should be sensitive to and address
herself to the hopes and fears of the Africans. That, as we
said above, is at a rudimentary stage. And the future of the
church in West Africa depends to a very large extent on how far
and how fast we address ourselves to the hopes and fears of West
Africans. I fear the rate of adaptation is rather slow and
sometimes half-hearted. Part of the trouble is that the Africans have learned their European lessons all too well, and that,
the worst aspects of Euro-Christian culture.

Two factors in the nineteenth century brought about a change
in the fortunes of the church: the new attitude to colonization,
and the evangelical revival. Now colonization was welcome; it
brought *pax et securitas,* the right condition for a mission.
The partition of Africa in part determined the denominational
structure of West Africa in at least two ways. First it determined which missionary could go where. After the revolution of
1789 in France, non-French citizens were prohibited from entering French territories. Only missionaries with French citizenship were allowed in French territories. Thus only the
Société des Missions Evangélique could work among the Wolof in
Dakar. American Presbyterians in Liberia who crossed into
French borders were driven out. Or again, when the Germans
annexed Cameroons in July 1884, the English Baptist Missionary
Society which had been working there for some 40 years before
the Germans had to move out and hand over their work to the
Basel Mission in 1886 (Steiner 1912). And when the Germans
were vanquished in the First World War and the Cameroons were
turned over to the French, the Paris Evangelical Society took
over the work of the Basel Mission, so that today the largest
Protestant Church in the Cameroun has grown out of that work
(Coxill and Grubb 1962:59). In June 1885 Father Weik of the
Congregation du Saint-Esprit et de l'Immaculé Coeur de Marie
(popularly known as the French Holy Ghost Fathers) was denied
permission by the German Foreign Office and Bismarck himself
to work in the Cameroons simply because his Order had a French
base. Later in 1890 they permitted the German Pallotine Fathers
or the Pious Society of Missions to work in the Cameroons, on
the condition that they did not trespass into Protestant territory, that only Germans served in the Cameroons, and that the
executive power resided locally in the colony. Here is the key
to the policy. Germany and for that matter France and Britain,
did not wish for any potential fifth-column in their territories. A missionary society went where her home country exercised political control and was deemed an interested party (see
also Der 1974; Debrunner 1965).

The partition of Africa, secondly, ensured that certain denominations predominated in some areas. Thus Elmina in Ghana
is very much Roman Catholic because that was where the Portuguese influence was great.

The other new factor in the eighteenth and nineteenth centuries was the rise of modern missionary societies: Baptist
Missionary Society (1792), London Missionary Society (1795),
Edinburgh and Scottish Missionary Society (1796), Church Missionary Society (1799), British and Foreign Bible Society
(1804), Basel Evangelical Missionary Society (1818), North
German Missionary Society (1836), Moravians, not to mention
quite a few from the U.S.A. On the Roman Catholic side there
was a similar development: the Societas Missionum ad Afros
(Society of African Missions) which worked in Southern Ghana
and Southern Nigeria. There was also the Society of Missionaries to Africa also known as the White Fathers, who worked
mostly in the savannah belt of West Africa--Upper Volta, Niger,
Northern Ghana, Northern Nigeria, etc., and the Society of the
Divine Word. This new development of a bevy of missionary
societies, all dedicated to the expansion of Christianity to
places outside Europe, meant an increase in the rate of evangelization of Africa. Thus by 1900 there was little of the coast
that was not evangelized and the onslaught on the interior had
begun.

What were the achievements of the mission? We have already
mentioned the achievement in education and also commented on
its strong points and weaknesses, so we shall not go over the
same ground again. The second achievement was the area of
medical work. But that has not been too impressive. At the
present time the Roman Catholics in Ghana have about 24 hospitals and 21 clinics; Methodists 1 hospital; Presbyterian 2
hospitals and 2 clinics; Anglicans 1 hospital. It is also the
achievement of the Presbyterian missionaries Mr. F. D. Harker
and Mrs. Margaret Benzies that the first blind school in West
Africa was set up at Akropong. More of such places are needed
because this provision has given otherwise socially useless and
neglected persons very meaningful and self-fulfilling lives.
For there they were taught not only arithmetic and English but
also craft-training such as basket-weaving, shorthand and
typing, etc. The church can do far more in the medical field
than she has done so far. She can establish more hospitals and
clinics. She can encourage good Christian men who are also
doctors to come out to West Africa to work to give a Christian
witness. In a country where doctors are very few, the medical
men have acquired scarcity value, with the result that all too
often doctors are interested in patients only as a source of
income; all human touch of a medic is gone. Maybe, good Christian men who are doctors can come out to live the human touch

of medicine and quietly effect a change in attitudes for the
better. Churches and churchmen can contribute drugs. The governments are not able to import enough drugs for the respective
countries. There are times when there are shortages of serum
for snake-bites in a country where snake-bites are an everyday
occurrence. It may be the churches in West Africa should take
stock of the medical needs of their respective countries and
then invite outside help. We need nurses and other medical
functionaries who have the human touch and therefore raise a
cheer in the faces of those afflicted by disease, pain, and
death. We need men and women with medical talents who are also
human.

One more plea: if the churches go into medicine and education, they should desist from seeing them as first and fore-
most catchment areas for disciples. We do these as acts of
charity, acts of love to bring liberation to the oppressed.

Here I wish to raise the issues of spiritual healing. In
West Africa it seems to be treated as the preserve of the independent churches. But the church as a whole has a healing
ministry. It may be the historic churches must revive the office of the healers. She must seek out those with that talent
and encourage them to use it in the womb of the church.

The third great contribution of the church to the development of *homo africanus* has been philological work. Christaller
reduced Twi to writing; Zimmerman Ga, Samuel Adjai Crowther
Yoruba, Goldin Efik, Henry Branton published a Grammar and
Vocabulary in Susu. These have been momumental and are still
unexcelled. That philological work still continues, though not
within the church. But if language is the soul of a people, an
instrument to support a whole culture, then the church has made
a contribution to the development of *homo africanus'* consciousness and development.

The work of the church in West Africa has not been unmiti-
gated success. First, the mission tended to divide African
society between Christians and pagans. Many were moved from
their homes to mission lands known as Topo in Yorubaland or
Salem in Ghana. This was the beginning of the disintegration
of African society. For those Christians in their enclaves,
believing themselves nearest the enigmatic wizard who was a
White Man, tended to renounce the authority of the chief. The
church sought to save *homo africanus* out of his society rather
than in his society, which is theologically not sound.

Secondly, especially in the nineteenth century they often
condemned everything African without any real effort to understand. In fact to become a Christian was to abandon African

initiation rites, dancing, traditional marriage, ancestral cult,
and even African names. In short, the abandonment of some of
the fundamental cohesive force of African society was a prerequisite to becoming a Christian. Today we are a little wiser
than our forefathers, but the mentality lingers on. For example, most Africans have two sets of names, a home name (e.g.
Papa Kofi Eduam) and a school/Christian name (e.g. John Samuel
Pobee). The same person bears the two names. And in crises
the home name will be used. Two worlds which never meet!

The main consequence of this, is to accelerate the process
of "acculturation" or Europeanization. It hastened the change
from African to the pseudo-European state which is still prominent. No wonder there is so much confusion in ourselves and
in our midst!

One last issue: A good deal of our confusion in Africa has
been blamed on politicians. I fear I must blame the church for
failing to be the conscience of society. Surely good Christians are in politics. And where have they been when evil has
been perpetrated? I believe part of the problem involves some
popular versions of Christianity, especially the impact of
Pietism and the Evangelical Revival: there has been a tendency
to treat sin only in its vertical dimension, i.e. in terms of
God and his laws and often to underplay the horizontal dimension of religion. One aspect of this is the tendency to say
"keep religion out of politics." Such reasoning, which is not
uncommon in Ghana, at any rate, amounts to a denial of the
sovereignty of God over all life. And such a society soon is
swallowed up in corruption, violence, in short in sin. There
can be no valid neutrality for the Christian in public life.
Christians have let down their countries. The church as an
institution must not be identified with any one group interest,
but remain the referee and linesman of the fight between the
warring factions of society. The church unfortunately has
sometimes given respectability to corrupt politicans by in-
viting them to chair harvest festivals, etc. The greatest problem of African states today is that of winning moral authority
for creating a new Africa. That is made more difficult partly
because the church has failed to give the proper moral leadership.

For all their faults, one looks at the sacrifices which missionaries made and their contribution to education, the foundation of our achievements, and development, and concludes that
West Africa owes a lot to missions. I quote again Mr. Nkrumah
who, addressing the Ghana Assembly of the International Missionary Council (Accra, December 28, 1957 to January 8, 1958),
said:

If you have time to visit more widely in this country, you will often find as you travel along the
roads, little cemeteries lost in the bush where lie
buried the brave men and women who, in bringing
the Christian faith to this country, gave the last
full measure of their devotion. They knew that they
faced the certainty of loneliness and imminent risk
of death. Yellow fever decimated them and their
families. But still they came. They belong to the
martyrs of Christianity as surely as those who faced
persecution for their faith. The fortitude which
they showed is the sure foundation upon which your
work has been based. Ghana salutes these men and
women who gave their lives for the enlightenment
and welfare of this land (Orchard 1958:148).

Today I stand before you a product of that sweat and labor.
And I am proud of it, for all the criticisms I venture. In my
society there is a proverb: *Nyimpa a ɔkɔ nsu, na ɔbɔ hyira,*
i.e. "It is the one whose duty it is to fetch water who breaks
the pitcher." In other words, in pursuing a good job, one is
bound to make mistakes. So I accept criticism of the church.
But I plead it is the criticism of one who cares deeply about
the church.

---

[1]Liberia was founded by the American Colonization Society
or more accurately the American Society for Colonizing the Free
People of Color of the United States in about 1820.

[2]For similar sentiments see Busia (1961); Williamson (1965:
175-176); Desai (1962).

[3]This is true even of Francophone Africa where there was the
separation of church and state after 1900. See also Benedict
Der (1974).

[4]The high mortality rate among the European missionaries and
its fear were an important factor in the evolution of this theory but not the only factor. The CMS was also in financial
crisis. Further, the Rev. Mr. Venn had also been impressed by
the success and effectiveness of Creole missions in Nigeria.

[5]The SPG, the Basel Mission, and the Methodists as well as
the Roman Catholics pursued this. Rev. M. Henry Thompson,
the first SPG missionary to the Gold Coast, sent three African
boys to London for training in the conviction that the future
of the African church depended on them. The Methodists brought
in the mulatto, the Rev. Mr. Thomas Birch Freeman.

Response #1
Dick Darr

Our brother, John S. Pobee, in his excellent paper *The Church in West Africa* did well early in his writing to remind us of the many diversities and differences not only in the vast area of West Africa but even within a country. Let me assure you there *is* a vast difference in the "geography, vegetation, temperament, culture and politics" of the Republic of Mali (where I served for 17 years) as compared to the coastal countries.

Much of what I say will concern the church in Mali because that is the country I know best. I believe that a great deal of what I have to say will apply, equally as well, to the inland Francophone countries whose borders reach up into the Sahara and who find themselves landlocked, as Mali does.

To understand the church in Mali, you must think of it in terms of its own cultural uniqueness. The cultural determinants and how they influence the Christian church must be recognized. Mali's history, its present economic and social problems and its political situation have determined to a great extent the development of the church to this point in history. And these factors will continue to affect its development in the years to come.

MALI HAS A RICH HERITAGE

Its people are proud of its history. The early missionaries were not as much aware of this factor as they should have been. Mali is heir to a succession of ancient African empires--the gold kingdoms of Ghana, Mali and Songhai--that ruled West Africa

from the Western Sudan to the Atlantic from A.D. 600 to A.D.
1500.

These kingdoms controlled the Sahara slave, gold, and salt
trade for almost 1000 years. The Mali empire came into promi-
nence during the 13th century. It was an impressive achievement in statecraft and the kingdom became one of history's
greatest empires.

Mansa Musa, who came to the throne in 1307, dazzled Africans
with his spectacular wealth. On his pilgrimage to Mecca he put
so much gold in circulation in Cairo that he almost ruined the
gold market. He brought 80 to 100 camel loads of gold dust each
weighing about 300 pounds! The fabled city of Timbuktu retains
much of its mysterious attraction today because of its former
trade in gold.

When France entered Mali in the mid-1800's, she faced one of
the strongest movements resistant to colonial rule in Africa.
It was not until 1895 that the resistance was crushed and the
area became the French colony of Sudan.

Malians identify with their past. When the French Sudan received its independence in 1960 the people reached back into
their past and chose "Mali" as their country's new name. The
memories of Gao, Timbuktu, and Mopti are indelibly implanted in
its national pride.

MALI HAS AN INADEQUATE ECONOMY

This is true of most of the desert, landlocked countries of
West Africa. The people yearn for a better life. But they face
staggering problems: under-developed mineral resources, limited
productive soil, an enervating climate, lack of a sea outlet,
and few industries. *Time* magazine recently rated Mali in the
lowest (fifth) category of the nations of the world. The per
capita income is $70 a year.

The economy depends largely on agriculture and livestock
raising. National income still depends on a few primary prod-
ucts--peanuts, cattle, rice and fish. The severe drought of
1973 was devasting to this area.

MALI HAS LIMITED SOCIAL ACHIEVEMENT

There are 26 different tribes in Mali. There is a wide
variety of peoples. Because of this Mali has been called
"Africa in microcosm."

The geography has been conductive to mobility and inter-
mingling of the population. French, of course, is the official

language of the country. Bambara is spoken by 80% of the
people and is one of the principle trade languages of West
Africa.

A greater problem than the multiplicity of the people is the
extremely high illiteracy rate of approximately 80%. Progress
is being made. The government has one of the best literacy programs in the world. But only 20% of the children aged 6-14
have an opportunity to attend school. Add to this the fact that
49% of the population is under age 15 and you can see how per-
plexing the problem is.

THE CHRISTIAN CHURCH IN MALI IS SMALL BUT STRONG

French colonialism kept Protestant missions out of the French
Sudan until a first survey trip by Rev. George Fisher and Rev.
George Reed came *in 1913*. They traveled from Dakar and St.
Louis, Senegal inland to Bamako, via the Niger, and north to
Timbuktu. They retraced their Niger waterway route back to
Bamako, and then further south into Guinea to the seaport of
Conakry. From St. Louis, Senegal inland as far as Timbuktu in
the Sudan and back to Conakry on the Guinea coast they did not
find one Protestant missionary at work. Not until a treaty
signed at the end of World War I opened the door did a mission-
ary take up residence in Mali: the year was 1919.

First, I wish to call to your attention the very important
fact that the gospel message came much, much later to the interior countries of West Africa than it did to the coastal
countries. The French were always suspicious of the American
missionaries, feeling that they were potential spies.

Secondly, you must understand that the predominant influence
in Mali, Upper Volta, Niger, as well as in Senegal, Guinea, and
Gambia on the coast, was the powerful force of Islam. The
Catholic Church which entered with the colonists in the 1890's
was closely associated with French colonialism in the eyes of
the African. After independence many of her adherents turned
to the Muslim faith.

The early missionaries and African converts concentrated on
evangelism and Bible translation. The entire Bible in Bambara
was printed by the early sixties. The rural areas were most
responsive to the gospel, but today the church is strongly
oriented toward the urban areas.

Thirdly, it is important to know that when compared to the
churches in the coastal countries of West Africa, the Mali
church is much *younger* and *smaller*. There are probably not
more than 30,000 Christians in the country today. This from a

population of nearly 5 million people. Believers in Christ are very much in a minority.

My fourth point is that the Mali church though small and young has incredible vitality. They are busy propagating their faith. They use an astonishing variety of methods to do this, radio (from Liberia), open air preaching, gospel recordings, literature production and distribution, fair evangelism, youth activities, camps, crusades, organized house-to-house visitation, and leadership training institutes. The result is a strong church--a growing church.

A second translation of the Scriptures in Bambara is well on the way. A concordance has been completed and the Bambara song book contains over 240 hymns written by Africans. Bible schools, reading classes, and literature ministries help reduce the illiteracy rate.

The church that came into being in 1961, as a result of Gospel Missionary Union work, chose the name Evangelical Protestant Church of Mali. The EPCM and the other three groups started by other missions societies are bound together in an Organization of Protestant Churches and Missions. The close unity and genuine Christian fellowship of this group has given the church a good image in the eyes of the government. The leadership is, of course, African. Praise God the Christian groups in Mali have few of the hang-ups that obstruct unity among the churches of the western world.

The call for a moratorium on missionaries is not heard from the struggling church in interior West Africa. Be very sure of one thing, however, the autonomous church will not tolerate the missionary or the mission with a paternalistic approach. They make it very plain that any missionary who comes to Mali and fails to cooperate with the church will pose a serious problem for the mission and will be in the eyes of the African Christian simply a tourist who is exploiting the missionary channel for his own ends.

The Christians who live along the edge of the Sahara desert are almost engulfed in a sea of Muslim people. How can the church grow in this condition? It cannot grow by isolating itself from the religious ideas and systems of those they are trying to reach. The simplistic approach that all that is needed is to preach the gospel is not enough. No one can preach the gospel if he is isolated from the religious ideas and systems of those he is trying to reach. The church *is* growing because it *is willing* to give a reason for the faith that is within. Dialog takes place because the Christians are willing to converse intelligently with those of other faiths. This is the testing ground for the young church in Muslim lands. This is the battle that determines the vitality of faith and commitment of the church.

It is my observation that the church in Mali knows full well, better than many missionaries or churches in America, that we cannot reach people with whom we do not talk. There can be no conversion to Christianity of those who do not hear its message. Consequently, they reach out to initiate dialog. They are not defensive. They are *going out* to make contact, to meet the Muslim face to face, to risk everything for Christ's sake. The African church believes very strongly in the finality of Jesus Christ. The core of the gospel is not bargainable. But this does not cause them to shrink from attempting dialog. They are good listeners, skilled to present their own case in love and urge a positive response to the message, and leave the hearer to his own ways, if he does not accept it.

The Church in Africa *needs the financial support of their brothers and sisters in Christ*. Just one example: there are four new congregations in Bamako which desperately need to build church buildings. Property has been granted by a government which is very friendly to them. Why would anyone consider this an unwise use of God's money? When the people are doing everything within their own means to help themselves it cannot be wrong to give liberally from out of the abundance that is ours in the western church.

The church asks for continued medical, educational, and agricultural assistance programs. They are very concerned that a high priority continue to be given to leadership training for the church.

The church that exists in the countries that are part of the Sahel where Islam is strong are young but growing. This can also be said of the coastal countries where the Muslims are predominant such as Senegal and Guinea.

The influence and ministry of EPCM reaches far beyond the boarders of Mali. The Church President, Kassoum Keita, was one of the featured speakers at the "Missions--1976" Conference at Lausanne, Switzerland, where over 3,000 young people from the continent of the Reformation gathered. The challenge to "go into all the world and preach the gospel to every creature" came to the European youth from an African (the dark continent) pastor.

I believe that the greatest thing I have to share with you as one who has worked in the inland Francophone area is that the autonomous churches of that area are reaching out with every means at their disposal to share the gospel of God's love in Christ Jesus. *The church is a missionary church.*

Response #2

Charles H. Kraft

We are indeed grateful to Prof. Pobee for this broad yet comprehensive survey of the Christian church in West Africa. As one dips back into the past like this and attempts to draw into one short presentation a phenomenon such as this, one can barely touch a few of the high points. And yet it becomes abundantly clear that Christianity in West Africa is and always has been a multifaceted, complex thing. When one considers the diversity of cultures, the varying backgrounds of the missionaries, the intensity of their dedication in the face of extreme risk and hardship and the tenacity of African Christians committed to even sub-ideal expressions of Christianity, one is forced to marvel at the grace and power of God to do the unexpected.

As I ponder this history--I who came upon the scene in the middle of the twentieth century--I am forced to ask myself what my involvement would have been like if I had arrived a century earlier. Would I have even taken the risk? Could I have endured the hardship? Would I have avoided the mistakes that my predecessors made? Probably not.

And yet, it is a different day today. Things are not as they once were, especially in Africa. And we would be foolish if we felt that the Christian cause in West Africa is well served by simply continuing to perpetuate uncritically the patterns of the past. I, with Prof. Pobee, am critical of the Christian church in West Africa. But, like his criticism, "it is the criticism of one who cares deeply about the church." It is analysis and criticism of the past and present of that church for the sake of a continuing and improved future for the church.

My involvement with the church in West Africa began in the
early 1950's when I began to train specifically to work in
Northern Nigeria. Anthropological and linguistic study in relation to Christianity in West Africa alerted me to a number of
potential problem areas in the interaction between a, Europeanized Christian message and methodology on the one hand and the
West African sociocultural context on the other. In 1957, then,
having learned Hausa, my family and I began pioneer missionary
service among a tribal people in northeastern Nigeria where
Christianity had barely gotten a toehold.

We were a part of a mission committed to the old "civilize
in order to evangelize" philosophy (called "the Bible and the
Plough" approach by Prof. Pobee). Our mission, therefore, ex-
pended most of its money and energy on starting and running
schools. A certain amount of money and energy, then, went into
medical work. Churchwork was a poor third priority for this
mission. Yet, largely because some dedicated Nigerian Christians got to our area before the mission did, we found a people
more turned on by the church than by the schools and medical
work. By working with, rather than against this indigenous
interest in Christianity, then, we saw marvelous (and, for this
area, untypical) things happen in the church. This experience
colors my whole approach to the issues raised by Prof. Pobee.

With this in mind, I would like to focus on four closely related issues raised by Prof. Pobee that I believe are of great
contemporary concern to the church in West Africa. Each of
these becomes pressing in these days because of what I deem to
be inadequate approaches in the past. The issues are: 1) Sensitivity to African culture, 2) The competitive posture that
has characterized Christianity vis-a-vis African religion,
education, medicine, and communicational techniques, 3) The
need to redefine education, and 4) The need for a more African
Christianity.

SENSITIVITY TO AFRICAN CULTURE

The first issue that I would like to address myself to is
that labeled by Prof. Pobee, "The failure of the earliest missionaries to be sensitive to African culture." Given my background training and my experience, the lack on the part of
Christian witnesses in this area is particularly appalling to
me. When, therefore, Prof. Pobee makes the statement, "The
Church and African society never really met or communicated,"
my mind fills with a host of illustrations of this point from
my own background. Intense dedication, even in the face of
incredible hardship, has not apparently been enough to overcome
this obstacle. Prof. Pobee mentioned the preaching of individualism to communal societies and the continued pride of many

Africans in their traditional cultures. I found the West Africans among whom I worked to be proud deep down but intimi-
dated in their contacts with Euroamericans. Both they and we
are impressed with the accomplishments of western culture.
There is, however, no excuse, especially in our day, for
allowing the impressiveness of one culture to blind us to the
fact that God seeks to use every culture for his purposes.

   David Barrett, in attempting to discover the root cause of
African independency, terms this lack of sensitivity a "failure
in love." He sees missionaries as magnificent in their por-
trayal of "love as service, love as sacrifice, love as forgiveness, love as caring, love as compassion, love as charity, love
in its social manifestation as peace" (1968:155). He sees
missionaries failing, however, in "love as close contact with
others involving listening, sharing, sympathizing and sensitive
understanding in depth as between equals" (ibid). This is a
failure in sensitivity. It is a failure to employ the golden
rule with respect to cultures. We from the West are anxious
that people around the world respect our culture. We have,
however, often been insensitive to the need of other peoples
to experience our respect for their cultures.

   We stand, therefore, condemned by our own Scriptures if we
do not rectify this lack of sensitivity to Africans in the cultural context in which they were born and in which they live
their lives. Many Africans are rejecting a Christianity that
does not square with its supposed biblical bases. If there was
ever a lesson we could learn from the past, it is the lesson
that all of us, no matter what our cultural background, are
accountable to present the Christian message *in Christian
ways*--in ways that show sensitivity and love toward those we
seek to reach. We of the West, and those who from African
backgrounds have converted to our ways, must learn this greater
sensitivity and love.

THE COMPETITIVENESS OF WESTERN CHRISTIANITY

   Stemming from this lack of sensitivity and from the deeply
ingrained competitiveness of our own cultures, we from the
West have gone about presenting Christianity in West Africa
as a competitor to African traditions. We speak of "winning"
the lost as if we were at war with them. Christianity has been
presented as a fully formed cultural system bent on replacing
much or all of the traditional cultural systems with which it
comes into contact. I, and I believe Prof. Pobee, question
this understanding of Christianity. The New Testament shows
that Christianity was not originally framed within European
culture. It entered European culture through the faithful witness of the members of the Jewish culture who early recognized

the fact that conversion to their culture was not an essential
part of the Christian message (see Acts 15). Western missionaries have not, however, always been so perceptive. Nor have
many African converts to Christianity who, for one reason or
another, converted to Christianity as a part of a larger conversion to western culture.

The fault lies, I believe, with those of us from the West
who have unconsciously seen Christianity merely as a religion
in competition with the religions of the people around us. We
are convinced that the one and only way to God is through Jesus
Christ. But we often unconsciously assume that that way lies
also through western religious forms that we have learned to
call "Christian". Africans, mistakenly identifying the impressiveness of western culture with the commitment of at least
certain westerners to God through Christ, have often inter-
preted the western concomitants of the Christianity presented
to them as requirements of faith. That is, they have opted
for the tribal religion of Euroamerica in place of their own
tribal allegiance. Much disaffection on the part of Africans
comes about, however, when the discrepancy between essential,
biblical Christianity and the western institutionalization of
Christianity becomes apparent to them.

In the *educational* efforts of the Christian church, likewise, the approach has been competitive. Every culture has
its own educational system that is highly effective in training
its children for participation in that culture. As westerners,
however, we only know and respect the kind of educational forms
designed to train people to participate in our culture. In the
name of Christianity, then, the church has set up the kind of
school system that has been familiar to us in the West. This,
then, has become around the world the greatest secularizing
force in all of history (see Kleinjans 1968).

Much of what we have done in missionary *medicine* also exem-
plifies this competitive approach. In many cases western medicine has been able to drastically alleviate human suffering.
But too often western structures have been set up in the name
of Christ without regard to the existing indigenous medical
system that has, in many ways, served indigenous peoples relatively well for many generations. Setting up a western system with little or no concern for what already exists gives
the impression that Christianity desires to compete with and
smash the system that traditional people have learned to trust.

We also often find the Christian church in competition with
indigenous *communicational systems*. Western communicational
systems are largely impersonal, often mechanical. They come
from outside of the experience of Africans who traditionally

employ largely person-to-person communicational techniques.
Western systems, such as writing and radio, virtually eliminate
the possibility of feedback and adjustment in the communication
process. As McLuhan has pointed out, though, the medium in
terms of which a message is presented has much to do with how
that message is perceived (Carpenter and McLuhan 1960).   Christianity has been closely associated with literacy, monologue
preaching, and western music. The use of indigenous music,
drama, storytelling, dialog, and other indigenous communicational techniques has been largely pushed aside within the
church by these foreign, less personal forms. I believe this
fact has much to do with indigenous perceptions of Christianity.

Does Christianity really require such competition between
European and African religious, educational, medical, and communicational techniques? Does the gospel require the destruction of these indigenous structures? I believe that our call
is not to compete with the cultural systems of the people to
whom the Christian message is presented, but to communicate to
them *within* those structures concerning that message. Jesus,
whom we claim to follow, worked within the cultural structure
of the people to whom he came (Phil. 2:5-8). He could have
attempted to extract the people to whom he spoke from their
culture into another. He did not, however. He, rather, identified with the people *in* their culture, seeking to win them to
Christian faith within that context. He respected them in their
culture and sought to bring about only a change of allegiance
with respect to God, not with respect to culture. The Apostle
Paul worked for a similar change of allegiance *within* the cultures of the people to whom he ministered. The African church
and those of us who attempt to assist it, must turn our backs
on the cultural competitiveness that has characterized the
church in West Africa and seek in a more concerted way to discover what it means for Christianity to function more completely
in and through African cultures.

THE NEED TO REDEFINE EDUCATION

In keeping with my above points and Prof. Pobee's comments
concerning the involvement in education of the church in West
Africa, I would call for a new concept of what education is all
about. The church in West Africa has been heavily involved in
starting, maintaining, and operating western schools. It has
been somewhat less involved in education. There is, I believe,
an important distinction to be made between schooling and education. Education may be defined broadly as the process by
means of which necessary techniques and strategies for successful functioning in everyday life are communicated to and received by people. Education is, therefore, intended to assist
people in the life that they actually live, not to divert them

from it. Education is, furthermore, more a matter of what the learner understands than of what the teacher intends.

People in one society are not greatly helped when the structures in which they are supposedly educated are designed to serve some of the needs of some of the people in another society (see Beals and Spindler 1973, ch. 9). The Nigerians with whom I worked found that the schools that they attended trained them either for a society that did not yet exist, or for a society that existed somewhere else in the world. The schools were, therefore, for them not educative but diversionary. Prof. Pobee suggests the need for vocational schools in greater numbers than heretofore. I see this as but a small part of the kind of revamping that would be required to make West African schools educational. Vocational schools ought certainly to be established. But vocations other than western vocations ought to be sympathetically dealt with as well. And techniques other than those that depend on literacy and other imported means of communication need to be developed.

I feel that studies of traditional education, many of which are already in existence,[1] need to be utilized to assist the church in involving itself truly in education, not simply in school-type diversions from education. The imagination of West African Christians has, I believe, often been crippled in this respect by the over-all commitment of missionary Christianity to western concepts and techniques. The wholesale commitment of western Christianity to salaried, white collar occupations has hurt the church both in Euroamerica and in Africa. Where is church endorsement of apprenticeship and discipleship as educational techniques more appropriate to person-to-person oriented societies than the impersonal western techniques?

The church should be particularly concerned, in this regard, with the education of its members specifically in the concepts vital to Christianity. Can techniques based on the unchristian competitiveness for grades so often exhibited in classroom situations be constructive for the development of mature Christianity? Can techniques demanding literacy in a world that seems less interested in literacy than heretofore, continue to be advocated as virtually the sole methods of Christian education? Perhaps the oft-repeated criticism of Christianity's lack of involvement in the real life of people should be heard as a criticism of school-based Christianity. I believe the need of the church to redefine education and to both give up control of schools and enslavement to the school concept of education is a crucial issue for the church in West Africa today.

THE NEED FOR A MORE AFRICAN CHRISTIANITY

All of this leads to the final issue that I would like to discuss. Prof. Pobee mentions the need for an Africanization of theology. I am strongly in favor of such a movement. I, like he, am encouraged to see Africans pioneering in this effort. I feel, however, that those of us in the West who are the successors of the missionaries who initiated policies that, in retrospect, appear to need undoing, should assist wherever possible in this process of moving towards greater indigenization. For I believe that we in the West have given the world the impression that Christianity was intended to be the ethnic religion of western culture. We have, therefore, produced and imposed an ethnic approach to every aspect of Christianity.

To me, the Bible demonstrates the possibility of doing theology from any of several Hebrew perspectives, including that of Hellenized Jews. Though the perspective of Hellenized Jews is moving in the direction of Europe, most of the cultural contexts in which the message of God exists in the Scriptures are closer to Africa. It is, therefore, a travesty to find a Europeanized Christianity imported into Africa at the expense of what might have been a much shorter bridge between biblical Christianity and African Christianity. Yet, what Robin Boyd calls "the Latin captivity of the church" (Boyd 1974), is a powerful factor to have to deal with in these days. Independent churches and a few creative minds both within and outside of African cultures are, however, showing us the way. If we will but analyze and follow the processes that we see going on in the New Testament, we will find a considerable amount of assistance in this task.

The early Greek churches were deominated by Hebrew theology just as African churches are now dominated by European theology. Their theology was "made in Jerusalem," just as Africa's is "made in Europe." God, however, led the Apostle Paul and others to struggle against the Hebrew Christians to develop a contextualized Christian theology for Greeks. Paul had to struggle, on the one hand, against the Judaizers, and on the other hand, against his own indoctrination. The one enemy was outside of himself, the other within himself. African Christian leaders are in a very similar position. In moving toward greater African expression of Christianity, therefore, Africans will need to struggle against both the enemy outside of themselves and the enemy within.

The New Testament, as Von Allmen (1975) shows, records for us the process of contextualizing. We see Paul on Mars Hill (Acts 17) starting with a God his hearers already knew. As Prof. Pobee points out, and as I have frequently discovered, many Africans when they get deeply into the Bible discover that the Christian God is the God whom they have already known, though imperfectly. For many, if not most, of the cultures of Africa, the contextualizing of Christianity can start with the God that they have traditionally known for some time.

We see in the New Testament, furthermore, the early Christian contextualizers employing and transforming indigenous words for Christian concepts. Contrary to the practice of many western missionaries in Africa, they saw no problem in adopting pagan Greek terms for God, church, conversion, repentance, sin, etc. They did not simply borrow technical theological terms for these concepts from Hebrew. They planted seeds of Christianity within the societies by employing and transforming these concepts into more adequate vehicles to convey Christian meanings. The New Testament churches knew that using foreign terms for Christian concepts stamps the church as indelibly foreign and that this is contrary to God's desire. Unfortunately, those who determine policy for African churches have not always been as wise. In Hausa, for example, foreign, rather than indigenous terms are used for such concepts as church, priest, yeast, prayer and many others.

We see the early church likewise, employing indigenous cultural forms from Greek culture. They adopted an initiation ritual (baptism) used both in Hebrew culture and in Greek mystery religions. They adopted speaking in tongues from the Greek mystery religions. They used Greek leadership patterns with Greek qualifications for appropriate behavior (1 Timothy 3). They employed Greek patterns for relationships between men and women, requiring Christian women to continue to be submissive to their husbands, to be silent and to keep their heads covered in public. These were the ordinary requirements of Greek culture that believed that women should never be noticed. What would African Christianity look like if it employed African rituals of initiation and consolidation (i.e. worship forms), rather than European forms? What would African Christianity look like if it, like New Testament Hebrew Christianity, employed visions, dreams, speaking in tongues, faith healing, and similar customs more appropriate to both Hebrew and African culture than to European culture? What would African Christainity look like if it employed African, rather than European requirements for church leadership? By and large, I believe not even the independent churches have begun to fully probe the extent to which African cultural forms should be used to express Christianity if we are to follow the process demonstrated for us in the pages of the New Testament.

Such a process is, of course, very risky. It is particularly risky to the orthodox Christians who were the instruments of God

to communicate the gospel to the people of new cultures. Those
most threatened by the Apostle Paul's innovations were the
Judaizers. Those most threatened by Jesus' innovations were
the Pharisees. Jesus and Paul had very little problem with
their enemies compared with the problems caused by those who
should have been their friends. The Pharisees and the Judaizers
wanted to see things remain as they were, using the sacred forms
of Hebrew culture. They were afraid to change those sacred
forms because they felt that pagan Greek culture could not adequately express the gospel. How similar this attitude seems to
the attitude of many of us as missionaries. We fear that com-
mitting Christianity truly to an African culture is likely to
result in unchristian syncretism. This is, of course, a very
real risk. There is, however, a much surer way of bringing
about syncretism. This is the way of the Judaizers and the
Pharisees who produced syncretism by refusing to adapt the
Christian meanings to new cultural forms. A similar thing
happened in later Christian history when the Roman Catholic
church produced syncretism by refusing to employ indigenous
cultural forms to express essential Christianity. Such foreign
domination is, I believe, a surer way to produce syncretism
that the path of indigenization, as risky as this latter path
is.

Essential Christianity is dynamic. It comes, furthermore,
with the power of the Holy Spirit. God, I believe, wants his
message to be put into every African language and culture to
transform each into a more useful vehicle for his glory. True
headway cannot be made on the problems that Prof. Pobee discusses unless this is taken as a given. The problems of for-
eignness, of lack of relevance, of lack of concern for pressing
social issues, and even of the broader worldwide relationships
between African Christians and those in other parts of the
world cannot, I believe, be adequately handled unless Christianity truly belongs to Africans in intelligible African cultural forms. The Nigerians with whom I worked felt that they
had to sell out culturally in order to gain a relationship with
God. They did not get this impression from the Bible, but from
those who brought the Bible. Islam is attractive to them not
because they feel it has a superior message, but because the
cultural requirements do not seem to be so unreasonable. It
will, I believe, take all of the energy we can muster to attempt
to reverse much of the history that Prof. Pobee points to for
the sake of a more vital African Christianity in the future.

CONCLUSION

I have not sought to deal with all of the issues raised by
Prof. Pobee. In a 15 minute response to a one hour presentation
this would, of course, be impossible. What I have tried to do

is, rather, to pick out four closely related issues that he
raised and to comment on them from my own perspective. The
overriding tone of my remarks has, I am afraid, been critical.
I ignore in this presentation the great strides that Christianity has made in Africa. I have not mentioned the large
number of African Christians who, though they have westernized
in order to become Christian, do not feel the least bit upset
by this. I have only mentioned incidentally the exciting independent church movement and have neglected Pentecostalism
completely. Experiments such as those of the Mennonites in
Ghana and Nigeria (Weaver 1975) and of Dr. Daneel in Rhodesia
in attempting to provide better theological training for independent church leaders are truly exciting. So is the rapid
growth of the church in many parts of Africa, including the
area in which I served where more than 2,000 were baptized in
the last year. There are experiments in theological education
by extension and communicating the gospel on tape that are
worth watching. Renewed interest in Bible translation in many
areas is also encouraging.

All of these things are going on and, if I chose to, I could
paint a very different picture of the church in Africa by fo-
cusing only on them. I have chosen not to, because I believe
the predominant concern in a conference like this should be for
what remains to be done, rather than for what has already been
successful. My concern is to challenge those of us committed
to assisting the church in Africa, rather than to risk the possibility that we might become complacent. My remarks, like
those of Prof. Pobee, though critical, come not from an outsider
seeking to disrupt the working of God in Africa, but from an
insider who has given and intends to continue to give a major
portion of his energies to the cause in which he sees some
things worthy of strong criticism.

----

[1]See the series of Case Studies in *Education and Culture*
published by Holt, Rinehart and Winston under the editorship
of George and Louise Spindler.

PART V

The Future of
the Church in Africa

The Future of
the Church in Africa

Norman E. Thomas

Can we prophesy with any degree of accuracy concerning the future of the church in Africa? Basil Davidson, the noted historian, titled his 1964 volume *Which Way Africa?* In it he concluded:

> The long-range answer to the question of Africa's future will depend on pressures that are probably beyond the reach of anyone's present understanding, and are certainly beyond mine (1964:214).

Perceptive analysts of African Christianity sound the same word of caution. According to Cecil Northcott, "It is always dangerous to prophesy about Africa as the continent, in spite of its obvious handicaps, is capable of producing something quite new in politics, citizenship, in government and in Church" (1963:117).

As for those who have attempted the impossible, their predictions differ widely.

Is the church in Africa growing so rapidly that the Christian community there by the year 2000 A.D. will exceed the continent's total population in 1970? That is the prediction of David Barrett based upon an analysis of population and church growth statistics (1970).

Others take a less sanguine view. Fifteen years ago Ram Desai surveyed the opinions of certain African intellectuals concerning Christianity and concluded:

Anyone acquainted with the developments in modern
Africa would agree that Christianity is facing a
crisis--its future is in doubt. While recognizing
that some students of African affairs believe Christianity "may yet regain its ascendancy in post-
colonial Africa," others "believe that Christianity,
along with colonialism, will eventually phase out of
the 'dark continent'" (1962:5).

Lest defenders of the church in Africa hasten to chastise
such prophets of doom, we should remember Christianity's check-
ered history on the African continent. St. Augustine wrote of
the *City of God* from Africa in the 4th century when Christianity was more firmly rooted in Africa than in Europe. Then
came the dark centuries of the advance of Islam. Again from
the 15th to the 17th centuries Catholicism appeared to advance
strongly into Africa before the ravages of the slave trade ended
that hope. The third period of Christian expansion in Africa,
of which we are witnesses, is by far the briefest. Such has
been the ebb and flow of the tide of Christianity on the continent.

"What prospect is there that this third phase of the total
movement will eventually survive the cataclysms of history
better than its predecessors?", Dr. C. P. Groves asks in the
closing chapter of his four volumes on *The Planting of Christianity in Africa*. "How far is the future course of events
predictable?" (1958:315).

The study of history provides a constant reminder of the com-
plexity of events and of the wide range of variables that exist
in any particular situation. One of these, and for us as Christians perhaps the most crucial one, is the human variable. We
are acutely aware both of human freedom as given by God, and of
its continuing misuse by sinful humanity. Therefore, it would
be folly to attempt to predict the exact course of Africa's
future.

Why then do we have the audacity to consider this topic,
"The Future of the Church in Africa"?

On the one hand, we can learn much from the past. A careful
analysis of the forces that have molded the past, and channeled
options for the present, leads us to indicate some of the developments that one might reasonably expect to occur in the
future.

On the other hand, we believe that although the alternatives
of action before us and our human capacities to respond to them
are limited by past events, nevertheless we have considerable
freedom to love or to hate, to build up or to destroy.

In this paper I have chosen to begin with an analysis of some of the forces of change (political, economic, and social) which may shape the world in which Christians will live and witness in coming decades. Then we shall consider the future of the church as the gathered community of believers in growth and renewal. Our analysis will next turn outward as the church relates to the potential forces of change. Finally, we shall consider briefly future patterns of relationship between the churches, and the need for interdependence.

FORCES OF CHANGE

1. Increased control over nature: progress or destruction?

Man's increased control over nature is the first force for change that we may expect.

Flying over Africa's vast spaces, one is impressed today both by seeming virgin lands waiting for development, and evidence of development already underway. New power lines bisect the forests often before roads are built. New railways open up remote lands and markets. Even the symbols of Africa's pristine beauty have been changed, as man harnesses for electric power part of the mighty "smoke that thunders" (Victoria Falls) and fences the Serengeti plains of Tanzania for settlement. With greater scientific knowledge and a more highly evolved technology it is reasonable to expect that Africans will achieve a greater control over their environment in the future.

Not all these developments, however, are likely to be beneficial. Just as the fabled gold of ancient Nubia was mined until worked out to glorify the rulers of ancient Egypt, Greece and Rome, so Liberia's sources of iron ore, Zambia and Zaire's of copper, South Africa's of diamonds, Mauritania's of phosphates, and Libya's of oil will one day be exhausted. Already Africa's leaders are asking: "For whose benefit are multinational corporations extracting as rapidly as possible Africa's mineral wealth?" Is this to be judged to be progress, or destruction?

2. Population growth: blessing or curse?

Africa's rapid population growth is a second force for change.

Present estimates are that from a mere 100 million in 1800, Africa's population grew slowly to reach 150 million in 1900. Thereafter the continent's population mushroomed once the ravages of wars and epidemics diminished and health services increased. By 1975 the population reached 355 million. At the present rate of growth Africa's people will increase sixfold in

the century to a total 800 million by the year 2000. Africa
will then have surpassed Europe, North and South America to
become the world's second most populous continent.

In traditional African culture children were the family's
primary wealth. They insured sufficient hands for cultivation
in the fields or for the herding of cattle. They were an in-
surance policy that the vital strength of the family would continue and hopefully increase in the next generation. If soils
were exhausted there were always other lands to request from
the chief. If population increased, some families could always
move a short distance across the hills or plain to a new lo-
cation.

Do large numbers of children continue to bring increased
prosperity for a family or nation? Increasing numbers of planners and parents are beginning to question that assumption.
Real limits have been reached. The marginal grasslands along
the southern edge of the Sahara desert (the region known as the
Sahel) cannot support more people and the flocks and herds which
provide their livelihood. An average peasant farmer in Rwanda
has less land to plow than his counterpart in crowded India.

Even in countries like Zambia with wide open spaces special
problems limit prospects for agricultural development. Only 6%
of the soil is arable. Despite plans for new mines and factories, the number of unemployed schoolleavers increases each
year. Within view of trainloads of copper ore, ten year old
children are told, "there are no places in grade one for you to
start school."

What alternatives are ahead? Short of a major change in the
systems of production and exchange they are few. Population
control, however, will take place in the years ahead--either by
the ravages of war, famine and disease, or by human efforts in
family planning.

Yes, Africa's population will increase rapidly, but will that
increase be a blessing, or a curse?

3. Burgeoning cities: the new Gomorrahs or Jerusalems?

A third force for change is the rapid growth of Africa's towns
and cities. In a world becoming increasingly more urban, Africa
has the highest urban growth rate of any continent. The number
of cities with 100,000 or more inhabitants increased 629% between 1900 and 1950.

Planners, however, view the burgeoning of towns with mixed
emotions. Words written 90 years ago by Josiah Strong are still

true: "The city is the nerve center of our civilization. It
is also the storm center" (Watts 1970:iv). In it gleam modern
skyscrapers, the dazzle of lights, and the brilliance of hundreds of aspiring musicians. But beside these are the darkness
and despair of increasing thousands of the homeless, destitute,
and aged without loved ones to care for them. All the vices
known to man flourish best in the city's crowded streets.

Side by side in Africa's cities can be found the luxury hotel
and mushrooming shantytown, the new university and thousands of
school push-outs (not drop-outs, it was not their choice). The
million-dollar teaching hospital may be close to open latrines
and rotting garbage and rampant venereal disease. Remembering
that ancient cities, once the jewels of empires, now lie in
ruins, we ponder on the future of Africa's pellmell rush to
urban living. Is the burgeoning city of Africa the new Gomor-
rah, or the new Jerusalem?

4. Wider social contacts: new loyalties or renascent tribalism?

Wider social contacts as a result of increased mobility of Africa's peoples is a fourth force for change. In Kitwe, Zambia
where we lived, the city rents houses when available to the
next person on the waiting list regardless of one's ethnic or
tribal background. A similar mixing of persons takes place in
schools and most types of employment. Even the highest barrier
to full social mixing, endogamy (marrying within one's own social group), is beginning to break down.

Many institutions work to build wider loyalties. "Harambee!"
(Let us pull together) and "One Zambia--One Nation" are current
political slogans. Children in schools learn to speak and read
a common language, be it English or Swahili, French or Hausa.
Christians by eating together help to break down long-standing
taboos.

But old animosities die hard. The massacres of Tutsis by
Hutus in Burundi, of Ibos by Hausas in Nigeria, and recently of
Langos and Acholis in Uganda--all since independence--give stark
testimony to this fact.

Will wider social contacts lead in the future to new loyalties, or a backlash of renascent tribalism?

5. Centralizing political power: for greater humanity or
   oppression?

A fifth force for change is the continuing centralization of
political power within nation states. Seldom has the constitution bequeathed by the colonial power at independence stood

the test of time. One-party states are numerous, with rule by
decree or assumed popular acclamation replacing the selection
by ballot of political leaders.

But pressures for political and social change remain, and
require channels for their expression. Where communication is
difficult between the people and those who govern, where political leaders are deaf to criticism, people are forced to seek
other means to redress their grievances. Then dissent is labelled "subversive" and suppressed, and violations of human
rights multiply.

Yes, political power is becoming more centralized in many
African states. The result could be a greater humanity as the
people are mobilized for human development, or greater oppression as the voice of opposition is silenced.

6. Competing ideologies: to illumine or escape reality?

The impact of ideas is a sixth force making for change in future
Africa. Those who would control political power know the importance of the mass media in building political loyalties. New
communication methods (TV communications satellites, programed
learning, etc.), however, also open channels by which ideas
generated in other continents enter African homes and schools.

Sources are multiple. Christianity and Islam win the loyalty
of increasing numbers. From poets and scholars come calls for
negritude, authenticity, and Black consciousness. Meanwhile
young Africans debate African socialism and capitalism, Marxism
and various brands of "democracy".

Already, however, can be discerned a growing frustration
with ideological debates. "Democracy" is a hollow word for
people who no longer have power to choose their leaders, and
"humanism" an idle slogan where the nation's wealth is increasingly concentrated in the hands of the few. People are asking:
"Are these competing ideologies designed to illumine us, or to
provide an escape from reality?"

7. Economic growth: human development or exploitation?

A seventh force for change exists in the world demand for primary products from Africa. This often stimulates economic
growth within many African countries, yet without commensurate
development. Consider Ghana and Ivory Coast, for example.
Both countries' exports of cocoa, coffee, and peanuts have increased greatly in recent years. With land diverted from food
to cash crop production more food has had to be imported. While
prices of exports fluctuate, those of imports tend to increase

steadily. Trade deficits necessitate the borrowing of large sums in lean years. The result for these countries, as well as for mineral exporters like Liberia and Zambia, can be an expanding GNP (Gross National Product) but a government deep in debt and a nation with very uneven distribution of wealth. A widening gap results between a small elite of politicans, managers, and skilled technicians on the one hand and the masses of un- or underemployed on the other (Davidson 1974).

The option of radical economic change will become more attractive in coming years. Changes already undertaken in Tanzania, Guinea-Bissau, Angola, and Mozambique will be watched by others with great interest. To each proposal for an economic panacea will be brought the searching question--will this change result in human development or continued exploitation?

8. Increasing prospects for violent conflict: a dying colonialism or escalating violence?

A eighth and final force for change in Africa is the increasing prospect for violent conflict.

The massacres in Soweto and Cape Town in South Africa and full-scale civil war in Zimbabwe (Rhodesia) lead many to predict increased bloodshed until every country is liberated from white minority rule. Church leaders at a recent consultation asserted:

Intensified brutality and satanic repressive measures applied by racist minorities against the vast Black majorities in Southern Africa, have marked a new chapter in the bloody struggle against the violation of fundamental human rights and God-given dignity (Consultation 1977).

Elsewhere on the continent the potential for violent conflict will continue. Within nations it will be found wherever dissent and change of leadership is thwarted. Leaders will be tempted to divert internal frustrations into hostility toward an "outgroup" either within or outside the country. It is hoped that Africa will be spared a xenophobia like that common to both Europe and Latin America during the rise of nation states there. Another threat to peace in Africa tomorrow will be the desire of big powers to export arms and have them tested in local wars, as the history of the Arab/Israeli and Vietnam conflicts reveal.

Some Christians may judge the examination of these forces as being too secular in content for inclusion in a consideration of "The Future of the Church in Africa." To do so, however, would be to ignore those very factors which will facilitate or thwart the church's mission in the future.

AUTHENTICITY AND CHURCH GROWTH

As we turn to focus on the future of the church in Africa, it
is appropriate to engage in a similar analysis of those forces
which have molded the church's mission in the past, as they may
indicate possible developments to expect in the future.

1. Church growth

The "meteoric rise of the church in Black Africa" since 1910
shines like a bright star in a period marked by the decline of
Christianity in the western and developed countries (Barrett
1970:51). In Africa the number of professing Christians grew
from a mere 4 million at the time of the Edinburgh Conference
in 1910 to reach 97 million by 1970. From almost nothing, the
church grew steadily until one-third of Black Africa's population claimed allegiance to Christ. It is David Barrett's judgment that "for sheer size and rapidity of growth, this must be
one of the most spectacular cases in history" (1970:51).

Can we predict an equally spectacular growth in the future?
Barrett anticipates a 4.5% annual increase in the Christian community in sub-Saharan Africa which would swell the total number
of Christians in Africa to 351 million by the year 2000. Although 2.7% of this ingathering would come through natural
growth of population, the balance would result from individual
and group conversions.

More is known today than ever before concerning both opportunities and obstacles to evangelization in Africa. MARC (Missions Advanced Research Communication) is attempting to use
advanced computer technology to file and disseminate information
on strategic evangelistic opportunities country by country.[1]

Evangelization will progress, however, at extremely uneven
rates across the continent. Old constraints remain, including
insufficient Bible translations and government restrictions on
missionary outreach. Committed Christians of one group may be
disinterested in carrying the gospel to unreached people living
side by side with them.

At this symposium we have become acutely aware of additional
barriers to the effective spread of the gospel. Has the gospel
message been the basis of relationships between westerners and
Africans? Is the missionary able to listen, to accept criticism? In South Africa, for example, evangelical Christians may
feel an urgency to witness for Christ, but their failures in
love between black and white leaders may cause the church to
stagnate.

We have also learned how persons sensitive to the cultural values of a people can witness for Christ in new and creative ways.

For one hundred years the Maasai peoples of Kenya and northern Tanzania (part of a total grouping of 1.5 million in East Africa) have largely resisted western education, civilization and Christianity (Barrett 1973:274). In 1966 the Holy Ghost Fathers (RC) began a radically new approach. They established no missions, built no schools, and even failed to carry relief supplies of food and medicine lest these be considered bribes to become baptized. Instead they offered only one thing--the good news of Jesus Christ. Daily the missionary spoke to the entire village at their invitation before the day's work of herding began.

Gradually "dynamic equivalents" for the central themes of the Christian faith became known within Maasai culture. The Church was called the "brotherhood"--akin to the last age set when both men and women covenant their mutual concern for each other in this life on earth and the life to come. Faith became understood not as the hunter's belief that the image in the sights of his gun is the animal he seeks, but as the leap of the lion who grasps the prey to itself.

Natural leaders begin to emerge. Even before conversion one person is asked to pray, another to teach, and still others to heal and prophesy. He who binds the whole village together, reconciles disputants, and makes the vital decision to move the entire village when grass and water supplies are depleted becomes the leader. He receives special training awaiting the day when together the entire village will be baptized. By this approach thousands already have been won for Christ.

The work of Brethren missionaries among the Higi people of Northern Nigeria is another example of working with the culture rather than against it (Kraft 1976). The church began there in 1953 as lepers who had been written off as dead by their own people returned to witness to them. The missionary who followed in 1956, when asked to preach, give an "authoritative" interpretation of Scripture, or select candidates for baptism, replied: "Anything you can do for yourself I will not do." The church grew rapidly as new converts, on fire with the faith, went as untrained evangelists to other villages. Now there are 75 village preachers and 2-3000 baptisms a year in a church of 12,000 members. The question remains: "Can the young church help so many to grow up into Christ while continuing to reach out to the more than 150,000 of their people who have not yet been won for Christ?"

2. Authenticity

Professor Harry Sawyerr of Sierra Leone, in his perceptive book
entitled *Creative Evangelism*, asks:

> Can Christianity take deep root in Africa, clothed as
> it is at present in western garb and with little or
> no Africanness? This is the fundamental question that
> has to be faced if Christian evangelism is to make
> full impact on African converts (1968:33).

Fr. Aylward Shorter out of his extensive experience at the Gaba
Pastoral Institute in Eastern Africa reminds us that "Christian
evangelization consists not only in proclaiming, but also in
listening--listening to the prophetical voice of Africa--so as
to know what Christ is saying to us in the African cultures, as
well as in the cultures of the Bible" (1975:113).

Consideration of these issues will lead to a deepening of the
church growth debate in coming years. Mere head counting could
be as fateful for the African church as for a farmer to estimate
his harvest on the basis of the number of plants that have
sprouted, or his flock on the number of chicks that have hatched.
David Barrett's statistic that there will be a 2.5% natural increase in the "Christian community" is deceptive. Will those
who joined the church for benefit of schooling without a deep
conversion be able to lead their own children to Christ? Will
the cultural forms in which the faith was presented to the first
generation of Christians in the colonial era be persuasive for
their children or grandchildren?

We can predict that the widespread revolt in Africa against
any form of domination by the West will lead many nominal Christians to reject Christianity if they link it with western culture and values. At the same time this challenge will become a
creative opportunity. Tomorrow the African church can be freer
than ever before to serve the gospel without the risk of confusion between that gospel and the "power" of the West.

The question for a rich African theology and for indigenous
worship and music will be pursued with vigor in coming years,
not only in African independent churches but in Catholic and
Protestant churches as well. Many will affirm with Dr. Fashole-
Luke that

> If Christianity is to change its status from that of
> resident alien to that of citizen, then it must be-
> come incarnate in the life and thought of Africa and
> its theologies must bear the distinctive stamp of
> mature African thinking and reflexion (1975:267-8).

Western Christians, however, must beware lest with their own cultural biases they condemn emerging African theologies and forms of worship as "syncretism". This term implies combining or reconciling differing beliefs in an "unacceptable" manner. On what basis, however, is this judgment to be made? Will it be on the basis of the gospel, or our own "Christian standards" which when examined closely prove to be ethnocentric?

For example, the traditional culture of the Shona people of Zimbabwe (Rhodesia) includes belief in the "living dead." It is believed that death is just a stage in a person's maturing. So far so good. But the Shona go on to believe that the "living dead" can influence for good or evil those of their kinsmen who honor or dishonor them, who pray to them or neglect them. A young African nun expressed it this way: "The European prays through his saints to God but I pray through my ancestors." A daughter grieving over the death of her parents in a road accident speaks directly to them in prayer. Could these be authentic African expressions of faith in the "communion of the saints"?

Jacob Loewen in his perceptive article, "Mission Churches, Independent Churches and Felt Needs" (1976) analyzes the deep psychological and spiritual felt needs which church leaders often disregard. To tell those who fear witchcraft or seek a personal cause of misfortune, or desire a direct authentic communication from God that they are asking the wrong questions is like giving a stone to one who asks for bread.

EQUIPPING GOD'S PEOPLE FOR MINISTRY

The quest for a meaningful African theology addresses both the challenge of a relevant evangelism which we have been considering and that of enabling the believer to "grow up into Christ."

Fifteen years ago the United Methodist Church in Southern Rhodesia faced a common problem for many church leaders in Africa. The church was vigorous with a growing membership of 20,000, the Methodist schools with more than 50,000 pupils were an even larger constituency. Could so many be led to maturity in Christ when workers are so few?

John Mbiti faced the same issue when he asked:

How does the church move to maturity beyond the point of evangelized peoples? Growth by evangelization has reached its peak; now comes the opportunity for growth by maturation, thus bringing to full fruition the redeemed people of God, for them to form a solid point

of reference and a living home for its members
(Barrett 1973:207).

Adrian Hastings, after predicting a massive threefold expansion from 28 million Catholics in 1965 to over 80 million by the
year 2000, admits that the figures are terrifying because the
church is not doing the planning that such an increase demands
(1967:100). The problem deepens as one major channel for Christian nurture, the school, passes from church to state control in
country after country.

Lest we despair, let us remember that the church has faced
and overcome similar challenges throughout its history. How did
the apostles instruct the 3,000 baptized on the day of Pente-
cost? When entire peoples have decided to follow Christ, as in
the mass movements in India, how did the church respond? Paul
in the letter to the Ephesians (4:11-12) gives one answer—that
God through the power of the Holy Spirit gives a variety of
gifts of leadership in his church to the end that all his people
(the "saints") may be equipped for their ministries ("work in
his service").

For the African church this implies a living out of the
"priesthood of all believers." The ministries of preaching and
prophecy, of pastor and teacher and healer can be shared among
the members of the community of faith. The church then would
experience the vitality of the "lay church" as Negash Kebede has
described it for Eastern Africa in his paper during the symposium.

Time permits only a brief outline of the implications of this
concept of a lay church for Christian education, theological
training, lay centers and the development of intentional communities in the African Church in the future.

Christian education programs will need to present a whole
gospel for the whole person in his/her whole world. The church
need not fear the transfer of schools to state control, if it
can continue to assist in presenting beliefs, values and standards by which the individual, community and nation may live.
A narrow sectarian approach will fail. Memorizing the cate-
chism will no longer suffice. There are hopeful signposts to
the future, however. One religious syllabus for schools was
prepared jointly by Catholics and Protestants in East Africa.
Teachers using it can present the faith not just as Bible
stories to be heard, or propositions of faith to be affirmed,
but as a living faith of prayer and praise to be experienced.

Theological education also must be radically changed if the
church is to realize its potential for growth.

For the past fifteen years the churches of Africa have faced a "crisis" in the Christian ministry. Church leaders warned us of an acute shortage of ordained ministers and predicted a stagnation of the church due to inadequate pastoral care (AACC 1964; Sundkler 1960; Hastings 1967). Meanwhile African independent churches with their numerous lay preachers, teachers, prophets and healers grew by leaps and bounds.

I believe that the "crisis" was misunderstood. One basic problem for the older churches was their misunderstanding of the primary function of the set-apart ministry--to equip all God's people for their work of ministry (Eph. 4:12). The salaried priest or pastor too often has looked upon himself more as a chief than as a servant of his people.

Tomorrow Africa will need a new style of theological training. I believe that it can best be conducted "in the world" combining action and reflection.

The church will need some highly trained leaders able to wrestle with such questions as the relation of the Christian faith with other religions, with political ideologies and economic theories, and with medical decision-making. Such training can best be provided in the university setting. Let ministers in training wrestle with problems of meaning and of national development together with other university students. Such training, however, should not be divorced from life in a praying, witnessing community.

The larger part of training for ministry will involve equipping far more persons than ever before for their ministries both in the gathered congregation and in "the world". Could the expensive residential college system be replaced with a decentralized training program using existing church and community buildings when otherwise vacant? Many persons receiving such theological training would continue in "tent-making ministries" of self-support both before, during, and after the special preparation for ministry. For example, the Anglican Church in Tanzania expects each rural priest to have another skill needed in the new *ujamaa* villages (teacher, agricultural demonstrator, medical assistant, etc.).

Lay centers will have a more important role in the future if the whole people of God are to be trained for their respective ministries both in the gathered Christian communities and in the scattered communities of work and witness. Such centers of necessity will be diverse in both program and participation. Some will be residential. Others will comprise mobile teams which stimulate study, training and action in the communities which they serve. Some will reach primarily members of one church.

Others will be broadly ecumenical in sponsorship and participation.

We have identified in this symposium several study areas in
which increasingly the locus of action should shift from the
West to the African continent. One is centers for research upon
evangelization and indigenization of the church. Another is the
important dialog with the other living faiths of Africa (traditional African religion and Islam). The Islam in Africa Project
has made a significant contribution already in view of the
church's task of interpreting faithfully in the Muslim world
the gospel of Jesus Christ; and to effect the research and education necessary for this.

Perhaps "center" conveys a false idea that bricks and mortar
are essential for an effective training program. Increasingly
issues of church renewal and leadership training will be carried
to the people by mobile training teams. Those concerned for urban community empowerment can meet in factories and homes, while
the work of rural transformation will take place at the new dam
site or in the fields.

During the symposium new opportunities have been shared to
assist the African independent churches. In Rhodesia a sociol-
ogist who wished to study and write a doctoral dissertation about
Zionist churches knew the frequent reaction to the researcher:
"You have taken even my soul from me; when will you give it back
to me?" He agreed to return to train their leaders. Mennonites
report similar invitation to several parts of Africa.

Some centers will be on the front lines of action for social
change in the years ahead. Will the institutional churches be
prepared to support programs of critical thought and action that
inevitably are controversial and may involve conflict? Past experience suggests that such centers need broad bases of support
and freedom from direct control by either church or state in
order to remain effective.

Intentional communities will spring up as renewal groups
within the older churches. Such "little churches in the Church"
(*ecclesiolae in ecclesia*) are signs of revival in the church.
In western church history we recall the monastic movement, the
house churches among German Pietists, and the Wesleyan class
meetings. In East Africa the Revival Fellowship continues with
many small groups for Bible study, testimony, prayer and witnessing. Catholics look for a new flowering of religious communities on the continent (Aquina 1975; AMECEA 1976).

Is the home and family the only "natural" community of Christian fellowship? Certainly not. If we believe that God empowers

us by his spirit to work and witness for him in all of life,
then we can anticipate that Christian students, teachers, businessmen, trade unionists, politicians, nurses, farmers, social
workers—each may desire to form their own Christian associa-
tions. Ideally they should be open to all seeking persons regardless of denominational loyalty. This is consistent with
the following statement by Catholic bishops of Eastern Africa
which has been described as "a decisive landmark in our pastoral
policy":

> Church life must be based on the communities in which
> everyday life and work takes place; those basic and
> manageable social groupings whose members can experi-
> ence real inter-personal relationships and feel a sense
> of communal belonging, both in living and working. We
> believe that Christian communities at this level will
> be best suited to develop real intense vitality and to
> become effective witnesses in their natural environment
> (AMECEA 1976:25).

JOINING THE AFRICAN REVOLUTION

Thus far we have looked inward at the possible future life of
the gathered church in witness and teaching and leadership. To
do so in an African context is not to retreat from contending
with those "secular" forces for change with which this paper
opened, but to equip a servant people. Those who teach that
religion and politics (or economics) should be kept apart import
an alien theology into Africa.

"In Africa, religion and culture are not two separate enti-
ties; they are interwoven," Musembe Kasiera of Kenya affirms.
He asks:

> How can an African Christian gainfully participate
> in the process of nation building when such a pro-
> cess takes the total life of the African societies
> seriously, while the Christianity he professes to be
> part of frowns upon that life? (1974:106).

The answer, and a major contribution of Africa to world Christianity, will be the development of what has been called "secular theology." It will be world-centered and pragmatic,
abolishing the old dichotomies between spiritual and material,
sacred and profane. It will affirm a religious outlook which
is fully integrated with every aspect of individual and social
life (Shorter 1975:34).

Is this possible? Can religion and culture be as harmoniously
integrated as Fr. Shorter and Mr. Kasiera imply? If so, religion

will function strongly to integrate society, to preserve order
and reduce hostility and social disruption. It may, however,
resist radical social change.

Other theologians predict a different future for Africa and
therefore affirm a quite different theology for the church's
mission in the world. They predict that the underdevelopment
will continue, and that a small African elite will connive with
outside economic interests in the systematic exploitation of Africa's considerable natural and human resources. Meanwhile,
according to this view, the rising expectations of the common
peoples will result in growing social unrest and political revolt against those in power. Rulers, supported by foreign
powers, may then establish military dictatorships, declare mar-
tial law, repress people's movements, and violate many human
rights. White oppression of blacks in South Africa today is
one contemporary example of this phenomenon, but the prediction
is that authoritarian rule will spread to other states as well.

These theologians now are asking: "What role will the church
play throughout such developments?" "What does past history
teach us?"

During the colonial era, the African churches achieved major
development projects (schools, hospitals, farms and community
centers) in close cooperation with government. Although at
times the churches criticized colonial policies, they did not
align themselves with those who wished to overthrow the system.
Sometimes missionaries to be sure were sympathetic with the
aspirations of African nationalists, but so were progressive
colonial administrators.

With independence Africans trained in large measure by the
churches emerged to lead both church and state. Thus the
churches continued to be the allies of the new ruling elites
in most independent African states. Old patterns continued.
African clergy were invited to grace political meetings with
their presence, and politicans reciprocated at large church
gatherings.

In the years ahead will the African churches mute their
criticisms of government failings so as to retain a favored
position, or will they take the risks involved in championing
the cause of the oppressed and their struggle for social justice? This will remain a key choice for the church in many
African countries.

According to a recent conference of Third World theologians
held at Dar-es-Salaam, "a new vision of a theology committed to
the integral liberation of persons and structure is now being

developed in the very process of participation in the struggles of the people" (Dar es Salaam Consultation of Third World Theologians 1977:6). Sensitivity at this point will enable African theologians concerned about authenticity to join together with those in southern Africa developing Black theologies of liberation.

THE DILEMMA OF VIOLENCE

Is a Christian justified to use violence in opposing a despotic state which is unresponsive to the welfare of its people? Southern Africa church leaders stated recently their struggle with this issue as they wrote:

> We must point out that the choice by the Black nationals to resort to armed struggle did not come as a first and easy choice. Those in Angola, Mozambique, Zimbabwe and Namibia who saw the armed struggle as the only means left for the restoration of their dignity, had done so when it seemed to them all else had failed to bring the White racists to the realization that discrimination on the basis of color was sinful. It is not easy to decide to lay down one's life for the salvation of a fellow man (Dar es Salaam Consultation of Third World Theologians 1977).

Bishop Muzorewa of Zimbabwe spoke for many Christians in that troubled land as he said:

> We have a dilemma . . . there are some of us in Southern Africa who strongly believe in non-violence so much that they are prepared to apply temporary righteous revolutionary violence in responsible love in order to eradicate the wicked violence now taking place . . . Admittedly it is the shortest way to end suffering and short cut creation of peace, but not the best way, and not capable of creating long lasting peace (1976).

Belief in non-violence, temporary use of violence, seeking a better way—these may serve as guideposts for African Christians as in the future they seek to be involved in the struggle against oppression yet with compassion and love.

THE CHURCH WITHIN AFRICAN SOCIALISM

Among the forces for future change in Africa noted above are competing ideologies and economic systems. Among them are those labelled "African socialism" which include increasing state control over both the economy and provision of social services.

Will the churches have a special contribution to make in the
building of African socialism?

New patterns developing in Mozambique and Angola today give
preliminary clues. At a recent Consultation on the Church and
Southern Africa, church leaders from Mozambique and Angola held
a positive view of future church/state relationships. Concerning Mozambique they declared:

> Church leaders see some new possibilities for them-
> selves to participate in nation building which does
> not pre-empt unique role of the government to mo-
> bilize the people of the nation. They are received
> by the government as citizens and collaborate in
> reconstruction of the nation with no wish to gain
> prestige for the church by so doing (NCC/USCC 1977).

Can we predict a vigorous Christian-Marxist dialog for Africa
in the future? If so, leaders of this continent may make a
major contribution to an ongoing worldwide debate. Already
there is evidence that Marx's anti-religious teachings gain
little support in Africa. African Christians and Marxists can
emphasize certain values in common—a mutual concern for a just
sharing of national resources, the ending of exploitation of man
by man, and the freedom in community for persons to realize
their worth and human potential.

TOTAL SERVICE TO THE WORLD

In other African societies the Christian church will continue
active in the years ahead in education, health services, rural
development, urban community building, Christian literature
production and distribution, etc.

Again and again, churches will be faced with a major choice:
shall we continue our historic institutional ministries or divert our energies and resources into new fields of service? A
realistic assessment of needs and available resources will often
lead church leaders to the conclusion that the time has come to
turn over schools, hospitals, and other institutions to the
state. Motives for retaining them should be examined critically.
Who are to be served—an elite or the more needy? Is the institution serving as a creative model which could be imitated by
others? Does it lead to self-reliance or instead to continued
dependency?

Many new options are ahead for the African church as it seeks
to participate in development. Leaders, however, should be
aware of three possible forms of Christian participation, the
limitations of each, and ask themselves:

1. Shall we concentrate on the giving of relief and aid to
the victims of disasters and to the underprivileged? Such action may save a life or alleviate suffering but cannot get at
the basic causes of the problem. It does not bring growth, or
a just social order, or self-reliance.

2. Should we concentrate on the development of local communities? Such projects as wells in the Sahel, agricultural coop-
eratives, and literacy programs are urgently needed. Often
spectacular results can be achieved, with a high degree of local
participation in decision-making and leadership. A major problem remains, however. How can we ensure that such progress continues and extends beyond local limits? Without a national effort, local efforts may weaken and even disappear.

3. Should we work for change of that very system which supports poverty and underdevelopment? To do so would involve a
program to bring the oppressed to a critical awareness of their
situation and to a desire to transform it. It would include
political organizing and action projects. Conflicts and possible violence may ensue (WCC 1975).

In each form of participation in development, Christians are
conscious of Christ's call to them to be the salt not of the
church but of the earth, and light not just to the believer
but to the world.

INTERDEPENDENCE

This brings us to a final issue—the future working relationship between churches. Christians outside of Africa are asking:
"What contributions should we make in the future to the life and
service of the church in Africa?" "How should such assistance
be organized and how should it relate to the African churches?"

THE MORATORIUM DEBATE

It is regrettable that the call from Africa for a moratorium
on aid received an instinctive negative response from donors
without a careful consideration of the issues involved.

The debate arose out of contemporary Africa in which sensi-
tivities to every form of neo-colonialism are on the increase.
While political independence has been achieved, African leaders
continue fearful that outside powers may exploit internal tensions to gain new influence. In economic life, continuing and
increasing financial dependence on international leading agencies and multi-national corporations breeds resentment.

The call for moratorium arose out of this environment. It
was not a call for isolationism, but for a restructuring of relationships in a serving and sharing fellowship. It was to be
one phase in growth through a time of independence to a new relationship of interdependence. Timing and implementation were
to be worked out carefully according to the needs of each church.
The possibility of future receiving of personnel and funds on a
new basis was accepted (Carr 1975). I believe that the option
of moratorium should continue to be discussed wherever African
churches seek for growth toward self-reliance to a new interdependence.

WIDENING CIRCLES OF INTERDEPENDENCE

Many forces of political, economic and cultural change will
continue to break down isolation, increase communication, and
promote mankind's interdependence. We can expect that a similar
trend will take place in inter-church relationships. Emphasis
will be placed upon a mutuality of giving and receiving between
partners of equal stature. Each must recognize, however, both
the strengths and limitations which they bring to their relationship.

For example, consider the issue of missionary participation
in evangelization efforts in Africa. Barrett has correctly observed that

> no people in history has been able to evangelize itself
> completely *ab initio:* outside agents of the gospel have
> usually assisted as initiators and catalysts until the
> numbers of local Christians have become large enough to
> enable evangelization to proceed under local momentum
> (Barrett 1973:286).

It is equally true, however, that primary face-to-face evangelism
will be most effective when done by those fluent in the language
and culture of the people to be reached. This would suggest a
partnership arrangement with African Christians from neighboring
peoples serving as **primary** evangelists, while financial support,
research facilities, literature production, and possibly training may be supplied from outside.

Some donors find the following guidelines useful as they work
for mutuality in relationships with African colleagues:

1. Channel financial support through a third party to reduce
control of the program by the donor group.

2. Determine priorities for support within Africa and adhere
to them in decision-making.

3. Second outside personnel to the receiving church as the employer, who determines conditions of service and to whom personnel are accountable.

The growth of global interdependence suggests for the church in Africa the importance of widening areas of cooperative effort. Within the continent closer working relations between Catholics, Protestants, and independent churches should be encouraged. In some countries (e.g. Lesotho and Swaziland) Catholics and Protestants have already joined together in a national council of churches. For others this may be a goal to be realized in the future.

Regional linkages between churches need careful development, especially across language groupings. Pan-Africanism, which captured the imagination of young Africans during the drive for political independence but receded during the initial years of nation-building, may assume increasing importance in African politics in coming years. The churches can play a significant role in building bridges of practical cooperation through joint action projects and sharing of personnel across national boundaries. The AACC should be strengthened to facilitate this.

Concerning relations between Christians in Africa, I would predict a wide diversity of responses to the need to affirm our oneness in Christ, to be in fellowship with one another, and to break down the walls that divide us one from another. Some organic unions of churches will take place, especially among churches of the same confessional family. Other Christians will respond: "God's call to witness and service in the world is so compelling that living under one church must wait. Besides, I cannot possibly in my lifetime achieve a roof big enough to cover all who in Christ are my brothers and sisters." Still others will respond: "If we profess one Father and one Savior let us form one united church of Christ in our land, with diversity of families within it, as in the Church of Christ in Zaire."

CONCLUSION

In conclusion I would remind you of the apostle Paul's assessment of the young church which he helped to establish in Corinth. The second letter reveals that he had to write a "severe letter" to the young church. Although Christians have received "the light of the knowledge of the glory of God in the face of Christ," they have this treasure "in earthen vessels" (4:6-7). God has given man freedom even in the precious body of his Son to honor or dishonor, to unite or divide, to build up or destroy. This freedom God gives "to show that the transcendent power belongs to God and not to us."

There are many parallels between the early church of the
first centuries and the church in Africa today. Dr. Kenneth
Scott Latourette gave this explanation of the vitality amid conflict and even persecution of the early church:

> The exceeding greatness of the power was displayed
> primarily in the transformation of those men and
> women who became followers of Christ, who put their
> trust in him. . . . It was chiefly through such
> lives that the creative impulse was released which
> produced the Church and Christian literature, the-
> ology and worship, which swept away the pagan
> cults. . . , which wrestled with the problems of
> war and with the relation to the state, property,
> marriage, and the popular amusements. . . . No
> individual attained fully to the "high calling of
> God in Christ." The churches were by no means
> identical with the city of God; there was in them
> much of the earthly city. Yet here, in earthen
> vessels, was a power at work which, in spite of
> what looked like chronic frustration, out of human
> material apparently hopelessly and basically marred
> and twisted was achieved the seemingly impossible,
> the re-creation of thousands of men and women un-
> til they displayed something of the quality of life
> which was seen in Jesus Christ. It was these men
> and women who were, to use the language of Jesus,
> "the salt of the earth" and "the light of the world"
> (1953: 263, 264).

In Africa today, God has implanted in the hearts and minds
of thousands of his children a like Spirit. Although tomorrow
they will be afflicted, perplexed, and persecuted, they who will
be the very body of Christ will live and grow. Therefore, we
say to them with the apostle Paul: "Be steadfast, immovable,
always abounding in the work of the Lord, knowing that in the
Lord your labor is not in vain" (I Cor. 15:58).

---

[1]Country by country profiles and data on unreached peoples
are available from MARC, 919 West Huntington Drive, Monrovia,
CA 91016.

Epilog

It is not my purpose to summarize at tedious length all that the symposium speakers have expressed so lucidly and forcefully. I would like, however, to isolate a few common themes that seem to me to tie together the diverse contributions, so as to bring the book to a fitting close.

But before doing this, I must express my regrets and apologies for the fact that there are in this volume no excerpts from the vigorous discussion that constituted so much of the symposium for those who were present. There was plenary discussion after each presentation and two responses, during which points were made or clarified. In addition, there were two impromptu evening discussions, one on the lessons to be learned from African independent churches, the other on moratorium. There was also discussion following the more popular lectures that the principal speakers gave on Saturday. The reason none of this potentially valuable material appears here is that it was not recorded; this was partly because my blank tapes were stolen at the last moment, but mostly because of the mechanical difficulty involved in picking up spontaneous speech in various parts of a large room and identifying speakers. In the end, we made a virtue of our failure, in that it permitted everyone to speak more frankly off the record.

Three major themes, it seems to me, run through all of these papers: that of dependence, independence, and interdependence; that of the creatively appropriate relation of the gospel to the African situation; and that of the unity of the church.

All the speakers in one way or another dealt with the shame-
ful continued dependence of African churches on non-African
churches and agencies, and the continued dominance of the latter
over the former. The areas in which this unwholesome asymmet-
rical relationship obtains run from the conceptualization of the
task of the church through liturgy and patterns of education; in
other words, all areas of church life and service. The forms by
which dominance is exercised run from more or less subtle "get-
ting our own way" via the purse strings all the way to gross and
overt racial oppression. It is no wonder that out of frustration bordering on despair, Africans among others have called for
moratorium. But that cannot be the last word, as Mr. Mutombo-
Mpanya points out. Neither practically nor theologically is it
sound for churches to be totally independent of each other;
ideally, we should be interdependent. But this implies a degree
of equality and mutual acceptance and respect which western
churches are seldom really prepared to practise. It involves
the recognition that spiritual maturity, wisdom, insight, and
vision are not certified by a school diploma, and that the non-
material contributions that African churches can best bring to
partnership are intrinsically more valuable than the cash which
we feel is so important because we contribute it. In other
words, true interdependence will involve a total reordering of
our values; I am not sure we will do what is needed, though I
continue to hope we will.

A particularly virulent form which our westernness takes as
it overshadows our Christian commitment is seen in our conniv-
ance, or at least in our acquiescence by silence, in the inhumanity of the racial system in southern Africa. Because the
oppressors are racially and culturally like us, and claim to be
acting from Christian motives, and to constitute the bulwark of
western Christian civilization against communism in Africa, we
at best give very low priority to the problem, and at worst give
our support to the oppressive system. It is time American Christians spoke out actively and directly against the perversion of
the gospel which the system entails, and worked through the political and economic processes to bring to bear upon the racists
in southern Africa the only kinds of pressure to which they may
be amenable.

The second major theme is that of a creative and relevant
interaction between the gospel and the social, political, economic, and cultural context in Africa. I will mention only two
lines of thought that emerged from the symposium.

Leeuw especially, but others as well, point to the need for a
new definition of the relation of church and state. Africans
find they have little in common with the history of Christendom
in the West; so that contemporary western ideas in this area,

arising as they did out of particular battles over establishment and the separation of church and state, can only lead to irrelevance if applied in the African context. Surely African Christians will find more fruitful ways, along lines suggested by our speakers, to bring the prophetic and redemptive voices of the gospel to bear on the political process and on the building of nations in the new Africa.

My second example in this area deals with cultural authenticity, growing out of insights into the dynamic relation which potentially can exist between the essence of the gospel and its multiple cultural forms and trappings. It was fascinating to listen to Vincent Donovan, out of his experience in pioneer evangelization among the Maasai, coming independently to insights developed by such missionary anthropologists as Nida, Smalley, Tippett, Kraft, and others, right down to the independent coinage of the term "supracultural" (see Smalley 1955; Kraft 1973). The adjustments in form run the full gamut from techniques of evangelism to the formulation of contextualized theology.

The third theme, which John Pobee emphasized particularly, is the need for the churches to recognize and give overt expression to their oneness as the Body of Christ in Africa, in the interests of credibility if for no other reason. It has been by now repeated *ad nauseam* that the fragmentation of the church is a scandal; and that the scandal is all the more heinous in places such as Africa, where the historic quarrels of the past in Europe and America have no bearing, and where the divisions are even more pointless than in the West. But the recognition of the scandal has not, by and large, led to action on a scale commensurate with the problem. Inertia, vested interests, the absolutizing of particular forms and formulations, all militate against the outward actualization of our spiritual unity; and everyone suffers.

Finally, it is my hope and prayer that, as readers acknowledge the validity of the descriptions and prescriptions offered by Africans in this book, they will also acknowledge that the Africans who offer them are members and leaders of a vital, mature, creative part of the whole Body, and may be disposed to act and to encourage others to act accordingly. For this book is only one token freshet of what should soon be a flood of contributions which Africans will make to the entire Church of Jesus Christ, not only in Africa but worldwide.

Bibliography

AACC, 1964. *The Crisis of the Christian Ministry in Africa.*
Kitwe: All Africa Conference of Churches

____, 1970. "The Church and Rapid Urban Growth in Southern
Africa," Report of the Southern Africa Urban Consultation,
Botswana. All Africa Conference of Churches

AFER, 1970. Manifesto presented by five Roman Catholic priests
to the hierarchy. AFER, Vol. 12, No. 2

Africa Now, 1977. Publication of the Sudan Interior Mission,
Jan.-Feb. 1977

Allen, Roland, 1965. *Missionary Principles: St. Paul's or Ours?*
London: World Dominion Press

AMECEA, 1976. "Building Christian Communities in Eastern Africa," AFER, Vol. 18, pp. 250-260

Aquina, Sr. Mary Weinreich, 1975. "An Aspect of the Development
of the Religious Life in Rhodesia," in *Themes in the Christian History of Central Africa,* ed. by T. O. Ranger & J.
Weller. London: Heinemann, pp. 218-237

Ayandele, E. A., 1966. *The Missionary Impact on Modern Nigeria.*
London: Longmans

Baëta, C. G., 1975. "My Visit to Lesotho," unpublished report

Barrett, David B., 1968. *Schism and Renewal in Africa*. Nairobi: Oxford University Press

____, 1970. "AD 2000: 350 Million Christians in Africa," IRM, Vol. 59, pp. 39-54

Barrett, David B., and others, 1973. "Frontier Situations for Evangelization in Africa, 1972," in *The Gospel and Frontier Peoples*, ed. by R. P. Beaver, South Pasadena: William Carey Library, pp. 233-310

BCC, 1970. *Violence in Southern Africa: A Christian Assessment*. British Council of Churches

Beals, A. R., Spindler, G., & Spindler, L., 1973. *Culture in Process*. New York: Holt, Rinehart and Winston

Becken, H.-J., ed., 1973. *Relevant Theology for Africa*. Durban: Lutheran Publishing House

Bonhoeffer, Dietrich, 1971. *Letters and Papers from Prison* (enlarged ed.). London

Bosch, David J., 1972. *Review of Essays on Black Theology*, in *Pro Veritate*, August 1972

____, David J., 1975. Article in *Theologia Evangelica*, 1975

Boyd, R., 1974. *India and the Latin Captivity of the Church*. Cambridge: Cambridge University Press

Bucher, Hubert, 1973. Article in AFER, Vol. 15, No. 4

Busia, K. A., 1961. "Has the Christian Faith Been Adequately Represented?" IRM, Vol. 50

Buthelezi, Chief Gatsha, 1975. "The Task of the Church in South Africa," *Missiology*, Vol. 3, pp. 31-32

Buthelezi, Manas, 1973. Article in *Pro Veritate*, September 1973

____, 1975. Lutheran World Federation Report, February 1975

Carpenter, E. & McLuhan, M., eds., 1960. *Explorations in Communication*. Boston: Beacon Press

Carr, Canon Burgess, 1975. "The Mission of the Moratorium," *Occasional Bulletin*, Vol. 25, No. 2, pp. 1-9

Carvalho, Emilio Julio Miquel de, 1974. "Politico-Socio-Religious Declaration of the United Methodist Church in Angola," tr. by L. W. Henderson

CCK, 1975. *Annual Report of the Christian Council of Kenya.* Nairobi

Chalfort, Lord, 1977. Article in *The Times*, London, May 30, 1977

Chipenda, José B., 1975. "Report of a Visit to Angola," Geneva

Costas, Orlando, 1973. "Mission Out of Affluence," *Missiology*, Vol. 1, pp. 405-423

Coxill, H. W. Wakelin & Grubb, Kenneth, eds., 1962. *World Christian Handbook*

____, 1968. *World Christian Handbook*

Dar-es-Salaam Consultation of Third World Theologians, 1977. "Theology from the Third World," *Grapevine*, Vol. 8, No. 7

Davidson, Basil, 1974. *Can Africa Survive?* Boston & Toronto: Little, Brown, and Co.

Debrunner, H., 1965. *A Church Between Colonial Powers.* London: Lutterworth

Der, Benedict, 1974. "Church-State Relations in Northern Ghana 1906-1940," *Transactions of the Historical Society of Ghana*, Vol. 15, No. 1, pp. 41-46

Desai, Ram, 1962. *Christianity in Africa as Seen by Africans.* Denver: Alan Swallow

DeVilliers, W. B., 1973. "The Future of the Missionary Enterprise," IDOC Report No. 3

Dickson, K. A. & Ellingworth, Paul, 1969. *Biblical Revelation and African Beliefs.* London: Lutterworth

Eby, John W., 1976. "The Institutionalization of the Church," *Mission-Focus*, Vol. 4, No. 4, pp. 1-9

EcuNews Bulletin, 1975. No. 25, August 13, 1975

Fashole-Luke, E. W., 1975. "The Quest for an African Christian Theology," *The Ecumenical Review*, Vol. 27, pp. 259-269

Findlay, G. G. & Holdsworth, W. W., 1922. *The Wesleyan Methodist Missionary Society*, Vol. 4. London: Epworth

Gensichen, H. W., 1976. "World Community and World Religions," in *Religion in a Pluralistic Society*, ed. by J. S. Pobee. Leiden: E. J. Brill

Goreham, Norman J., 1975. "Towards an African Theology," *Expository Times*, Vol. 86, No. 8

Groves, C. P., 1948-1958. *The Planting of Christianity in Africa*, 4 vols. London: Lutterworth

Gruchy, John W. de, 1974. "The Identity of the Church in South Africa," *Journal of Theology for Southern Africa*, No. 8

Hastings, Adrian, 1967. *Church and Mission in Modern Africa*. London: Burns and Oakes

Hodges, Melvin, 1953. *The Indigenous Church*. Springfield, MO: Gospel Publishing

Hoernle, R. F. Alfred, 1945. *Native Policy and the Liberal Spirit*. Johannesburg: Witwatersrand University Press

IDOC, 1976. IDOC Bulletin No. 41-42, March-April 1976

Idowu, E. Boladji, 1965. *Towards an Indigenous Church*. London: Oxford University Press

Ilogu, E., 1974. *Christianity and Ibo Culture*. Leiden: E. J. Brill

Journal of Theology for Southern Africa, 1973. Article in No. 2, March 1973

Kane, J. Herbert, 1971. *A Global View of Christian Missions*. Grand Rapids: Baker

Kasiera, Musembe, 1974. "The Cultural Issue in East Africa," in *In Search of Mission*, IDOC Bulletin No. 63

Kato, Byang H., 1975. "Evangelism Opportunities and Obstacles in Africa," in *Let the Earth Hear His Voice*, ed. by J. D. Douglas. Minneapolis: World Wide Publications, pp. 155-158

Kealy, John P. & Shenk, David W., 1975. *The Early Church and Africa*. Nairobi: Oxford University Press

Kendall, R. Elliot, 1972. *Politics, Mission and Church Aid.*
Sweden

Kimble, D., 1963. *A Political History of Ghana 1850-1928.*
Oxford: Clarendon Press

Kinuthia, Mary, 1973. *Deliverance Church--The Study of an
African Independent Church.* Nairobi

Kleinjans, E., 1972. "Communicating with Asia," lecture at
East-West Center, University of Hawaii (Jan. 1968), reprinted
in *Intercultural Communication.* Belmont, CA: Wadsworth

Kraft, Charles H., 1973. "Toward a Christian Ethnotheology,"
in *God, Man and Church Growth,* ed. by A. R. Tippett. Grand
Rapids: Eerdmans

_____, 1976. "Cultural Concomitants of Higi Conversion,"
Missiology, Vol. 4, pp. 431-442

Lamont, Victor, 1971. "African Independent Churches," *Risk,*
Vol. 7, No. 3

Latourette, Kenneth Scott, 1953. *A History of Christianity.*
New York: Harper & Row

_____, 1971. *A History of the Expansion of Christianity,* Vol. 7.
Grand Rapids: Zondervan

Lewis, I. M., ed., 1966. *Islam in Tropical Africa.* London:
Oxford University Press

Loewen, Jacob A., 1976. "Mission Churches, Independent
Churches, and Felt Needs in Africa," *Missiology,* Vol. 4,
pp. 405-425

Loffler, Paul, 1962. *The Layman Abroad in the Mission of the
Church.* New York: Friendship Press

Machel, President Samora, 1975. Inaugural Speech at Independence of Mozambique, June 25, 1975

Makhathini, D. D. L., 1973. "Black Theology," in *Relevant
Theology for Africa,* ed. by H.-J. Becken. Durban: Lutheran
Publishing House, pp. 8-17

Matthews, Basil, 1960. *Forward Through the Ages.* London:
World Dominion Press

Mbiti, John S., 1971. *New Testament Eschatology in an African Background.* London: Oxford University Press

_____, 1976. "Some Concerns of African Theology," *Expository Times,* Vol. 87, No. 6

Moffet, J. P., ed., 1958. *Handbook of Tanganyika.* Dar es Salaam: Government Printing

Morrison, Lionel, 1977. "My Return to South Africa," *The Sunday Telegraph,* May 29, 1977

Mulago, Vincent, 1965. *Un visage africain du christianisme.* Presence Africaine

Muzorewa, Abel Tendekai, 1976. "The Righteous Violence," unpublished sermon

Naylor, Wilson, 1905. *Daybreak in the Dark Continent.* Illinois

NCCK, 1974. Report for 1974 of the National Christian Council of Kenya. Nairobi

NCC/USCC, 1977. Draft Report of the Consultation on the Church and Southern Africa (Marcy, N.Y., March 7-11, 1977). National Council of Churches and U.S. Catholic Conference

Neill, Stephen C., 1966. *Colonialism and Christian Mission.* New York: McGraw Hill

Nkrumah, Kwame, 1958. Speech at the Conference of Independent African States. Accra, April 15, 1958

Northcott, Cecil, 1963. *Christianity in Africa.* Philadelphia: Westminster Press

Oduyoye, Amba, 1976. "The Church in Youth Education--Years Ago, Years to Come," in *Religion in a Pluralistic Society,* ed. by J. S. Pobee. Leiden: E. J. Brill

Oldham, J. H., 1974. Quotation in *Focus on Southern Africa,* Vol. 1, No. 2, p. 2, from *Christianity and the Race Problem* (1924)

Oliver, Roland, 1967. *The Missionary Factor in East Africa.* London: Longmans

One World, July-August 1976

Orchard, R., 1958. *The Ghana Assembly of the International Missionary Council*. London: Edinburgh House Press

Pobee, John S., 1975. "Church and State in the Gold Coast in the Vasco de Gama Era 1492-1947," *Journal of Church and State*, Vol. 17, pp. 217-237

____, 1976. "Church and State in Ghana 1949-1966," in *Religion in a Pluralistic Society*. Leiden: E. J. Brill

Randall, Max Ward, 1970. *Profile for Victory*. South Pasadena: William Carey Library

Ranger, T. O., 1970. *The African Voice in Southern Rhodesia*. London: Heinemann and Nairobi: East African Publishing House

Risk, 1971. Vol. 8, No. 3

Sales, Richard W. & Mbali, Z. E., 1976. "Botswana Theological Training Programme," unpublished report

SANRC, 1908. *The South African Native*. London: The South African Native Races Committee

Sawyerr, Harry, 1968. *Creative Evangelism*. London: Lutterworth

Setiloane, Gabriel M., 1974. "The State of the Church and Mission in Botswana," unpublished report

Shorter, Aylward, 1975. *African Christian Theology*. London: G. Chapman

Sithole, Ndabaningi, 1959. *African Nationalism*. London: Oxford University Press

____, 1970. *African Nationalism*, 2nd ed. New York: Oxford University Press

Smalley, William A., 1955. "Culture and Superculture," *Practical Anthropology*, Vol. 2, pp. 58-71

Smith, Ted, 1975. "Special Report to the South African Council of Churches," *EcuNews Bulletin*, No. 35

Stark, Louise & Morton, Don, 1976. *Torment to Triumph in Southern Africa*. New York: Friendship Press

Steiner, P., 1912. *Kamerun als Kolonie und Missionsfeld,* 2nd edition

Sundkler, Bengt G. M., 1960. *The Christian Ministry in Africa.* London: S.C.M. Press

____, 1961. *Bantu Prophets in South Africa,* 2nd edition. London: Lutterworth Press

Taylor, John V., 1958. *Processes of Growth in an African Church.* London: S.C.M. Press

____, 1967. *The Primal Vision.* London: S.C.M. Press

Taylor, John V. & Lehmann, Dorothea, 1961. *Christians of the Copperbelt.* New York: Friendship Press

TEF, 1976. *Ecumenical Responses to Theological Education in Africa, Asia, Near East, South Pacific, Latin America and Caribbean Progress Report on the T.E.F. Third Mandate Programme.* Heathfield: Errey's Printers Ltd.

Tillich, Paul, 1964. *Theology of Culture.* New York: Oxford University Press

Trimingham, J. S., 1959. *Islam in West Africa.* London: Oxford University Press

Von Allmen, D., 1975. "The Birth of Theology," IRM, Vol. 44, pp. 37-55

Vos, A., 1976. "Rapport over een bezoek aan de Lesotho Ev. Church (LEC)," unpublished report

Wakatama, Pius, 1976. *Independence for the Third World Church.* Downers Grove, IL: Intervarsity Press

Ward, W. E., 1958. *A History of Ghana.* London: Allen & Unwin

____, 1967. *Emergent Africa.* London: Allen & Unwin

Warren, Max A. C., 1976. "Political Realities and the Christian Mission," in *Religion in a Pluralistic Society,* ed. by J. S. Pobee. Leiden: E. J. Brill

Watts, Hilston, ed., 1970. *Focus on Cities:* Proceedings of a Conference, University of Natal (July 8-12, 1968). Pietermaritzburg: Natal University Press for the Institute of Social Research

WCC, 1975. *To Break the Chains of Oppression.* Geneva: World
   Council of Churches

____, 1976a. "Two WCC Staff Members Visit Mozambique." Geneva:
   World Council of Churches

____, 1976b. "WCC Delegation Visit to Angola." Geneva: World
   Council of Churches

Weaver, Edwin & Irene, 1975. *From Kuku Hill.* Elkhart, IN:
   Institute of Mennonite Studies

Welbourn, F. B., 1965. *East African Christian.* London: Oxford
   University Press

Williamson, S. G., 1965. *Akan Religion and the Christian Faith.*
   Accra: University of Ghana Press

Winter, Ralph D., 1970. *The Twenty-Five Unbelievable Years.*
   South Pasadena: William Carey Library

____, 1974. "The Two Structures of God's Redemptive Mission,"
   Missiology, Vol. 2, pp. 121-139

Yamamori, Tetsunao & Taber, Charles R., eds., 1975. *Christopaganism or Indigenous Christianity?* South Pasadena:
   William Carey Library

Zorn, H. M., n.d. *Viability in Context.* Heathfield: Errey's
   Printers Ltd.